WITHDRAWN

Troop Morale
and Popular Culture in the
British and Dominion Armies
1914–1918

Troop Morale and Popular Culture in the British and Dominion Armies 1914–1918

J. G. FULLER

CLARENDON PRESS · OXFORD
1990

Oxford University Press, Walton Street, Oxford OX2 6DP
Oxford   New York   Toronto
Delhi   Bombay   Calcutta   Madras   Karachi
Petaling Jaya   Singapore   Hong Kong   Tokyo
Nairobi   Dar es Salaam   Cape Town
Melbourne   Auckland
and associated companies in
Berlin   Ibadan

Oxford is a trade mark of Oxford University Press

Published in the United States
by Oxford University Press, New York

© J. G. Fuller 1991

British Library Cataloguing in Publication Data
Fuller, J. G.
Popular culture and troop morale in the British Dominion
armies, 1914–1918
1. World War 1. British soldiers. Attitudes
I. Title
940.48341
ISBN 0–19–820178–8

Library of Congress Cataloging in Publication Data
Fuller, J. G.
Popular culture and troop morale in the British and Dominion
armies 1914–1918 / J. G. Fuller.
p. cm.
Includes bibliographical references and index.
1. Great Britain. Army—History—World War, 1914–1918.
2. Commonwealth of Nations—Armed Forces—History—World War,
1914–1918.   3. Great Britain. Army—Military life.   4. Commonwealth
of Nations—Armed Forces—Military life.   5. Soldiers—Recreation.
6. Morale. I. Title
D546.F94   1990
940.54' 12' 41–dc20
ISBN 0–19–820178–8

Typeset by Wyvern Typesetting Ltd,

Printed and bound in
Great Britain by Bookcraft Ltd,
Midsomer Norton, Bath

For Gabriella and
my family

Contents

Abbreviations

AIF	Australian Imperial Force
ASC	Army Service Corps
BEF	British Expeditionary Force
CEF	Canadian Expeditionary Force
CO	Commanding Officer
MO	Medical Officer
NCO	Non-Commissioned Officer
OC	Officer Commanding
PSC	Passed Staff College
RAMC	Royal Army Medical Corps

Introduction

How was it, asked many who served in the British and Dominion forces in the First World War, that 'the unmilitary amateur British outlasted friend and foe alike' so that the war, in the end, 'was chiefly won on the ground by a huge crowd of young Britons who never wanted to be soldiers, hooted at all traditions of military glory, but went on and on, when American forces were still not fully deployed and the French were fading out'?[1] How could it be that, having 'no real imperialism in them, none of the highfalutin' Deutschland über Alles, none of the French or Italian bitter revengefulness, nor peasant hunger for acquisition', it was yet the case that 'the unmilitary British lasted out until the enemy caved in and gave up'?[2]

There is much, no doubt, of chauvinism in these claims, but historians too have been interested by the question of morale in the improvised British Empire forces. Uniquely among the combatants they lacked any sizeable core of Regular officers, NCOs, and men, or any experience of conscript soldiering on the part of the wartime recruits who now joined the colours. The war was not fought on their soil and, by comparison with Wilhelmine Germany, theirs was not a militaristic society. Yet their performance, and above all their endurance in a war where the immobility of fronts made this a quality of prime importance, were astonishingly good. The armies of their French, Russian, and Italian allies tumbled into large-scale mutiny or military collapse in 1917. By the following autumn the resistance of Germany's allies was disintegrating and the great German army itself, the engine of the war, was cracking under the strain. Yet the British and Dominion forces kept going, withstood the mightiest blows that the German army could deliver in spring 1918 and took the leading part in the great war-winning offens-

1 J. B. Priestley, *Margin Released* (1962), 130, 137.
2 R. H. Mottram, *The Spanish Farm Trilogy* (1979), 514; R. H. Mottram, *The 20th Century: A Personal Record* (1969), 49.

ives of that autumn.[3] At no time did discipline collapse. The
Fifth Army staggered under the weight of the greatest German
assault of the latter part of the war in March 1918, but no
Caporetto-style collapse ensued.

Historians have speculated as to the reasons for this endurance.
Many British and Dominion units came to the war later than
their French or German counterparts (as did the whole of the
Italian army). They did not suffer casualties in quite the same
proportion as the French or Germans (although this was certainly
not true for all units, and overall the British and Dominion troops
suffered more heavily than the Italian). Antagonism towards the
Germans was, according to some, kept high by an aggressive
policy of trench raiding (although the evidence suggests that this
costly policy was far more likely to inspire antagonism towards
their own staff and that, in so far as hatred could survive between
front-line soldiers facing common perils and seeing the same
enemies in profiteers and jingoists at home, hatred of *les Boches*
was more lively among French troops).

All these arguments will be explored in more detail, but com-
parisons are in many ways less interesting, because of their
imprecision, than the question of what made this particular army
work. How did the British and Dominion troops regard their
plight? What was their attitude to home and what did they think
they were fighting for? What, in turn, can these attitudes tell us
about the societies they came from and the impact upon these
societies of their return?

The whole area of morale is pregnant with interest, but
historians have been handicapped by the limitations of the available sources. The materials available, most obviously in the form
of official documents, letters, diaries, and memoirs, are certainly
vast, but they all have their shortcomings for the subject. There
is relatively little in the great corpus of official papers which bears
directly on morale: the British army of the next war was to pay
much greater attention to education in war aims and monitoring
the mood of the troops, but in this war reports on morale as
revealed by the men's letters were infrequent and calculations
about relative rates of manpower attrition paid little attention to
the fact that the basis of these optimistic calculations might be

---

[3] J. E. Edmonds, *History of the Great War Based on Official Documents* (1920
onwards), 1918, ii. 483–4, iv. 510.

overturned by a refusal to continue the fight. Letters, diaries, and memoirs are necessarily subjective, and letters in particular were written, through the filter of the censorship, for a home audience, which might lead to the truth being softened or alternatively dramatized according to the circumstances of the case. The magazines produced by the troops on active service overseas poked fun at the prevalence of exaggeration in letters:

> The Editor says he would like to get
> Some of the contents for his Gazette:
> Those tales of things that have never been
> And horrible sights that nobody's seen.[4]

Memoirs too have to be treated with similar care because of the risk that time has worked its distortions on memory, particularly where the subject is so evanescent as mentalities. The memoirs of a private who served in the Northumberland Fusiliers at the Somme, at Third Ypres, and in Italy, record his reaction on hearing a 1960s' radio broadcast about the war:

when I heard one of the survivors in the broadcast assert that at the outset of the great battle, the authorities had stationed Military Police to shoot anyone who refused to go over the top, I felt that something had gone wrong. Such an idea was completely alien to the spirit of that army. In any case, even had such an idea been projected its realization would have proved impossible under the conditions of the Somme battlefield . . . I never saw a Military Policeman in the trenches, although this is not to say that they did not appear from time to time in the course of duty.[5]

In such a case, where does the truth lie?

This study attempts to deal with the problem of sources by tapping for the first time on any significant scale the large archive of magazines produced by front-line units in all the major theatres of war, whose production is in itself an intriguing phenomenon. Their existence is fairly well known through a number of post-war reprints of the most famous, the *Wipers Times*. What is not generally appreciated is the extent of this activity and the character of its productions. This study has drawn on over a hundred such magazines, produced usually on a

[4] *The 5th Glo'ster Gazette*, 6 (Sept. 1915), 6. Similar comments were made in *The Brazier*, 5 (Aug. 1916), 67 and *Another Garland from the Front* (Dec. 1916), 47.
[5] E. N. Gladden, *Ypres 1917* (1967), 11.

rough monthly basis by units of all types but predominantly by
the infantry. Moreover, from the references to others no longer
extant it is apparent that, as with their French counterparts, 'les
collections conservées ne sont que les débris d'une production
nettement plus vaste dont il est très difficile d'apprécier l'ampleur
avec précision'.[6]

Chapter 1 investigates in more detail what moved men confronted by appalling hardships to devote so much effort to these
journalistic outpourings and exactly what is their value as
sources. However, briefly stated, they claimed a great value for
themselves as the imaginative shards from which a world might
be reconstructed by 'that future Macaulay who writes the history
of the great European War 1914– ',[7] and there is much to bear out
this claim. They are not coloured by subsequent experience and
they represent a collective rather than an individual commentary,
validated to a large extent by their soldier audience. In addition,
they deliberately set out, in many cases, to capture the spirit of
the army. They addressed themselves directly and continuously
to a task which letters and diaries tackle only peripherally and
randomly. Even without this purpose, the journals were themselves an expression of the collective culture which this study
attempts to describe. They served, moreover, as a means of intra-
unit communication, with the result that there lodge in their
pages not only essential details of unit administration, but also
many details of the jealousies and feelings otherwise perhaps too
trivial to be generally recorded, but important to the historian
none the less.

Using these magazines in conjunction with the more familiar
sources, this study deals with the experience of troops from the
British Isles and the Dominions of Australia, Canada, and New
Zealand who served on the main active war fronts in the First
World War (the Western Front, Egypt/Palestine, Salonika, Gallipoli, Italy, and Mesopotamia). It concentrates on the infantry
because the material conditions of their lives were generally
worse than those for other arms, and the sacrifices demanded of
them greater. In all armies they constituted a diminishing proportion of the total strength—only 32 per cent of the BEF by

[6] S. Audoin-Rouzeau, *14–18 Les Combattants des tranchées* (Paris, 1986), 11.
[7] *The Incinerator*, 2 (June 1916), 17.

November 1918[8]—but they dominated movements of unrest. In the French mutinies of 1917, 100 of the 113 worst outbreaks took place in the infantry, twelve in the artillery, and one in the dragoons.[9]

It was of course on the Western Front that the preponderant part of the British and Dominion infantry served, but, whilst allowing this theatre the prominence it deserves, other areas of the war will not be ignored. Morale could also be under severe strain elsewhere. The French mutinies were not confined to the armies in France, but broke out also in the only major expeditionary force which the French maintained for any long period upon another front: the Salonika force.[10] The strains on morale might be to some extent different in theatres other than the Western Front, with casualties generally lighter, and the problems of boredom, isolation, and maintaining a sense of purpose rather greater. However, the backgrounds of the men did not vary between theatres, and the varying problems of morale drew forth a remarkable and illuminating uniformity of response.

The period of the war on which this study concentrates is the time from mid-1915 onwards, when the mass army was taking over the main burden of continuing the struggle from the old Regular army which had been all but exterminated in the earlier battles. Conditions thereafter were of course not constant. The weight of weaponry deployed grew continuously, and tactics were adapted in response to try to protect the infantry from ever-increasing shell-fire. At the same time, behind the line, systems evolved and conditions of life became on the whole more ordered as the war progressed. The picture is one of gradual and continuous change, but without any sudden discontinuity. Thus, although the Somme offensive is often in retrospect pictured as a watershed, when earlier idealism gave way to stoical endurance, many non-Regular units had already suffered a year or more overseas before the offensive opened, and survivors saw grounds for reckoning these times among the most depressing experienced. Even at the end of their participation in the Somme battle, when they found themselves 'stuck fast in the autumn's

[8] *Statistics of the Military Effort of the British Empire during the Great War 1914–1920* (1922), 65–6.
[9] P. M. de la Gorce, *The French Army*, trans. K. Douglas (1963), 127.
[10] A. Palmer, *The Gardeners of Salonica* (1965), 140.

mud', the 24th Canadians' trench magazine carried a poem to
'The New Spirit':

> How different from that long and dreary time
> Of warfare in the trenches when the slime
> Of Flanders mud clung to our feet, and when
> Defensively we fought—raids now and then!
> But at the Somme the wind of victory blows
> Success our way, confusion to our foes.[11]

The pattern of the war was more complex than modern percep-
tions often admit. Within a slowly changing continuum, conditions of life varied, unit by unit, according to such factors as the
theatre or the section of front where one was serving, the
attitudes of the authorities at each level in the hierarchy, the
weather, military success, or the proximity of civilian services.
Whilst being aware of the two contrary trends over time towards
worsening conditions in the line and better conditions behind it,
it makes little sense to chop this complex continuum into chrono-
logical sections. The experience of the mass army is best treated
as a gradually evolving whole.

Finally, this study also attempts to give time behind the lines
its full place within this whole. Historical analyses of the British
and Dominion soldiers' experience of the Great War have concentrated attention overwhelmingly on the world of the trenches.
The titles of such recent studies as E. J. Leed's *No Man's Land* or
Tony Ashworth's *Trench Warfare* are sufficiently revealing of
their content.[12] Little attention has been paid to the roughly
three-fifths of the infantryman's service overseas spent in the rear
of these lines, but as this study will show, the phases of active
service life overseas were in fact so interlinked as to make it
difficult to understand any part of the picture in isolation from
the rest.

J.G.F.

---

[11] *The Vic's Patrol*, 3 (Dec. 1916), 24.
[12] E. J. Leed, *No Man's Land: Combat and Identity in World War I* (Cambridge, 1979); T. Ashworth, *Trench Warfare 1914–1918: The Live and Let Live System* (1980).

I

Trench Journalism

The British and Dominion armies overseas in the First World War were swept by a remarkable 'trench newspaper fever' which saw units of all types on all fronts producing their own company, battalion, or brigade magazines in a way not paralleled in previous wars.[1] Other armies were similarly gripped, at least on the Allied side.[2] The historian of French troop journals estimates that some 400 such journals were produced by French army units between 1914 and 1918, of which rather less than 200 have survived.[3] This study draws on some 107 produced by the smaller British and Dominion armies overseas, details of which are listed at Appendix A.

Of the 107 journals listed, sixty-one represent units wholly or predominantly of infantry. Of the other forty-six, only ten are really productions of base units, the remainder serving artillery, cavalry, engineers, signals, field ambulances, and transport in the zone immediately behind the front line. Base units apart, in many cases the distinction is not a sharp one. The infantry journals tended to be produced when units were withdrawn into rest or reserve. Their readership certainly overlapped unit bounds, and took in men from the other arms among whom they found themselves billeted. Similarly, letters and contributions in non-infantry journals show that infantrymen were among their readers.

The journals appeared on all active war fronts. The predominant numbers were produced on the Western Front, paralleling the distribution of forces. Of the seventy-four British and Dominion Divisions which served in active war theatres, only thirteen (or 18 per cent) spent the larger part of their over-seas service elsewhere than on the Western Front. The propor-

---

[1] *Dead Horse Corner Gazette*, 2 (Dec. 1915), 22.
[2] Audoin-Rouzeau, *Les Combattants*, p. 7.
[3] Ibid. 11.

tion of the 107 journals listed produced in these other war theatres was some 19 per cent.

The journals were representative of the various types of infantry division from which the British and Dominion forces were formed. The Regular Divisions were created from the units of the peacetime army, brought up to strength with reservists. The first-line Territorial Divisions were formed from the battalions of part-time soldiers of pre-war days, brought up to establishment where necessary with a small number of rejoined men: in this category can also be included the single Yeomanry Division. The New Army, or Kitchener, Divisions were improvised from civilian volunteers after the outbreak of war, and the Australian, Canadian, and New Zealand Divisions, formed from successive waves of volunteers, were also broadly of this type. Finally, the second-line Territorial Divisions were another wartime creation, competing with the Kitchener units for recruits, but originally intended only for home service and drafting of replacements to first-line Territorial units.

There was some interchange of battalions between the Regular and Kitchener Divisions, for the purpose of stiffening the latter, but so few were the Regulars that, even though they used a quarter of their strength to this end, that still meant only a contribution of thirty-four battalions for the thirty Kitchener Divisions, which contained 360 battalions in total.[4] This small dilution apart, divisions remained almost entirely composed of units of a single of the four types.

Only three infantry divisions fall outside this general scheme: the Guards (a mixture of Regular battalions with newly raised), the Royal Naval Division (Regular marines, naval reservists, and a variety of army troops) and the 75th (a late creation in Egypt, combining stray battalions of first- and second-line Territorials sent there from India). To these might be added the British troops serving in Indian Divisions, of approximately three divisions aggregate strength, to get an overall view of relative proportions within the British infantry (see Table 1).

All these types of unit supported troop journals. The exact provenance of non-infantry journals is in many cases not clear, but looking at infantry journals alone, there are only two cases

---

[4] H. Green, *The British Army in the First World War* (1968), 64.

TABLE I. *Categories of British infantry serving in all major theatres (France, Italy, Salonika, Gallipoli, Palestine/Egypt, Mesopotamia)*

Category	No. of infantry divisions serving in major war theatres	% of total	Average time there served (months)
1. Regular	11	14	49
2. First-line Territorial	13	17	38
3. Kitchener	30	39	38
4. Dominion	10	13	29
5. Second-line Territorial	7	9	23
6. Other	3	4	28
7. British troops in Indian Divisions (Categories 1, 2, and 4)	3*	4	22

*Aggregate strength, excluding British units in Indian Divisions created out of other category divisions in the reorganization of March 1918, to avoid double-counting.

Sources: Statistics of the Military Effort, opp. p. 28; E. A. James, *British Regiments 1914–1918* (1978), 131–2.

where the parent unit cannot be precisely identified. Leaving these aside, production appears to have been broadly in line with the relative size of the different unit types, although with the Dominion troops markedly over-represented, bearing out the magazine of the 58th London Division's description of them as 'the most prolific of trench journalists'.[5] (See Table 2.)

Most journals are represented by only a handful of issues. Forty-three out of the surviving sixty-one infantry journals have five extant issues or less. This is probably close to the truth of the picture. Journals that did endure showed a tendency to increase their circulation over time. Magazines usually started out to serve a single battalion, but often progressively enlarged their constituency, even to the point where the magazine of the 7th Manchesters, for example, was selling 26,000 copies in Egypt and the magazine of the 7th Canadians almost 20,000 on the Western Front.[6] These were extraordinary figures, but other journals boosted sales to as many as 5,000 copies.[7] With most of the

[5] *The Direct Hit*, 1 (Sept. 1916), 2.
[6] *The 7th Manchester Sentry*, 5 (May 1916), 4; *The Listening Post*, 19 (Oct. 1916), 118.
[7] *The Switchboard*, 2 (Aug. 1916), 2; *The Outpost*, 4/2 (Feb. 1917), 156.

TABLE 2. *Infantry journals according to type of unit*

Type of unit	No. of journals	% of total infantry journals	% of total infantry divisions in active war theatres
Regular First-line	5	8	14
Territorial	10	17	17
Kitchener	19	32	39
Second-line Territorial	3	5	9
Dominion	18	31	13
Other	4	7	8

Sources: See Appendix A.

journals where five issues or less are preserved, however, it is a single first issue or a run of early issues which survives. It therefore seems likely that in many cases this was all that was produced.

The fact should not be surprising. Production of troop journals represented a considerable outlay of effort in a life which was already exhausting. As the editor of *The Moonraker* commented, 'more than one sentence has been interrupted by a crump, and every page represents what might have been a pleasant sleep'.[8] Moreover, upheavals caused by advances or retreats sometimes caused manuscripts or equipment to be lost. Moving spirits, too, were lost. Nine of the fifteen staff of *The 7th Manchester Sentry* died in the Dardanelles. On its first anniversary, only two members of the staff of *The Mudhook*, the magazine of the 63rd Division, remained. Six of the fifteen contributors to the first issue of *The Moonraker* were lost before the second issue appeared six months later.[9]

The magazines were not, however, the exclusive production of any particular period of the war. The first seem to have started in 1915, but new journals were begun in each succeeding year. The

[8] *The Moonraker*, 1 (Apr. 1917), 1.
[9] *The 7th Manchester Sentry*, 3 (Mar. 1916), 1; *The Mudhook*, 7 (Sept. 1918), 1; *The Moonraker*, 2 (Oct. 1917), 47.

TABLE 3. *Appearance of infantry journals and arrival of infantry divisions in active war theatres*

	New infantry journals	Infantry divisions arriving overseas
1914	–	10
1915	21	43
1916	16	14
1917	13	7
1918	8	–
Not known	3	

Source: Appendix A and James, *British Regiments, passim.*

numbers of new titles declined, but so did the number of divisions arriving overseas (see Table 3).

Nor were they unique to any single rank within the army. Some details of the rank of the editorial staff can be gleaned for sixty-six out of the 107 journals. Thirty-five identify a single editor, and thirty-one an editorial team. According to these identifications, twenty-seven seem to have been edited by officers only, twenty-five by other-ranks only, and fourteen by a combination of the two. The pool from which the journals drew was not, however, limited to the editorial staff. The contributions of all ranks were invited, and the lists of contributors, where available, suggest that there was a good response.

Some of the magazines were printed or cyclostyled by the troops themselves, using abandoned French presses and paper or army equipment.[10] Others were printed by agents in France or England to whom copy was sent.[11] The authorities gave some limited help in several cases. *The 20th Gazette*, for example, stated that without the accommodation which the battalion adjutant placed at its disposal, it could not publish. The editor of *The Leadswinger*, taking his cue from the magazine's title, claimed that its production functioned as 'neither more nor less than an excuse by means of which the staff could evade some irksome parade or fatigue'. *The Middlesex Yeomanry Magazine,*

[10] *The Wipers Times* (1930 fac. edn.) p. v; *Aussie*, 3 (Mar. 1918), 1; *The Mudhook*, 5 (May 1918), 1.
[11] *The Outpost*, 4/6 (Apr. 1917), 228; *The Mudhook*, 7 (Sept. 1918), 1. (*The Mudhook* changed to this system following the loss of its equipment as a result of the German offensives in spring 1918.)

on the other hand, found itself initially hindered by 'unsympathetic' authorities.[12] Most journals seem in fact to have survived first and foremost by their own efforts. Before the adjutant took an interest in *The 20th Gazette* (shortly after it became officer-edited in May 1916), the other-rank editors of the magazine had earlier recorded that the only concession they had so far been granted was to be once excused a route march.[13]

In the circumstances, it may well be asked what it was that impelled men to sacrifice their free time in this way. Sometimes they were clearly concerned to produce a journal which was a message to those at home. The *Christmas Garland* of the 5th Canadian Battalion, for example, was 'an effort to answer a demand for something distinctive of the Battalion which at this particular season of the year would be suitable for all ranks to send from the trenches to friends and relatives in the British Isles and Canada'.[14] This motive seems to have had particular force with the Dominion troops, cut off from home more than their British fellows. The magazine of the 24th Canadians gave as its *apologia pro sua vita* 'its ability to portray for our friends at home the conditions under which we live and to show them that it takes more than Flemish mud and German shells to quench the spirit of the 24th'.[15] More simply, the journal of the 23rd Australians recorded in January 1918 that 'the first issue of the battalion paper has reached its intended destination, Australia'.[16]

The sentiment was rarer, though by no means absent, among British journals. The editor of the magazine of the 56th London Division gave as one of its objects to 'show the good folk at home what we are thinking and doing . . . [for] we can't tell them much in our letters and one leave a year'.[17] Troops further afield than the Western Front often felt themselves to be every bit as remote from home as the Dominion troops. The editor of the magazine of the 2/4th West Kents in Palestine reflected in the third issue how 'the magazine is playing the part designed for it originally. It

---

[12] *The 20th Gazette*, 2/2 (July 1916), 5; *The Leadswinger*, 2 and 3 (1919, fac. edn.), p. iii; *The Middlesex Yeomanry Magazine*, 2 (Oct. 1917), 1.

[13] *20th Gazette*, 1/9 (Mar. 1916), 46.

[14] *A Christmas Garland from the Front* (Dec. 1915), 7.

[15] *The Vic's Patrol*, 1/1 (June 1916), 1. Cf. *The Trench Echo*, 1 (Dec. 1915), front cover; *The Sling*, 1 (Jan. 1917), 4; *M & D*, 1 (July 1917), 3.

[16] *23rd: The Voice of the Battalion*, 8 (Jan. 1918), 5.

[17] *The Dagger*, 1 (Nov. 1918), 2.

is becoming the medium by which those at home can realise, far better than from the ordinary press, exactly what we are seeing and doing in the "Land of Promise" so far away.'[18] Journals with this purpose often sprang up very early in a battalion's service overseas, sometimes reporting first impressions and then, apparently, no more.[19]

Quite different was the case of, for example, *The Mudhook* of the 63rd (Royal Naval) Division, which was started after the division had been almost three years overseas, and which therefore served a real and inward-looking community. The first issue proudly proclaimed 'we shall cater for no tastes but our own'.[20] *The Mudhook* was a success, but where it reflected an existing *esprit de corps*, many other journals had first to try to create this feeling. Sometimes this was an official effort. The magazine of the 13th Cheshires, for example, edited by the adjutant, was designed 'to be a history of the Battalion, a chronicler of its doings and sayings, a creator and a cherisher of love of Regiment, of esprit de corps, of pride in its short but glorious history'.[21] None of the productions with avowed aims of this grandiose sort seem, however, to have been long-lived. More sustaining was a simple concern with the battalion as a practical community, evolved in training and quickly bound by experience. *The Vic's Patrol*, for example, aimed 'to bring the different units within the Battalion into a more intimate relationship'; *The 20th Gazette* to bring 'officers, NCOs and men of the 20th battalion CEF into closer touch with one another'.[22] Both enjoyed long runs.

Each battalion had numerous petty jealousies between NCOs and other-ranks, new drafts and old, specialists and the rank and file. Often the journal was intended to serve as a means of venting these jealousies along with other grievances, humorously defusing them, and thereby binding the battalion more closely together. *The R.M.R. Growler* of the 14th Canadians, for example, advertised that 'as the name will suggest, our columns are open to every grouch in the Battalion, and a growl on any subject,

---

[18] *Chronicles of the White Horse*, 3 (1917), 8.
[19] Examples of this are *The Judean*, *The Quaysider*, and *The Dud* of the 14th Battalion Argyll and Sutherland Highlanders: see Appendix A.
[20] *The Mudhook*, 1 (Sept. 1917), 2.
[21] *The Cherrybuff*, 1 (Sept. 1917), 3. Cf. *Stand To*, 1 (May 1916), 1.
[22] *The Vic's Patrol*, 1/1 (Mar. 1916), 4; *20th Gazette*, 1/1 (Apr. 1915), 1.

whether the grievance be either real or fancied, will be joyfully
received and have immediate insertion'.[23] Other journals had
similar names and intentions, such as *The Growler* of the 16th
Northumberland Fusiliers, *The Strafer*, and *The Incinerator*.
They sought to give 'a good healthy criticism of the things going
on around us' and 'to provide a medium through which we can
vent our little grousings'.[24] Many ran specific columns of complaints: 'Bricks from the Editor's Pack', 'We Wonder Why',
'Kicks and Growls', 'Ricochets from the Sniper', 'Our Strafe
Column', and so on. Here, as *The Iodine Chronicle* commented,
'officers and privates find scope for criticism which is often dar-
ingly outspoken'.[25]

The light-hearted way in which these kicks were presented was
characteristic. The prevailing tone of all the journals was
humorous. *The Enfield Express* described *The AOC Workshops
Gazette* as 'a happy blend of *The Sporting Life* and *Punch*',[26] and
this description could be aptly applied to many other troop
magazines. *The Times Literary Supplement* in October 1916 described the trench journals overall as 'miscellanies of personal
chaff, old Service jokes, crude parodies, rude drawings, spoof
examination papers and bogus advertisements'.[27] This tone
remained constant throughout the war: there is no detectable
darkening.

In a sense, this is not surprising. One of the primary purposes
of the journals was to amuse. Several stated their intention to
'give the boys something to make them forget their surroundings', or to be 'the means of bringing a little pleasure in this none
too gay life'.[28] Others, however, had far less self-conscious
purpose. They presented themselves as merely a response to
boredom, initiated 'to provide a pastime for myself and a few
comrades during our slack periods on active service' or 'to while
away the tedium of the evenings of a winter in Flanders'.[29] Some
were the fruit of a desire to 'burst into print' or a need for 'an

[23] *The R.M.R. Growler*, 1 (Jan. 1916), 1.

[24] *The Open Exhaust*, 9 (Sept. 1916), 5; *The Rum Issue*, 1 (June 1917), front cover.

[25] *The Iodine Chronicle*, 15 (Easter 1918), 4.

[26] *The AOC Workshops Gazette*, 11 (July 1916), 8.

[27] *The Times Literary Supplement* (12 Oct. 1916), 481.

[28] *The Forty Niner*, 1/4 (Jan. 1915), 16, 25–6. Cf. *The Mudlark*, 1 (Apr. 1916), 3;
Dead Horse Corner Gazette, 1 (Oct. 1915), 1.

[29] *The Leadswinger*, 2 and 3 (1919), p. iii; *Mules Monthly*, 1 (1916), 1.

outlet for volumes of penned-up gems of thought'.[30] Others saw themselves as part of the 'fad', a product of the vogue for unit magazines inspired in many cases by former civilian journalists who now found themselves in khaki.[31]

However, the fad itself, and the form chosen for the response to boredom, owed something to the fact that men were aware of taking part in great events. They wanted to preserve a record of their thoughts and experiences, both for themselves and for history. The value of the magazines as souvenirs is constantly emphasized. They would record the human side of the war in a way that nothing else could. Their tone was held to be not a consciously assumed pose but a reflection of the reality: 'the history of the Aussie Army is being given by the Official War Correspondents. *"Aussie"* wants to give its spirit.'[32] In this endeavour they claimed a high degree of success. *The 7th Manchester Sentry* declared that, 'the whole series when completed will form a unique record of the life and thought, work and aspirations of a typical battalion of Manchester Territorials during the Great War. Macaulay's New Zealander may well trace the aptest expression of the ideals of our generation in the columns of the Sentry.'[33]

To what extent are these claims justified? How useful are the troop journals as sources? Certainly in the area of mentalities, they have a number of advantages. They attempted to set down the mood of the moment and, unlike letters, they did so publicly and, in most cases, with a soldier audience primarily in mind. The journals were to a large extent responsive to this audience. As ventures which operated to cover their costs or, in some cases, to earn profits for unit funds from which comforts could be bought, they had to command a readership. Staff and contributors, producing for a unit audience with whom they were inescapably in daily contact, had an added reason to be sensitive to the views and criticisms of comrades. As the historian of French troop newspapers comments,

[30] *The Canadian Sapper*, 1 (Feb. 1918), 10; *The Shell Hole Advance*, 1 (Feb. 1917), 1.
[31] A. J. Sansom, *Letters from France* (1921), 195; *Dead Horse Corner Gazette*, 2 (Dec. 1915), 22; E. Townshend (ed.), *Keeling Letters and Recollections* (1918), 147, 202.
[32] *Aussie*, 2 (Feb. 1918), 1.
[33] *The 7th Manchester Sentry*, 4 (Apr. 1916), 1.

Les rédacteurs vivaient au milieu de leurs lecteurs et ne pouvaient ignorer leur état d'esprit. Ils avaient nécessairement très vite et très directement connaissance des réactions que suscitaient leurs articles. C'est pourquoi la plupart des journaux de tranchées ont su évoluer dans le sens d'une authenticité croissante. Censure et autocensure ne pouvaient empêcher la presse de tranchées de rejoindre peu à peu les préoccupations, les interêts, les rancœurs et les espoirs de ses lecteurs et de s'en faire l'écho. Tout journal qui aurait durablement ignoré cette 'demande' se serait condamné à la disparition.[34]

The result should not be surprising. *The Leadswinger* found that it was losing readers because it had strayed from its original format of 'bright, brief and topical' articles, and forthwith promised to change back. *The Middlesex Yeomanry Magazine* adopted a lighter tone for its second issue because the first was criticized on the grounds 'that it was too academical, too serious, and not representative of the regiment'. Conversely *The Wiggle Waggle* was set up 'with the sole intention of providing its readers with a little wholesome amusement', but soon found that 'more serious notes seem to have crept in . . . evidence that among some of our contributors there is a desire to express some of the feelings which lie deeper than laughter'.[35]

The journals were also of course aware of their second audience, the audience at home. For all the progressive sundering of civilian and military worlds, the soldiers still cared passionately what the Home Front thought of them. The artillery, ASC, or RAMC journals would launch verses appealing against what they felt to be unfair public neglect. British journals would complain of the excessive publicity given the Dominion forces, county regiments of the attention lavished on the London Territorials, first-contingent Canadians of the unjust lionizing of the second-contingent men. The armies in the Salonika and Palestine theatres in turn resented, and protested, the public image of these sectors as 'cushy'. Every branch and every unit trumpeted its merits, and pushed its competitive claim for attention.

Given this intense desire for their sacrifices to be appreciated, the troops were understandably angry at the extent of civilian incomprehension and complacency. A standard scene in the

[34] Audoin-Rouzeau, *Les Combattants*, p. 34.
[35] *The Leadswinger*, 2/7 (Feb. 1918), 381–2; *The Middlesex Yeomanry Magazine*, 2 (Oct. 1917), 1; *The Wiggle Waggle*, 2/3 (Nov. 1916), 17.

journals presents the returned front-soldier subjected to a barrage of idiotic civilian questions: was he not anxious to get back to France; were not the troops 'all right' because they had gas-helmets and dug-outs; was he not thrilled by the music of the guns; was it not fun splashing about in the trenches?[36] Nor was satire so far from reality. Basil Peacock recalls, from his first leave, his mother's expectation that hostilities would cease on Sundays, or the neighbour's anxiety to know what his mother thought of him getting home at past midnight.[37] One private on leave remembers being asked 'do you like it over there?'[38] Another was dining with a relative who proclaimed himself to be 'dying to go out and see the fun': 'at the word "fun" . . . I had an almost irresistible impulse to stand up and strike him across the face. But it was a public restaurant and I controlled myself.'[39]

The journals were cheerful, but they tried hard to ensure that this cheeriness should be seen in its true light as something that had to be struggled for:

some people at home have got the idea that officers and men alike are having a very pleasant holiday—Rations free too—in France etc. Sir William Robertson is reported to have said that when he wanted a holiday he went to France owing to the cheeriness of the British colony there, which forms a contrast with the long faces sometimes seen at home. The truth is of course that were it not for the spirit of bonhomie and cheerfulness, we should find it very hard to keep going.[40]

Similarly, the magazine of the Welsh Division declared:

to the casual stranger . . . who happens upon this Souvenir of ours we would say just this . . . do not therefore conclude that when a man becomes a soldier he develops into a queer type of being who lusts alternately for battle and for beer . . . Do not salve your conscience by pretending that he likes it. Nothing is further from the truth—for all that you read in newspapers.[41]

A tag from Kipling was repeatedly applied, in the hope of reminding people to see beyond the surface cheerfulness:

[36] *The Outpost*, 4/6 (April 1917), 197–8; *The Leadswinger*, 2/5 (Oct. 1916), 280; *The 5th Glo'ster Gazette*, 22 (Mar. 1918), 9; *Aussie*, 9 (Dec. 1918), 23.
[37] B. Peacock, *Tinker's Mufti* (1974), 62.
[38] M. Brown, *Tommy Goes to War* (1978), 225.
[39] F. A. Voigt, *Combed Out* (1920), 132.
[40] *The 5th Glo'ster Gazette*, 19 (June 1917), 21.
[41] *A New Year Souvenir of the Welsh Division* (Jan. 1918), 7.

I have written the tale of our life,
For a sheltered people's mirth,
In jesting guise; but ye are wise,
And ye know what the jest is worth.[42]

The journals had no desire to perpetuate the distortions of the home press and quite to the contrary, one of the aims commonly expressed was to provide the people at home with a true picture of life on active service.[43] To do so, they did not shrink from shattering illusions, albeit politely:

people are frequently asking us how we 'enjoy' life out here. I don't know whether the following is a general opinion, but at least this remark made by one of our attached men, after reading about a man being sent to prison for a month's hard labour, gives an idea of the extent of his 'enjoyment': 'Blimey, who wouldn't do a month in quod after this lot. A bloomin' pinch ain't it'.[44]

As well as the prevalence of malingering, and the front-line troops' desire not to provoke the enemy opposite, fear and physical wretchedness were constant themes of their humour. Mock advertisements begged for a means of escape, or for someone to change places with the front-line soldier. Stories were told of the man who, by one ingenious device or another, 'worked his ticket'. The men were fed up with the whole business, and said so: they were suffering from 'exhaustion' and 'war weariness', pondering 'who will give first?'[45] The 'Amateur's Alphabet', in the magazine of the 6th Battalion South Lancashire Regiment, had it that

U is the uniform he donned at first with glee,
But the pride and glamour's faded now, 'fed up', 'sheer fed' is he
V is the valley of abuse he'd like to pour
On decrepit politicians who caused this blanky war.[46]

The journal of the 27th Canadians requested:

[42] *The Whizz Bang*, 7 (July/Aug. 1916), 1; *The Vic's Patrol*, 2 (July 1916), 9; *The Canadian Sapper*, 9 (Oct. 1918), 51.
[43] *The Dud* (Argyll and Sutherland), 1 (Nov. 1916), 1; *Chronicles of the White Horse*, 3 (May 1917), 8; *23rd: The Voice of the Battalion*, 8 (Jan. 1918), 5.
[44] *Stray Shots*, 7 (June 1916), 2.
[45] *The Outpost*, 6/3 (Jan. 1918), 90.
[46] *The Mesopoluvian*, 1 (June 1917), 3–4.

In that unhealthy land where nightmares crop,
Put some nice brown crosses and write up on top,
They were all fed up and they wanted to stop.[47]

Of course, there was a censorship, exercised for some journals at battalion level and for others at divisional level, which placed some constraints on what the journals could say. However, in most cases it operated with surprising liberality. According to *The Minden Magazine*, 'we are not allowed to insert the names of the various places we go to; neither are we allowed to discuss too minutely the ins and outs of our prolonged misunderstanding and unpleasantness with the Germans. Neither are we permitted to criticise too freely our political enemies or friends.'[48] Within these limits, however, considerable freedom was allowed, as it had to be if the journals were to fulfil the 'grousing' purpose for which they had often been set up. As in the French army, 'le commandement comprenait que la survie de la presse de tranchées, jugée souhaitable, imposait des compromis quant au contenu faute de quoi, vidée de sa substance, elle ne pourrait que disparaître'.[49] As a result, one finds *The Dead Horse Corner Gazette*, for example, able to ask 'whether the officer of a certain Canadian battalion who ordered one of his men to pick up scraps of paper from the top of a communication trench in broad daylight attended the man's funeral?', or *The Swell* to enquire 'who were the 3 Non-coms who suddenly got an attack of "cold feet" when the bombardment started, and left their men to find their own way around'.[50]

Quite apart from what can be gleaned of mood and morale from the journals, there is a wealth of innocuous but invaluable factual information about organization behind the lines. The censorship did not worry about details of the soldiers' daily lives, their recreations, and societies, but this information is useful to the historian trying to reconstruct a picture of the soldiers' experiences, and cannot be adequately duplicated from any other source. As we shall see, many observers attributed to recreations in particular an importance which, if justified, makes them a key feature in understanding the character of this army and even its performance.

[47] *The Trench Echo*, 4 (Dec. 1917), 3.
[48] *The Minden Magazine*, 2 (Dec. 1915), 1–2.
[49] Audoin-Rouzeau, *Les Combattants*, p. 25.
[50] *Dead Horse Corner Gazette*, 1 (Oct. 1915), 5; *The Swell*, 2 (Jan. 1916), 1–2.

The evidence of the troop magazines certainly needs to be used with circumspection. They represent battalions of every type, but in each battalion they would tend to be the product of the most articulate sections, albeit influenced by the remainder. A large part of their function was to amuse and entertain. Sometimes they sought actively to boost morale. Yet they did seriously aim at being representative, they contained much incidental material which neither the writers nor the authorities had any motive to distort, and they were allowed considerable freedom to speak outside matters of military intelligence. They were not invented at divisional or even brigade level as an instrument of man-management, but came into being in response to innumerable individual initiatives. For the ephemeral, they provide invaluable contemporary testimony, validated to a great extent by their soldier audience and uncoloured by subsequent experience or by selective memory. For all these reasons, they are not lightly to be discounted and, used in conjunction with other sources to serve as a check and balance, can make a valuable contribution to our understanding of the First World War.

2

Morale

Morale is an elusive subject and it may be as well, before turning to an examination of its functioning in the British and Dominion forces, to attempt some definition of the concept. Modern writing on military effectiveness and the causes of its disruption tends to divide principally into two schools. These might be termed, for convenience, the 'primary group' and 'legitimate demand' schools. Broadly, the first maintains that the main influence on the soldier's willingness to fight is the capacity of his immediate social group to supply his material and psychological needs, and so engage his loyalties, irrespective of commitment to any larger cause. The seminal study for this school, the American examination of morale in the German army in the closing stages of World War II, concludes that, 'where conditions were such as to allow primary group life to function smoothly, and where the primary group developed a high degree of cohesion, morale was high and resistance effective or at least very determined, regardless in the main of the political attitudes of the soldiers'.[1] 'Legitimate demand' theory, by contrast, holds that the soldier's impulse to fight hinges more upon an underlying commitment, however little articulated, to the legitimacy of the ends in view, and to the validity of the military hierarchy's methods in pursuit of those ends. Even in circumstances where military primary groups cannot cohere, for example where the turnover of personnel is very rapid, the individuals who make up those groups will still be motivated to combat if they believe in the worth of the socio-political system to which they belong, the necessity for its defence, and the legitimacy of the commands which they are called on to obey as a means for that defence.[2]

[1] M. Janowitz and E. A. Shils, 'Cohesion and Disintegration in the Wehrmacht in World War II', in M. Janowitz (ed.), *Military Conflict* (1975), 216. Cf. R. W. Little, 'Buddy Relations and Combat Performance', in M. Janowitz (ed.), *The New Military* (New York, 1967), 195–233.

[2] S. D. Wesbrook, 'The Potential for Military Disintegration', in S. C. Sarkesian (ed.), *Combat Effectiveness* (1980), 244–78; C. Moskos, 'Behavior of Combat Soldiers

The two schools are not of course exclusive. As a student of combat behaviour in Vietnam observed, 'the ideological and primary group explanations are not contradictory. Rather, an understanding of the combat soldier's motivation requires a simultaneous appreciation of the role of small groups and underlying value commitments as they are shaped by the immediate combat situation.'[3] A member of the historical division of the American army in the Second World War reached the same conclusion on the basis of the numerous post-combat interviews he conducted:

when the chips are down, a man fights to help the man next to him, just as a company fights to keep pace with its flanks. Things have to be that simple . . . Yet above and beyond any symbol—whether it be the individual life or a pillbox commanding a wadi in Sahara—are all of the ideas and ideals which press upon men, causing them to accept a discipline and to hold to the line even though death may be at hand.[4]

The evidence of the First World War mutinies certainly does not support any simple assumption that military collapse can be equated with failure of the primary group. Undoubtedly there was a fierce loyalty to the 'mates' of one's section or platoon, an almost religious sense of comradeship, the passing of which was to be regretted by many veterans. This, according to C. M. Bowra, was 'what held soldiers to their work'.[5] An ex-private remembered: 'many of us wish to run, but there is a restraining force stronger than the fear of Redcaps; a power outside the bonds of patriotism even—the inner knowledge that we should be letting down the others and ourselves'.[6]

Yet the comment 'and ourselves' is significant. Primary group theory seems, on the evidence of troop behaviour in the First World War, to have more to do with the reason why a man will support his fellows in a course of action, than with the explanation of why a majority of those fellows should have chosen the course of action in the first place. Primary group solidarity, in other words, cuts both ways. It may produce common obedience

in Vietnam', in C. Moskos (ed.), *The American Enlisted Man* (New York, 1970), 134–56.
    [3] Moskos, 'Behavior of Combat Soldiers', pp. 135–6.
    [4] S. L. A. Marshall, *Men Against Fire* (New York, 1947), 161.
    [5] C. M. Bowra, *Memories* (1964), 90.
    [6] W. V. Tilsley, *Other Ranks* (1931), 180.

or common rebellion, but the choice between these two seems to be determined less by an impulse towards solidarity, than by the whole structure of prejudices, beliefs, and loyalties which society sets up in the minds of individuals.

The capacity for group solidarity to facilitate, quite as readily as to interdict the emergence of indiscipline, is perhaps best seen in the Australian disbandment mutinies of 1918. The units of the AIF enjoyed an intense camaraderie among the rank and file. 'Mateship', as the historian of the AIF has written, was 'a particular Australian virtue, a creed, almost a religion'.[7] In the conditions of trench warfare, mateship came to apply to all members of one's platoon rather than to a particular individual: one had to be able to trust implicitly whomsoever one was with. The intensity of the resultant group bonding was heightened by the distance from home in space and time, and the impossibility (until September 1918, when the first leave boat sailed) of home leave. In the words of one former ranker, 'we Diggers were a race apart. Long separation from Australia had seemed to cut us completely away from the land of our birth. The longer a man served, the fewer letters he got, the more he was forgotten. Our only home was our unit.'[8] A similar view was expressed by an ex-ranker of the 56th Battalion:

to every Australian soldier, his company, his battalion was his home. Here lived our truest and most trusted friends and companions, brothers who would share their last franc or crust with each other, bound together till victory or death. Home and civilian associates were only misty memories . . . It seemed as if we in the company had always been soldiers and cobbers. Away from the company one of us felt like a lost dog.[9]

Consequently, Australian units enjoyed a depth of human loyalties unknown in the British forces.[10] This was one of the reasons for their superior fighting record, which made them the shock troops of the army, but it was also one of the reasons why they alone of the units under Haig's command suffered serious mutinies of formed units whilst the war was still raging.

[7] B. Gammage, *The Broken Years* (Canberra, 1974), 101.
[8] G. D. Mitchell, *Backs to the Wall* (Sydney, 1937), 168.
[9] H. R. Williams, *The Gallant Company* (Sydney, 1933), 146.
[10] Ibid. 131.

In the British army, private soldiers were painfully aware of their own vulnerability before authority. As a private in the Guards wrote, 'wherever one more rash and intemperate than the rest has rebelled against a superior officer, the wiser and more experienced have said to him: "don't be a fool, if you go against the army the army will break you" '.[11] Australian soldiers, though, knew that their comrades would support them, and that the army could not 'break' hundreds or thousands of men. Beyond their own units, the freemasonry of the Australian forces, which bound all to answer a 'coo-ee' call for help in a brawl, worked also on a larger field. When the disbandment of the 37th Battalion was ordered in September 1918, officers and sergeants fell out from the disbandment parade according to orders, but only one private and one corporal obeyed: 'the remainder were told that, if they did not join their new units that afternoon, they would be posted as absent without leave. Being left to themselves they at once re-established strict military form in the battalion, choosing from their own number commanders to carry on temporarily the absent officers' duties.'[12]

Each of the other six battalions whose disbandments were ordered followed this example. Men from other units of the AIF supported the strike by keeping the strikers supplied with stolen rations, or with boxes of food 'lost' from their own waggon-loads as they passed near-by.[13] In the face of such solidarity, the commanders had to climb down. One of the battalions had at length been persuaded to disband by its popular brigadier, but the other six were reprieved.[14]

Examination of the two Australian mutinies not connected with disbandment, which also took place in September 1918, bears out the importance of solidarity. In one case elements of the 59th Battalion refused an order to return to the line, and in the other parts of the 1st Battalion refused an order to attack. In each case the mutiny began with one company refusing solidly to obey. The loyalties of the other companies then split, with some men joining the mutineers and others remaining obedient to their

---

[11] S. Graham, *A Private in the Guards* (1919), 7–8.
[12] C. E. W. Bean, *Official History of Australia in the War of 1914–1918* (Sydney, 1921 onwards), vi. 938–9.
[13] Williams, *Gallant Company*, pp. 290–1.
[14] P. A. Smith, *The Anzacs* (1978), 150.

officers.[15] The first step into mutiny was so momentous that it could perhaps only be undertaken by the united 'soldiers and cobbers' of a company. To join such a mutiny then became a less terrifying act.

If the mutineers did count upon members to secure them from punishment their hopes were not disappointed: both groups did in fact escape serious consequences. The exhausted men of the 59th, having rested for some hours, were then persuaded by their brigadier to march up to the line, and no subsequent action seems to have been taken against them. The 119 men of the 1st Battalion who refused to attack, were recommended by the battalion commander for the 'severest punishment'.[16] The authorities fought shy, however, of bringing this number of men to trial for mutiny, punishable in the AIF as in the British forces by the death penalty. Instead they were tried for desertion, and with one exception found guilty. However, 'fortunately the ending of hostilities caused General Monash not to enforce the penalties'.[17]

The details of the escape may have owed something to luck, but the men cannot have been unaware of the generally lax attitude towards disciplinary offences shown by the authorities in the AIF. Sympathy, shortage of men, fear of civilian reaction, and perhaps fear of the reaction of the troops themselves, all worked in this direction. The CO of the 1st Battalion, in recommending harsh measures, offered his opinion of the consequences of leniency:

I consider the lightness and suspension of sentences in the past for desertion as greatly responsible for the trouble ... Capt. Moffat informed me he had traced it all to one man in his Coy. who was a suspended sentence man and I think the same will be found in other Coys., namely men with bad records have induced the others to leave [the front line] and others have been too weak not to follow.[18]

Where one escaped so lightly, many together might escape scot free, and even the suspended sentence man might not suffer the

[15] War Diary of the 59th Bn. AIF, WO 95/3652, 5 Sept. 1918; War Diary of the 1st Bn. AIF, WO 95/3217, Sept. 1918, Appendix 'C.O.'s report to Bgd. 20.9.1918'.
[16] War Diary of the 59th Bn., Sept. 1918; War Diary of the 1st Bn., Sept. 1918, Appendix 'CO's report'.
[17] Bean, *Official History*, vi. 940.
[18] War Diary of the 1st Bn., Sept. 1918, Appendix 'CO's report'.

consequence of his actions if he could persuade others to join him.

The link between unit cohesion and the ability to organize mutiny had long been perceived by the colonial powers. Their native African units, like many Indian army regiments, deliberately mingled different, and even antagonistic, tribes and sects.[19] Similarly, were group solidarity and indiscipline truly antitheses, as primary group theory maintains, the French mutinies of 1917 would have been a strange anomaly. After more than two years in the field, units and sub-units were tightly bonded groups, like the squad depicted in Henri Barbusse's classic memoir.[20] The early casualties of the Nivelle offensive were not such as to shatter these groups. Rather it was units acting together, and not a mass of disorganized individuals, which crippled for a time the French war potential.[21] Similarly, in the Russian army in 1917, 'une solidarité de groupe unit entre eux les combattants. Ils basculent de l'obéissance à l'indiscipline par unités entières. Les actes individuels sont rares.'[22]

It is therefore only in the round that the mutinies can be understood. The French mutinies of 1917, for example, rested on a base of discontent which included anger at the military organization's failure to meet the soldier's needs. Rest and leave were inadequately provided, rations poor, monotonous, and carelessly prepared, cantonments behind the line were of the very worst sort, and officers were neglectful of that paternal solicitude which plays a large part in cementing the military group. Yet 'il est probable que ces sources de mécontentement n'eussent point donné naissance au torrent des mutineries si la méfiance de la désillusion des hommes à l'égard des méthodes offensives qu'on leur avait imposées jusqu'alors n'avait atteint un point de rupture après l'échec d'avril et du début de mai.'[23] The demands of the mutineers, the timing and location of the outbreaks, all reveal the movement as fundamentally one of protest 'contre une certaine forme de guerre'. Orders were no longer obeyed because they

[19] V. G. Kiernan, 'Colonial Africa and Its Armies', in B. Bond and I. Roy (eds.), *War and Society*, ii (1977), 34.

[20] H. Barbusse, *Under Fire*, trans. W. F. Wray (1926), *passim*.

[21] G. Pedroncini, *Les Mutineries de 1917* (Paris, 1967), 311 and *passim*.

[22] M. Ferro, 'Le Soldat russe en 1917: indiscipline, patriotisme, pacifisme et révolution', in *Annales ESC*, 26 (1977), 37.

[23] Pedroncini, *Les Mutineries*, p. 311.

were perceived as illegitimate. The '*poilu*' remained committed to the basic necessity for the war: 'les mutins en general ont . . . accepté ou promis de garder les tranchées. Ils ne voulaient pas, hors quelques exceptions, que les Allemands puissent passer.'[24] However, this necessity did not justify orders to attack under the conditions of May 1917: 'il devenait évident qu'on ne gagnerait pas la guerre en continuant de la sorte'.[25]

Pétain, when he set about restoring discipline, recognized this dual nature of discontent. On the one hand, he ensured that future offensives would not be lightly undertaken, would have realistic goals, and would be painstakingly organized with heavy weight of supporting artillery and tanks. On the other hand, he greatly increased the entitlement to leave, instituted periods of total rest, improved the food situation, and reformed the cantonments, and, not least, called upon officers to be more attentive to the welfare of their men.[26]

A sense of immunity may have helped call them forth, but the same mixed background underlay the Australian mutinies. In action almost without respite in the continuing offensive which began on 8 August 1918, the troops, by September, were close to exhaustion. In the 5th Australian Division,

men were breaking under the strain; men who had been decorated and redecorated for acts of the highest courage were now deserting it: if, that is, to creep away for a week and sleep in some dingy cellar and then to return to battalion headquarters and say, 'I was knocked up. I have been away for a sleep and a rest. I'll take whatever punishment is coming to me. I'm all right for the line again now'—if that constitutes deserting.[27]

The military group was ceasing to provide adequately for the individual, and dissatisfaction was rife throughout the division. Sergeant Stevens of the 58th Battalion recorded in his diary:

3 Sept: our strength is now very low.
6 Sept: we move on forward tomorrow. All the boys full up and done up. Hope they do not refuse to go forward.[28]

In fact, though, it was the 59th Battalion which mutinied. The

[24] Ibid.
[25] Ibid.
[26] Ibid., 235–50, 277-8.
[27] A. D. Ellis, *Story of the 5th Australian Division* (1920), 362–3.
[28] Smith, *The Anzacs*, p. 319.

battalion's medical officer reported that 'the men are one and all
suffering from excessive fatigue, loss of sleep and nervous strain.
In my opinion the limit of endurance has been reached for most
of the men.'[29]

The whole division was exhausted, but, for this battalion,
added to it was a feeling that the command was calling for
unjustifiable and fruitless sacrifices. The order to return to the
line came when the troops had experienced a thoroughly disillu-
sioning day. Having first been set 'an impossible proposition', an
attack with inadequate barrage into heavy frontal and flanking
machine-gun fire, they were set to hold a position under direct
observation, suffering gas shelling and enfilading fire. According
to Corporal Skinner,

the most disappointing feature throughout our operations so far as we
were concerned was that we were under heavy fire and suffered casualties and hadn't a sporting chance of getting into close quarters or a
suitable position to deal effectively with our enemy. Our men have good
heart for their job but these conditions were more than trying and had
an unhappy effect on the morale of men already tired through a long
period of fighting. With a fighting chance over the top and at the Hun
the spirit of troops would have been good indeed, but they found it hard
to accept our position and see the good of the work in very much of our
operations.

Sergeant Hamilton agreed: 'the most disappointing feature of the
operations was the heavy shelling the battalion was subjected to
. . . without a sporting chance of dealing with the enemy'.[30] Now,
no sooner had they arrived at their billets than they were ordered
back into the line. It seemed that they were not being treated
fairly. Only 'after the situation had been explained to them' did
they consent to obey.[31]

Similarly, in the 1st Australian Division, the mutiny of the 1st
Battalion represented only to a limited extent the consequences of
fatigue, and much more the sense that the demands being made
were unfair. The battalion commander recorded that, 'the men
have not had a hard time as we have known hard times in the
past, but shelling has been fairly constant near their dugouts and
their nerves seemed on edge and they made themselves believe

[29] War Diary of the 59th Bn., Sept. 1918, Appendix 12, p. 76.
[30] Ibid., Appendix 10, pp. 64, 71–2.
[31] Ibid., 5 Sept. 1918.

they were not fit to take part in an attack.' This state of mind brought to a head the sense of grievance at their over-use: 'I had a talk with the men, but the feeling existed that they were "not getting a fair deal" and "were doing other people's work".'[32]

The pattern appears in other armies on a larger scale. The German and Italian armies suffered a degree of disciplinary breakdown in late 1918 and late 1917 respectively. Certainly, the privations of the troops were extreme, but discipline had remained constant under these strains until a perception of futility took hold, whether in the face of the ever-growing strength of the Allies, or as a result of eleven barren battles on the Isonzo, which had only sufficed to call forth a crushing offensive to reveal the incompetence of the High Command.[33] Similarly, the disintegration of the Russian forces came not in consequence of an urgent desire to escape from the dangers and discomforts of the front, but from a growing distrust of the officer corps and a sense that the war was being continued less for defence of the homeland than to serve counter-revolutionary ends.[34]

Morale, then, was much more than the group; its constituents much more than adequate food, weapons, and comradeship. Perhaps the best definition, persuasive because of its recognition of the complexity of the subject and the infinity of variables which made morale never constant, was provided by S. L. A. Marshall on the basis of his interviews of American soldiers at every stage of active service in the Second World War:

morale is the thinking of an army. It is the whole complex body of an army's thought: the way it feels about the soil and about the people from which it springs. The way that it feels about their cause and their politics as compared with other causes and other politics. The way that it feels about its friends and allies, as well as its enemies. About its commanders and goldbricks. About food and shelter. Duty and leisure. Payday and sex. Militarism and civilianism. Freedom and slavery. Work and want. Weapons and comradeship. Bunk fatigue and drill. Discipline and disorder. Life and death. God and the devil.[35]

Well as this definition would seem to fit the facts, it is worth briefly considering two more simplistic explanations of morale

[32] War Diary of the 1st Bn., Sept. 1918, Appendix 'CO's report'.
[33] H. Dalton, *With British Guns in Italy* (1919), 138.
[34] Ferro, 'Le Soldat russe', pp. 14–39.
[35] Marshall, *Men Against Fire*, p. 158.

which crop up from time to time in writing about the First World War. Marshall's definition omits any direct reference to the question of casualties, except in so far as a unit's experience may have an impact on the way men think about the subjects which Marshall enumerates. However, there has at times been a tendency for historians of the war, speculating broadly, to assign to the record of casualties a grand causal role in mutiny which would make morale at this level a subject unrelated to the field studies of Marshall and others. John Keegan, for example, plays with the idea of a simple equation whereby an army will tolerate casualties up to a specific, predetermined limit, and then will throw over the bounds of discipline when that limit is reached. He says of First World War armies that 'collapse, mutiny, call it what you like, occurred when the number of battle deaths equalled the fighting strength of the armies at the outbreak of war. The British Army achieved its full fighting strength in 1916. It ought by rights to have collapsed in the summer of 1918. It did not. The reasons are worth exploring.'[36] John Baynes, conversely, suggests that, leaving aside episodes of incompetence or catastrophic peaks of losses, a generally high casualty rate may actually have contributed to maintaining unit morale in the First World War by ensuring a steady turnover of personnel and thereby averting a wholesale build-up of combat weariness.[37]

In fact, there is little to suggest that casualties operated so simply either steadily to destroy or to reinforce morale. They were a factor in the overall equation of morale, but only one among many. The Regular Divisions, for example, remained the best and most reliable in the British armies throughout the war, notwithstanding the fact that they served the longest and suffered the most. The 29th Division suffered a total of 94,000 casualties, enough to replace every man in its infantry and artillery about seven times over, as against an average of 39,000 for the first wave of Kitchener Divisions. Yet the 29th remained an élite division, 'the incomparable 29th . . . the most famous division in the British Army', whilst the quality of the Kitchener Divisions became distinctly uneven.[38] Similarly, no simple formula could deduce from the tale of army casualties given in Table 4 that

---

[36] *The Daily Telegraph*, 9 Sept. 1986.
[37] J. Baynes, *Morale* (1967), 100.
[38] Green, *The British Army*, pp. 2–3, 7–8, 38–9.

TABLE 4. *Battle casualties suffered 1914–1918*

Army	Total mobilized army strength	Casualties 1914–18 (excluding sickness)	% casualty rate
Germany	13,387,000	7,231,283	54.0
France	8,194,150	4,235,000	51.7
United Kingdom	5,704,416	2,535,424	44.4
Italy	5,615,000	2,197,000	39.1

Source: A. G. Butler, *The Australian Medical Services in the War 1914–1918*, iii (Melbourne, 1943), 868–80.

French and Italian disciplinary crises would precede any weakening of the cohesion of the German army. The striking feature, in fact, is the relatively small difference in casualty rates given the markedly different disciplinary histories of the armies.

Time served in an active theatre of war provides no more accurate guide. Almost two-thirds of divisions sent to active war theatres by Britain and the Dominions were serving there by September 1915.[39] By spring 1918 when the last great German offensives were launched, their service was therefore at least equal in length to that of the French armies which mutinied in spring 1917, and in many cases they had served up to a year more than those armies. Yet there was no collapse then or later.

Despite the occasional *obiter dicta* of historians, there is no short cut to understanding the morale of First World War armies. To begin to understand them, it is necessary to study the whole range of subjects which Marshall's definition of morale suggests, from the parent society and the place of the army within it to the organization of that army and the methods by which it was led.

[39] *Statistics of the Military Effort*, p. 64.

3

Patriotism and the Place of the Army in British Society

The British mass armies which in the course of four years were built up overseas were the first of their kind in history. Never before had British subjects, from the home islands or the Empire, served in such numbers. They had no tradition of conscript service which might have prepared them to accept its imposition as unexceptionable, as one of the recognized burdens of citizenship. The army, at least below officer level, had long been outside the mainstream of society, a mercenary caste in the hands of the ruling élite.[1] Distrust of this potential enemy of liberty traditionally ran strong. The growth of the popular press and, with it, of interest in the imperial campaigns; the creation of the Volunteers; and the popular nationalism of the music halls had all gone some way towards building a more popular image of the army. However, there was nothing to compare with the great national myths of 1793 in France and 1813 in Germany, which associated these armies with popular liberty and defence of the homeland; nothing either to compare with the role of the army in these States as the crucible of nationality.[2] For Britain, the Royal Navy was the bulwark against foreign oppression, as well as the friend of the people since the Civil War.

For a volunteer army, low prestige coupled with arduous foreign postings to the stations of the Empire and poor pay meant a generally poor standard of recruit, which diminished the public standing of the soldier still further. Even the poorest of civilians could feel contempt for those who wore khaki. In the slums of Salford, 'neither victory nor national pride could alter the common soldier's status one iota. With us, as with the rest of the working class, "regulars", ex-regulars and their families, stayed

[1] E. M. Spiers, *Army and Society, 1815–1914* (1980), 206; H. Cunningham, *The Volunteer Force* (1975), 95; A. R. Skelley, *The Victorian Army at Home* (1977), 243–6.
[2] E. Weber, *Peasants into Frenchmen* (1977), 298.

unquestionably "low".[3] In rural Gloucestershire, too, girls who were seen walking with a soldier might be said to have 'lost their character': soldiers might be turned away from pubs with the warning that 'we don't serve soldiers here; this is a respectable house'.[4] It is hardly surprising that, as an Inter-Departmental Committee on Physical Deterioration reported with regret in 1904, 'under present conditions, largely those who have failed in civilian life offer themselves as recruits'.[5]

The wartime volunteer and the conscript enlisted, therefore, with no very high conception of the military life. Their donning of uniform was unlikely to give them a thrill of pride; they had no great romantic commitment to the idea of soldierly duty or bearing, no passionate devotion to national icons of *élan* or *gloire*. They were unlikely, in short, to give themselves up to their role, but would remain 'individualists', 'civilians in uniform'.[6] In this they were at a great disadvantage. According to Lord Moran, the high prestige of the military way in German society helped to bolster morale when sections of that society found themselves in *feldgrau*, for 'the German soldier is considered by himself and by the nation a member of a privileged brotherhood'. For the British soldier, however, 'this pride in arms . . . was of course an abiding source of strength in the regular army in the early part of the last war. But it never took root in the citizen force upon which the burden of the struggle fell later.'[7] Military life was simply an evil to be borne, and with the coming of the Armistice, British troops could not be free of it fast enough: 'we've all had enough of this bloody war and this bloody army' was the feeling.[8] Significantly too, in the years after the war, British veterans were to form no such self-conscious grouping as the French or German: they remained 'citizens first. The military mystique in Britain, if it ever existed, lost its charm during the Cromwellian era.'[9]

In France, it is true, antimilitarist sentiment had been noisily vocal almost to the eve of the Great War. For twenty years, the

---

[3] R. Roberts, *The Classic Slum* (Manchester, 1971), 145.
[4] *The 5th Glo'ster Gazette*, 12 (May 1916), 11.
[5] Skelley, *Victorian Army*, pp. 238–9.
[6] A. Thomas, *A Life Apart* (1968), 71; R. Keable, *Standing By* (1919), 149.
[7] C. M. W. Moran, *The Anatomy of Courage* (1945), 172–3.
[8] A. Rothstein, *The Soldiers' Strikes of 1919* (1980), 55.
[9] S. R. Ward, *The War Generation: Veterans of the First World War* (New York, 1975), 34.

army had been under attack from its political masters and from the radical Left. The prestige of a military career, for officers and NCOs alike, had stood very low and, as with the British Territorials, it had proved impossible to recruit reserve officers up to strength.[10] However, there were definite limits to 'la vogue intellectuelle de l'antimilitarisme'.[11] Even within the Left, deep patriotism and an ever present awareness of the German threat curbed the vehemence of its proponents. The nation in arms, the *levée en masse*, remained a powerful and appealing image: the army had been, and might be again, much more than an instrument of oppression and reaction.[12] Moreover, it is questionable how far the vogue, which owed much to the abolition of bourgeois exemptions, extended beyond the bourgeoisie and the ideologues of the Left. Its exponents 'made but a weak impression in the working class population they aimed to convert', and among the peasants of the provinces conscript service retained on the whole a positive image.[13] Like the intense nationalist revival which superseded it after about 1911, antimilitarism remained essentially a phenomenon of the élite. Throughout the period when it demanded most attention, 'l'action de l'enseignement primaire s'est traduite au contraire, de 1879 à 1914, par une diffusion de plus large de l'idée patriotique'.[14] Patriotic sentiment had remained strong in the teaching profession, through the influence of an older generation of teachers appointed in the years after 1871, and through the work of pressure groups like the Union des Instituteurs Patriotes.

Fertile ground for this teaching was provided by the revolution in communications, which had brought the provinces out of their immemorial isolation and into the main current of French life.[15] Peasants with a dawning sense of nationality were taught that the army was the creator of the nation, its expression and its defence:

sans cette action en profondeur à laquelle l'école et le service universel

---

[10] D. Porch, *The March to the Marne* (Cambridge, 1981), 79–102 and *passim*.

[11] R. Girardet, *La Société militaire dans la France contemporaine, 1815–1939* (Paris, 1953), 245.

[12] D. Porch, 'The French Army and the Spirit of the Offensive 1900–14', in Bond and Roy (eds.), *War and Society*, i (1976), 117–20.

[13] Girardet, *La Société militaire*, pp. 213–16; Porch, *March to the Marne*, p. 113; Weber, *Peasants into Frenchmen*, p. 298.

[14] Girardet, *La Société militaire*, pp. 224–6.

[15] Weber, *Peasants into Frenchmen*, pp. 493–4.

ont simultanément contribué, sans ce reserrement constant depuis 1870 des liens de la collectivité nationale, le reveil patriotique des années 1911 et 1912 n'aurait probablement pas suffi à assurer la ferveur, l'unanimité avec lesquelles, au mois d'août 1914, l'opinion française est entrée dans la guerre.[16]

In the four years to follow, the peasants who made up the majority of the rank-and-file French infantry, and their spouses on the farms, 'like the daughters and sons of the American immigrants, would face the challenge of the First World War with a resignation born of their condition, but also with the firm certitude of neophytes'.[17]

Observers were very struck by the difference in overt patriotic sentiment between French and British troops. To an Italian observer of the French forces on the Salonika Front, it appeared that 'patriotic feeling was extremely developed among all'.[18] Similarly, for British and Dominion observers, to hear the French singing a patriotic anthem was to be impressed by their 'extraordinary passion and abandonment'; to realize 'something of what France means to Frenchmen. It is no vague abstraction, as with us, but a vivid reality.'[19] Patriotism was also strongly evident in the French troop journals, in contrast to the British.[20] The behaviour of the troops offered the same contrast. Coming out of the line, according to one British ranker,

the French . . . had their own distinctive ways; we once lay near them off Houthulst Forest, and when the French came out they would be met a mile or so back by the band and the Marseillaise and the sacred Tricolour and all that. They'd sing too, and very patriotic it sounded. Once one of our younger officers copied the idea, and we were to sing; and then about a minute later we were to stop singing. We had not got the thing right, it seemed; we had no word about the Patrie or Glory or the Fun of Dying for the War Office. We all sang with extremely improper variations to the tune of 'We Wanted to Go Home'.[21]

All the forces under Haig's command seem to have displayed

[16] Girardet, *La Société militaire*, pp. 245–6.
[17] Weber, *Peasants into Frenchmen*, p. 94.
[18] L. Villari, *The Macedonian Campaign* (1922), 66.
[19] O. E. Burton, *The Silent Division* (1935), 15; V. J. Seligman, *The Salonika Sideshow* (1919), 180.
[20] Audoin-Rouzeau, *Les Combattants*, pp. 203–8.
[21] J. Gibbons, *Roll On Next War* (1935), 92.

this markedly sceptical attitude towards patriotism. The Canadian Expeditionary Force would sooner sing anything than patriotic songs.[22] The AIF was 'too British' to base its battle spirit, like the French, upon patriotism.[23] The BEF had no 'self conscious patriotism among the rank and file . . . The word itself meant nothing to them.'[24] The journal of the 7th Canadians satirized this silence: 'nobody seems to have the nerve to admit that he enlisted for patriotic reasons; but the party who said he joined up to get a clasp knife and razor must have been pretty keen.'[25]

Patriotism there was, of course, but more often it took the form of a deep if quiet affection for the localities from which men came, and for the symbols of their culture. Philip Gibbs noted that, 'any allusion to "The Empire" left them cold, unless they confused it with the Empire music hall, when their hearts warmed to the name.'[26] Their 'Anglia Irridenta' lay in 'the football fields and factories, the music halls and seaside excursions that they talked of, and now hoped to see once again'.[27]

But if the British and Dominion troops did not wear their patriotism on their sleeves, in large part this was because they were so secure in their feelings of national superiority. General Ironside wrote of them that their 'kindly but marked contempt for all "foreigners" provided [them] with an armour which it is difficult to pierce'.[28] Similarly, an officer of the 17th and 51st Divisions considered that 'they had implicit belief in their own superiority over every other country in the world. This was the one great factor in their make-up as soldiers.'[29]

Many elements contributed to this assumption of superiority: the insularity of an island people; the generations of economic pre-eminence under Victoria; the influence, however imperfectly transmitted, of Whig teachings about the special providence at work in British history; an awareness of the Empire and of military success, fostered by boys' papers and the popular press.[30] In

[22] *The 20th Gazette*, 4 (May 1915), 13–14.
[23] Williams, *Gallant Company*, pp. 272–3. Cf. Bean, *Official History*, vii. 36.
[24] P. Gibbs, *Realities of War* (1929), 57.
[25] *The Listening Post*, 29 (Dec. 1917), 30.
[26] Gibbs, *Realities of War*, p. 57.
[27] Mottram, *Spanish Farm Trilogy*, p. 515.
[28] E. M. Halliday, *The Ignorant Armies* (1961), 116.
[29] W. N. Nicholson, *Behind the Lines* (1939), 147.
[30] P. Howarth, *Play Up and Play the Game* (1973), 73–5; P. A. Dunae, 'Boys'

the Dominions, schools vigorously preached the message of pride in race.[31] The settler societies saw themselves as living exemplars of the Anglo-Saxon (sometimes amended to Anglo-Celtic) 'civilizing mission' and destiny for rule. At the same time, as small and isolated communities which felt themselves to be under threat, they embraced the more enthusiastically reassuring notions of innate superiority. But above all, at least in Britain itself,

it was at the halls you learnt your patriotism, were told you had a navy, a British Navy, which kept your foes at bay, that a Little British Army went a damned long way, that the soldiers of the Queen (or later the King) always won, and that you couldn't beat the boys of the bulldog breed who made Old England's name. And you believed it all.[32]

Night after night they put over their creed that 'ours was the finest country in the world; one Britisher was equal to half a dozen foreigners, the British soldier and the British sailor were the salt of the earth and "we don't want to fight but, by Jingo, if we do!" '[33]

All this might not be sufficient to take in the working classes and make them imperialists against their interests, but it did represent a sustained inflation of the national self-esteem. And if the music hall stereotype of the Briton coloured his perception of himself, equally inevitably the comic stereotypes of foreigners helped to establish his attitude toward them. The 12th Battalion East Surrey Regiment, on its way to join the Italians after their disaster at Caporetto, regaled itself on the journey south with the song of Antonio and his ice-cream cart, a music hall hit, and great was the surprise and disappointment of the men to discover, upon arrival, that the country was not peopled by the ice-cream sellers and chestnut vendors of popular conception. For others, the move was only rumoured, so the image of the Italians as a race of Antonios remained undispelled, and the reaction to

Literature and the Idea of Empire 1870–1914', *Victorian Studies*, 24 (1980), 105–21; J. Morris, *Heaven's Command* (1973), 431.

[31] S. G. Firth, 'Social Values in the New South Wales Primary School 1880–1914: An Analysis of School Texts', *Melbourne Studies in Education* (Melbourne, 1970), 123–59; E. P. Malone, 'The New Zealand School Journal and the Imperial Ideology', *New Zealand Journal of History*, 7 (1973), 3–12; J. N. I. Dawes and L. L. Robson, *Citizen to Soldier* (Melbourne, 1977), 44–6, 55.

[32] W. M. Pope, *Carriages at Eleven* (1947), 211.

[33] J. B. Booth, *A Pink 'Un Remembers* (1937), 118.

Caporetto was to look forward to giving 'those ice-cream men the bird'.[34]

It remained to be seen whether a patriotism so unrealistically based could provide a strong sustaining force. The reality of war would chip away the jingoistic veneer from any creed, but still the patriotic creed in the French forces was a consciously articulated, socially enforced and fostered one, with its codewords and anthems which brought it vividly to mind. Moreover, the facts of the situation gave strong reinforcement to the frame which it provided for the struggle and suffering. According to the historian of the French troop journals, 'leur patriotisme a poussé dans l'expérience quotidienne de la guerre des racines nouvelles qui donnent une spécificité certaine au sentiment national des combattants. La défense d'un sol, d'une terre avec laquelle ils se sentent en communion presque charnelle fait partie des éléments qui ont donné un sens aux souffrances endurées.'[35]

The French troops stood amid the ruins of their northern *départements*, fighting to liberate their fellow countrymen and expel an invader who had brought destruction on them for the second time in half a century. The British and Dominion troops had no such clear reason to fight. A ranker in the 55th (West Lancashire) Division speculated 'how much more seriously the company would take the war were the Salient round Preston, or Bolton, or Manchester',[36] but it was unalterably around Ypres. The importance of the distinction can hardly be exaggerated:

on attaquait votre pays, vous le défendiez. Idée simple, mais idée forte . . . Cette réponse au 'Pourquoi tient-on?' si peu belliqueuse qu'elle n'est que l'autre face du goût commun de la paix, n'est peut-être méme plus la réponse à une question. Elle remplace la question elle-même. Mais elle en pose aussitôt une autre, celle que le même auteur se posait à propos des Anglais qui se battaient à côté de nous, mais en terre étrangère . . . Comment . . . peuvent-ils continuer? . . . Ceux qui n'ont pas senti cette différence-là, n'ont pas compris la guerre.[37]

Few of the front-line troops, French or British, could share in

[34] J. A. Aston and C. M. Duggan, *The History of the 12th (Bermondsey) Bn. East Surrey Regt.* (1936), 180; A. Smith, *Four Years on the Western Front* (1922), 283.

[35] Audoin-Rouzeau, *Les Combattants*, p. 204.

[36] Tilsley, *Other Ranks*, p. 202.

[37] J. Meyer, *La Vie quotidienne des soldats pendant la grande guerre* (Hachette, 1966), 263–4.

the extravagant Germanophobia of the civilians. The similarities in the plight of the infantrymen of both sides made it all too easy to sympathize with the plight of the man opposite. The sight or sound of the enemy going about everyday tasks, seeking amusement, singing, or talking, confirmed the impression of common humanity, which press and cartoonists at home were doing everything to deny. The discovery in army life of new enemies of the infantrymen—the staff, the supply troops, the military police, even the civilians themselves—and the awareness that the soldiers in the trenches opposite were similarly victimized, added to the sense of fellow-feeling. On top of all this, there was the sheer impossibility of acting upon any sense of burning hatred in a situation where, if life was to go on at all, provocation had to be avoided for the greater part of the time, and even tacit agreements worked out with 'Incarnate Evil'.[38] Understandably, hatred withered.

Still, a residual hatred was present in the French troop journals which was not to be found in the British. Reviews of the journals commented on the fact, noting that, in contrast to the French productions, 'the British trench journalist has as little to say of the Boche, generally speaking, as of mud, blood and khaki'.[39] On the French side, 'certes, l'image de l'adversaire s'améliore de façon continue dans la presse des tranchées entre 1914 et 1918. Celle-ci se montre beaucoup moins sévère à la fin de guerre qu'au début, mais en dépit de cette modération, une image negative de l'ennemi prévaut jusqu'à la fin du conflit.'[40] On the British side, *The Outpost* noted in 1917, 'the Hun' was 'a popular word with the pulpit and with part of the press'; 'the Bosche' was 'a word much affected by the officers'; but among the men the talk was of 'Johnny' or 'the Allemand', or quite kindly of 'Old Fritz'.[41] Far from vituperation, the British private soldier was apt to speak of the German 'almost affectionately; Old Fritz, or Old Jerry! Might be an ally!'.[42] There is some evidence that more of the Dominion troops, particularly among the Australians, retained an active hostility towards the Germans, untempered by respect

---

[38] Ashworth, *Trench Warfare, passim.*
[39] *The Times Literary Supplement*, 12 Oct. 1916, 481–2; *Iodine Chronicle*, 15 (Easter 1918), 4.
[40] Audoin-Rouzeau, *Les Combattants*, p. 204.
[41] *The Outpost*, 5/4 (Aug. 1917), 121.
[42] Tilsley, *Other Ranks*, p. 8.

because of their own prowess.[43] The bulk of the British Empire armies, however, 'had no feeling of hatred for their enemies', and in the absence of such feeling were the more likely to question whether the struggle was worthwhile.[44]

[43] Gammage, *Broken Years*, p. 225.
[44] R. Aldington, *Death of a Hero* (1929), 291; W. H. A. Groom, *Poor Bloody Infantry* (1976), 71; C. Dawson, *Living Bayonets* (1919), 32–3.

4

Organization of the British and Dominion Forces

Britain entered the war with nothing approaching the 3.5 million trained men of France, or the 4 million of Germany. Even counting the amateur Territorials, army and reserves came to hardly 750,000 men.[1] Bearing the brunt alone while new units trained, this small asset rapidly diminished to the point where it was almost completely wiped out.

The effect was to give the British and Dominion forces the demoralizing sense of being amateurs up against professionals.[2] Their own lack of training, and that of their officers, put a brake upon their offensive success, and led to costly mistakes, most notoriously the first day on the Somme. Even when all went smoothly, German infiltration tactics were beyond them, and they had to be committed to the attack in vulnerable masses. In defence too they were slow to abandon a strongly held front line in favour of more flexible defensive systems, and they paid the price in casualties.[3]

No less serious, British units lacked any significant core of Regular soldiers around which to cohere. This was a serious handicap for, with their coolness, their military skills, their paternal authority, their habituation to army ways, and their knowledgeability about how to make the best of conditions, veterans were an invaluable leaven to the whole. The professional German NCOs, in contrast, were to remain throughout the war the backbone of that army.[4] In the British armies, the small residue of Regulars, and the spirit they passed on, was sufficient to preserve for the Regular Divisions their superiority over other

---

[1] Edmonds, *History of the Great War*, 1914, i. 15; *Statistics of the Military Effort*, p. 30.

[2] Tilsley, *Other Ranks*, p. 202.

[3] Edmonds, *History of the Great War*, 1915, vol. ii, p. viii; 1916, i. 490–2; 1916, ii. 570–1; 1917, i. 554–5; 1918, i, p. vii; 1918, ii. 479–82.

[4] J. Terraine, *White Heat: The New Warfare 1914–1918* (1982), 51.

divisions, and to indicate how much was lost by the shortage of trained men.

The absence of such natural shapers of opinion might perhaps be counteracted, to some extent, by the importation of civilian structures of authority, and this was a feature of a proportion of both Kitchener and first-line Territorial Battalions. Among the first-line Territorials, there might be battalions like the 1/5th Royal Warwickshires which 'had a B.S.A. Company and a Mitchell and Butler's Company with the chief salesman as its colour-sergeant'. Such a situation was by no means unique, but it 'was the ideal and was all too rarely attained'.[5] Some basis of common experience outside the army may explain the reputation of first-line Territorial units for a friendlier spirit and more human relationship between the ranks, but the men of the second-line Territorials had far less in common. From the outset, many such units had only the most notional links with their theoretical locality. The 2/4th (Ross and Cromarty) Seaforth Highlanders, for example, was formed with 460 citizens of Manchester in its ranks.[6]

In the Kitchener Divisions, the units which embodied some element of the civilian community structure were the locally raised battalions, bringing together neighbours, workmates, or friends, officered by prominent local men. In all, 142 of the 557 Kitchener 'Service' battalions formed to fight overseas were locally raised.[7] However, by no means all of these were truly local in character. The 14th (Carnarvonshire and Anglesey) Battalion Royal Welch Fusiliers 'typifies the "local" battalion which lowered its standards to fill its ranks. When it embarked for France that December [1915] only 24 per cent of its personnel came from Canarfonshire, 9 per cent from Anglesey, 26 per cent from other areas of North Wales, 20 per cent from South Wales and 21 per cent from England.'[8] As for the battalions raised by the War Office, these had in theory a geographical basis of recruitment, although too broad to give them the community character of a genuine Pals battalion. In practice, however,

[5] C. E. Carrington, *Soldier from the Wars Returning* (1965), 101.
[6] M. M. Haldane, *History of the 4th Bn. Seaforth Highlanders* (1928), 316.
[7] C. Hughes, 'The New Armies', in I. F. W. Beckett and K. Simpson (eds.), *A Nation in Arms* (Manchester, 1985), 106–7.
[8] Ibid. 116.

county affiliation was, even from the outset, little respected. A recruit to the 6th Battalion Duke of Cornwall's Light Infantry, for example, found himself reporting at Bodmin 'with a hundred nice quiet country lads from Poplar and Fulham and other remote West Country villages'.[9]

Counting in all the first-line Territorials with the locally raised Kitchener units, this most generous estimate would put the battalions with a true sense of civilian community at less than 30 per cent of all those British and Dominion battalions serving in active war theatres. In fact, though, such an estimate would be misleading, for it takes no account of casualties. There was not a separate reserve battalion for each battalion in the field. Originally it was intended that the third-line Territorials should supply drafts to the first line and second line whilst a handful of Reserve and Special Reserve units kept up the strength of all the other battalions. Inevitably, therefore, replacements even from the outset often did not share the particular characteristics of the original formations.

Moreover, as time went on, demarcation became even less rigid. After the opening of the Somme offensive, even cross-drafting between regiments became common. The staggering losses suffered by many battalions in the assaults of 1916 brought home to the authorities the drawbacks of organizing units on so narrow a social or geographical basis: whole communities saw their menfolk decimated. Drafting policy began deliberately to 'nationalize' the army. From September 1916, the New Army reserves at home were reclassified as training reserve battalions, shorn of regimental connections. All recruits under the Derby Scheme and subsequent Military Service Acts were recruited for general service and allocated as required.[10] The sheer difficulty of administering any segregated system of reinforcement, with the teeming population of the base camps and the pressing needs of front-line battalions, accentuated the trend. A London first-line Territorial Battalion, the Queen Victoria Rifles, was rebuilt after a tour of duty on the Somme with drafts from seventeen different units.[11] The distinctive character of battalions like the 1st Brad-

[9] *The Red Feather*, 1 (Dec. 1915), 9.
[10] I. Beckett, 'The Territorial Force', in Beckett and Simpson (eds.), *A Nation in Arms*, 137–8, 146–7.
[11] F. Hawkings, *From Ypres to Cambrai* (1973), 103.

ford Pals disappeared: 'we had so many casualties that we were all strangers after that. The new men who came were fed up, they were conscripts, they didn't want to come, and they didn't want to fight. Things were never the same any more.'[12]

For all battalions, Territorial or Pals, the effect on cohesion and *esprit de corps* was deleterious. By 1918, 'in every platoon different dialects could be heard, so that . . . even the company lacked cohesion'.[13] In the 1st Battalion Kensington Rifles, 'except between the few original Kensingtons left, the old esprit de corps was practically non-existent, and even these few of us were now war-weary'.[14] An identity founded upon locality was uniquely susceptible to destruction by these means.

The British and Dominion forces seem to have gained relatively little, then, from the peculiarities of the Pals battalions and the first-line Territorials. By contrast, they suffered much from the improvised nature of some two-thirds of all battalions. These lacked any tradition as units, and the authorities sought to compensate by associating at least the British units with the great historic regiments. The British regiment was unique in that, because it was not a tactical unit, it was capable of indefinite expansion to incorporate all the wartime recruits in new battalions. All British infantrymen therefore found themselves included in one of the old regiments, and associated with the traditions by which each proclaimed its present uniqueness and links to glorious predecessors. According to the advocates of this system, it added to the obligation of not letting down present comrades the charge of not disgracing those previous generations, who had each in turn handed down as a trust the honour of the regiment: the soldier was to belong to and be bound by a historical, as well as a physical, community. At the same time, possession of distinctive traditions was to heighten present *esprit de corps*.

Front-line battalions of all types established journals with the explicit aim of promoting regimental esprit. Only in the journals of the Regular battalions, however, was this effort at all sustained. Otherwise, after a nod towards regimental traditions in the first-issue editorial or the CO's introduction, these

[12] Brown, *Tommy Goes to War*, p. 194.
[13] H. Hill, *Retreat from Death* (1936), 340.
[14] J. F. Tucker, *Johnny Get Your Gun* (1978), 110.

magazines in practice concerned themselves exclusively, in their grievances, jokes, and praise, with the community of the battalion.

This was inevitable. The New Army battalions had small cadres, and later none, from the Regulars. They might, like the battalion Guy Chapman describes, have no officers who had ever served with the regiment: 'in consequence it learned nothing of the traditions of its name—few could have told you anything of Alma or Albuera'.[15] Even in war, the men of the citizen army were not fertile ground to receive the teaching. Territorial and Kitchener alike, they had neither the professional pride, nor the sense of army community, which had fed the rivalries of the old army: 'had they been soldiers an appeal to the "glorious traditions of the regiment" might have got them . . . But they were not soldiers. They were, as the sergeant-major never tired of pointing out, civilians in uniform.'[16]

The regimental system had worked in the old army, where there was time for its principles to be inculcated, and where the battalions of the regiment (normally two) had a real association. It seems to have worked even in the wartime Regular battalions, where the surviving 'Contemptibles' passed on the spirit to the Kitchener men who came to fill the ranks.[17] But it could not work in the majority of units in the new conditions, where some regiments might swell to thirty battalions or more, most of which had never seen each other. To the new recruits, the creed of regiment was hardly more than a fiction, and this, says Moran, was their great point of difference from the Regulars, who had 'implanted in the very marrow of the men the creed of the Regiment which blossomed into a living faith till nothing else mattered'.[18] In the absence of this 'living faith', 'a dull spit and polish discipline was our principal inheritance from Regular Army and regimental traditions'.[19]

There was one further peculiarity of the British and Dominion

[15] G. P. Chapman, *A Passionate Prodigality* (1965), 4. For the paucity of Regular officers see K. Simpson, 'The Officers', in Beckett and Simpson (eds.), *A Nation in Arms*, pp. 71–4.
[16] A. Thomas, *A Life Apart* (1968), 71.
[17] R. Graves, *Goodbye to All That* (1980), 78; P. Croney, *Soldier's Luck* (Ilfracombe, 1965), 93.
[18] Moran, *Anatomy of Courage*, p. 171.
[19] Hill, *Retreat from Death*, p. 340.

forces, arising from the late introduction of conscription everywhere but Australia, where it was never introduced at all. All units had started out as units of volunteers, but it is questionable whether this fact had any very significant effect upon morale and discipline one way or the other. There were forces working in both directions. In a sense, the volunteer had entered freely into a contract, and might therefore feel himself constrained to hold up his end of the contract, but he might equally feel entitled to take action if the army did not do likewise. The Australians certainly give the lie to any idea that volunteers are necessarily obedient, but the British record shows that neither need they be rebellious.

Equally ambiguous in effect was the fact that the late introduction of conscription tended in at least some cases to sour relations within units once conscripts started to arrive. Like the home press, the troop press had for two years been inveighing bitterly against the shirkers, labelling them as cowards, and calling for them to be put at the posts of greatest danger in order to save the lives of 'better men'.[20] Now volunteers and conscripts had to live and work together in situations of the greatest stress. Understandably there was hostility and mistrust,[21] but the significance of this was mitigated by the fact that at the same time that discontent was increased and commitment undermined, the solidarity essential to action was weakened. The late introduction of conscription, in short, cannot be said to have given any clear impulse either to discipline or to indiscipline. The reasons for the disciplinary record of the British and Dominion forces need to be sought elsewhere than in the peculiarities of their organization.

[20] *The Minden Magazine*, 1 (Nov. 1915), 13–14, and 3 (Jan. 1916), 13; *London Scottish Regimental Gazette*, 235 (July 1915), 162; *The New Church Times*, 1/1 (Apr. 1916), 8.
[21] W. L. Andrews, *Haunting Years* (1930), 242–3; C. E. Montague, *Disenchantment* (Westport, Conn., 1978), 98–9; A. D. Haslam, *Cannon Fodder* (1930), 190.

5

Discipline and Relationships between the Ranks

For all that pre-war Regular soldiers in the British and Dominion armies were very thin on the ground relative to the situation in the other combatant armies, the influence of Regular army ways was very strong among British troops. Loyalty to the idea of the regiment may have been too arcane a tradition to communicate itself readily to wartime soldiers, but more practical traditions made themselves felt from the outset. Many of these sprang from the peculiar nature of the pre-war army.

As an all-volunteer force, raised by a society in which the private soldier was still something of a pariah, the British Regular army before 1914 had to rely for most of its recruits on the least able, the social misfits, and the most disadvantaged. In the period 1907–13, 70 per cent of recruits had been unable to pass the educational standards normally set for 11-year-old children.[1] For the management of this material, the army had evolved its characteristic disciplinary code, based upon the precepts of cleanliness, total obedience, and keeping the men always busy. As applied to the citizen army of the Great War, however, this appeared to many men 'a travesty of discipline . . . a notorious tragic farce'.[2] The army continued to behave 'as if a small gentlemanly officer class still had to make soldiers out of undergardeners' runaway sons and slum lads known to the police'.[3] New officers in training were taught the old system with all its 'total lack of comprehension of the ordinary man's psychology; in an army where all the ranks were criminals or seducers, and the officers all bloody bullies, the regiment could only be kept up like

---

[1] Spiers, *Army and Society*, p. 64. According to a former officer in the Cameronians, rank-and-file recruits to the regiment in the years before 1914 had an average mental age of 10; Baynes, *Morale*, p. 157.

[2] H. D. Gauld, *Truth from the Trenches* (1922), p. 31.

[3] Priestley, *Margin Released*, pp. 134–7. Cf. C. Packer, *Return to Salonika* (1964), 35.

this; nowadays such treatment engenders sheer hatred and makes men give the smallest they can without being caught'.[4]

It was not in its recourse to field punishment or the firing squad that this discipline was unique. The French, for example, were not markedly less severe, and the total of 346 British and Dominion military executions during the war must be set in the context of expeditionary forces overseas almost three million strong at their peak.[5] The threat of the death penalty did not deter the French mutinies, and British and Dominion memoirists overwhelmingly assert that it played no part in holding them or their comrades to their duty: 'the rest of us did not need the example, and the poor fellows who were shot for the most part could not help what they did. I doubt if any man ever did his duty from fear of being shot.'[6] Certainly the German army was able to turn in a most impressive performance, despite all privations and an increasingly unfavourable balance of *matériel*, whilst carrying out only forty-eight death sentences in the course of the war.[7]

British Regular army discipline was more uniquely characterized by its constant emphasis upon spit and polish, 'bull', and the rigid separation of the ranks. Other armies lacked the peculiar social background which had given rise to this tradition. In the French army, the British obsession with 'bull' was almost entirely lacking. An English subaltern remembered watching its crack XX Corps, 'the Iron Corps', march past, with its ramshackle transport and its tatterdemalion men, hardly any two dressed alike: 'to the British soldier, trained in tidiness, order and discipline of spit and polish, their ways were a revelation and a constant source of amusement'.[8] The *poilus* were literally the 'hairy ones', while the British army insisted on daily shaving. Yet, funny as the apparition might be when encountered on line of march, the effect of the British army's faith in spit and polish was greatly to antagonize the ordinary infantryman: 'it never

[4] A. G. West, *Diary of a Dead Officer* (1919), 38.

[5] Pedroncini, *Les Mutineries*, p. 3; *Statistics of the Military Effort*, pp. 64, 648–9.

[6] E. G. Black, *I Want One Volunteer* (Toronto, 1965), 28–9; R. Feilding, *War Letters to a Wife* (1929), 375; Gladden, *Ypres 1917*, p. 11.

[7] M. van Crefeld, *Fighting Power: German and U.S. Army Performance 1939–45* (1983), 113.

[8] R. B. T. Kelly, *A Subaltern's Odyssey* (1980), 88–9. Cf. Villari, *The Macedonian Campaign*, p. 65; D. V. Kelly, *39 Months with the Tigers 1915–1918* (1930), 17.

failed to annoy the rank and file who believed it made no contribution to winning the war and was designed only to rile them'.[9] It was symptomatic of an approach to leadership which placed heavy emphasis on strict control from above even at the cost of alienating the sympathies of the led.

The contrast with French practice was observed by the troop journals. According to *The Invicta Gazette*, 'the French army is trained on quite a different system from the British. The French, perhaps the most truly democratic race on earth, have nothing in their methods to correspond with the strict etiquette obtaining in the British army, nor is there so great a gap between their commissioned and non-commissioned ranks.'[10] A British ranker, who served six months in a French camouflage section, reported in *The Outpost* that

rank has no barrier in this army, and, from Papa Joffre down, the commanders are all fatherly towards their men . . . The officer [is] smart in appearance, polite, ready to listen, ready to help. If you are a ranker you are made welcome right away by the friendly handshake, and rank stands aside. If you meet him on business, you will be asked to dine with him. Try this in our army—![11]

One should beware of the tendency to set up an idealized comparison in order to highlight the perceived deficiencies in the British army. The *poilus* certainly did not feel that their officers fully shared their lot, or that there was a perfect comradeship between them.[12] But still there does seem to have been less of the caste spirit in the French army. Even the comparatively free and easy Canadians were struck by the egalitarianism of the French forces: 'there was here none of that class distinction which had galled free-born Canucks . . . The poilu would address his superior officer as mon colonel or mon capitaine and was addressed in return as mon vieux, mon brave or mon enfant—and we never noticed anything disrespectful or patronizing in the relationship.'[13]

[9] E. N. Gladden, *The Somme 1916* (1974), 81. Cf. A. Lambert, *Over the Top* (1930), 70; J. T. Biscoe, *Gunner Subaltern 1914–1918* (1971), 62.

[10] *The Invicta Gazette*, 4 (Oct. 1916), 8–9.

[11] *The Outpost*, 7/2 (Aug./Sept.) 1918, 65.

[12] D. Englander, 'The French Soldier, 1914–1918', *French History*, I (1987), 59–60.

[13] F. W. Noyes, *Stretcher Bearers at the Double* (Toronto, 1936), 164.

The British soldier did not have to look so far for a comparison. Almost all Australian officers were promoted from the ranks, and no marked privileges or code of military etiquette divided them from their erstwhile equals:

'Journey's End', with its five company officers sitting together in a front-line dugout could never have been written of an Australian company. Rather would you have seen each platoon officer glumly feeding from his mess tin among his men, the company commander sitting in solitary glory. I have often had my rum issue swiped by some dissolute private when my back was turned. And cigarettes—blazes! While I had one left, the platoon considered that they had an option on it.[14]

Discipline was equally different from that of the British forces. When the Australians

came out of the line they came out like tired men who had finished a job of work; you would find them dropping out independently, and sleeping by the roadside in twos and threes just as they fell. Then in the next day or so they would get up and stroll along and rejoin their units. But we had to come out like imitation Grenadier Guards, all in our proper fours and all rifles at the correct slope. They used to make public fun of us, and we used to hurl back insults at them.[15]

Not only would they not stand for seeing their own men tied up on Field Punishment Number One, but they would set free any Tommies whom they found undergoing this 'crucifixion'. Not only would they spurn spit and polish on rest, but they might liberate their more passive British comrades from like suffering by disrupting their parades.[16] All this their own officers learnt to accept:

after breakfast I put my head outside my hut and rap an order. Do I see men running to obey? No. We are Australians. There are curses and growls everywhere . . . and in about a half-hour the men are on parade. I know all about it so I always call out half an hour before I really want them. Then a job is given them. Do they smartly obey? No. They gather in cliques and finally slouch off, swearing and smoking.[17]

When the British infantryman looked at his Dominion com-

[14] Mitchell, *Backs to the Wall*, p. 122; Bean, *Official History*, iii. 53–4.

[15] J. Gibbons, *Roll On Next War* (1935), 91–2.

[16] D. Black, *Red Dust* (1931), 227; Tilsley, *Other Ranks*, pp. 233–4; L. Macdonald, *They Called It Passchendaele* (1978), 68–9.

[17] Gammage, *Broken Years*, p. 121.

rades, he was understandably struck by these differences. A ranker in the Royal Welch Fusiliers, on first encounter with Australian troops, noted 'the excellent spirit of comradeship between officers and men'.[18] When Anzacs or Canadians appeared in the British troop journals, it was in stories illustrative of their free and easy attitude towards discipline: the officer bucked to receive an Anzac's salute, the Canadian soldier touched for a loan by his major, the Australian officer briefing his men: 'Now boys, these English staff officers are coming to size us up today. So look smart . . . And look here, for the love of Heaven, don't call me Alf.'[19] Consequently, when the British troops sought for an explanation of the greater success of the Dominion forces, which had established them as the army's shock troops, they found it in this feature. The variance was explained as arising from the 'ample communication between officers and men' in the 'practically classless Commonwealth forces': 'they did not pretend to have any discipline; they did not submerge their identity in rules and regulations; they simply fought'.[20] And when they fought, they fought superbly: 'in action there were no finer troops in the world, for the simple reason that their spirit and initiative had full play and were not curbed and twisted and beaten down within the narrow compass of pre-historic rules that men of sense and intelligence openly jeered at'.[21] The Anzacs themselves were only too ready to confirm this condemnation of the old system.[22]

There were those who held the opinion that, for all its inanities, this discipline of unthinking obedience lay at the root of the British, and to a lesser extent Dominion, armies' endurance.[23] Certainly the disciplinary record of these armies, set against that of most of the other armies that fought in the war, was remarkable, and there was inevitably a temptation to connect this peculiarity with the peculiarities of the disciplinary systems. The

---

[18] F. Richards, *Old Soldiers Never Die* (1933), 251.

[19] *The Invicta Gazette*, 10 (Apr. 1917), 16; *F.S.R.*, 1 (Sept./Oct. 1915), 15; *The 5th Glo'ster Gazette*, 6 (Sept. 1915), 2.

[20] Groom, *Poor Bloody Infantry*, p. 24; F. Gray, *Confessions of a Private* (Oxford, 1920), 42.

[21] Gauld, *Truth from the Trenches*, p. 31.

[22] Bean, *Official History*, ii. 1081–8; Gammage, *Broken Years*, pp. 239–41; F. M. Cutlack (ed.), *War Letters of General Monash* (Sydney, 1935), 66; Burton, *Silent Division*, p. 193.

[23] For example, Graham, *Private in the Guards*, pp. 17–20.

Australian mutinies apart, the remainder of the British and Dominion armies did not suffer the mutiny of a single formed military unit in any active theatre in the course of the war. The only collective indiscipline on any scale, on which in consequence great attention has been lavished and a popular mythology erected, were the riots staged by the amorphous drafts at the bases against the conditions experienced there or against transfer from their parent formations.[24]

Moreover, whereas the French mutinies of 1917 had been prefigured by a rising wave of indiscipline, which already in 1916 had seen serious cases tried by courts martial almost double, and desertions more than treble, over the previous year,[25] the statistics of British military crime show no such clearly developing trend. Indeed, the rate of courts martial per thousand men overseas actually fell over time.[26] As Haig noted in 1918, 'really the absence of crime in this army is quite wonderful'.[27] It becomes clear why the disciplinary record of the Australians, who had nine times as many men in prison per thousand as the British in March 1918, so vexed and angered him, and one may see in it a sign of the trouble to follow.[28]

One can understand the search for explanations, but if there was a connection between the army's harsh disciplinary code and its good disciplinary record, then it was certainly a limited and ambiguous one. The argument is to some extent circular: it says in effect that discipline did not collapse because discipline would not allow it. But discipline is essentially a matter of consent. S. L. A. Marshall, whose field researches as a member of the American army's historical division in the Second World War gave him a uniquely valuable body of evidence and experience, concluded that it is 'one of the oldest myths in the military book that morale comes from discipline . . . The process is precisely the reverse . . . true discipline is the product of morale.'[29] This was most

[24] D. Gill and G. Dallas, 'Mutiny at Etaples Base in 1917', *Past and Present*, 69 (Nov. 1975), 88–112; Calais Base War Diary, PRO, WO 95/4018, 3 Apr. 1918.
[25] G. Pedroncini, 'Le Moral de l'armée française en 1916', in *Verdun 1916: actes du colloque international sur la bataille de Verdun* (Verdun 1976), 159–73; de la Gorce, *French Army*, p. 127.
[26] *Statistics of the Military Effort*, pp. 64, 643, 661, 663, 666.
[27] R. Blake (ed.), *The Private Papers of Douglas Haig 1914–1918* (1952), 291.
[28] Bean, *Official History*, v. 30.
[29] Marshall, *Men Against Fire*, pp. 158–9.

clearly shown by the soldiers' strikes which broke out after the
Armistice, among battalions which had been loyal throughout the
war, occasioned by parades, route marches, the state of men's
boots, in fact by any minor thing.[30] Obedience had been given by
consent as long as the war lasted, and now that consent was
withdrawn. The real question is why consent had been given.

There were those who, applying the old comforting aphorism
about Waterloo and the playing fields of Eton, saw the answer in
the role of the public-school subalterns. According to R. C. Sherriff, 'without raising the public school boy officer onto a pedestal,
it can be said with certainty that it was they who played the vital
part in keeping the men good humoured and obedient in the face
of their interminable ill-treatment and well-nigh insufferable
ordeals'.[31] Public-school officers were, however, in a poor position to judge their own importance to their men. Firstly, they
were predisposed to take a particular view. The public-school
man's carefully inculcated belief in 'school' ran deep. A creed had
been preached to him throughout his formative years, with an
intensity and pervasiveness which has been compared to the tech-
niques of brainwashing: the public school was an educational
cynosure, a nursery of leaders of men who effortlessly stood out
above their fellows, of men reared to give the rule to their social
inferiors and to the world.[32] This came on top of the normal
tendency, revealed by statistical studies of the American army in
the Second World War, for officers to be confused by enforced
deference and to build up an exaggerated impression of the
esteem in which they were held by the ranks.[33] The immense gulf
which separated officers and men in the British army of the First
World War can only have reinforced this tendency to misjudge.

Some other-ranks certainly saw little special about public-
school officers:

there was one rather queer thing that struck me about officers. They
used in the old days to say of the Public Schools that, while they might

[30] T. H. Wintringham, *Mutiny* (1936); Rothstein, *Soldiers' Strikes*, pp. 68–75;
H. M. Urquhart, *The History of the 16th Bn. (Canadian Scottish) C.E.F. in the Great
War 1914–1919* (Toronto, 1932), 326; D. Morton, '"Kicking and Complaining":
Demobilisation Riots in the Canadian Expeditionary Force 1918–1919', *Canadian
Historical Review*, 61 (1980), 334–60.
[31] G. A. Panichas (ed.), *Promise of Greatness* (1968), 152.
[32] R. Wilkinson, *The Prefects* (1964), 5, 42.
[33] S. A. Stouffer (ed.), *The American Soldier*, i (Princeton, 1949), 395–7.

turn out a lad unfit to earn a living and ignorant of almost everything beyond the classics and Kelly's Keys to the classics, at least that lad would be of the officer caste; and that if ever the Great War came, there amongst the old Public School ties would be our natural officers. So they were; and then they got killed off, and we got officers exactly as good for all purposes from an entirely different sort of school and an entirely different sort of tie.[34]

To many, the most notable thing about officers from the public schools, especially as the war wore on, was their youth: mere schoolboys were sent 'straight from England, without any war experience, to take charge of as hard-bitten and experienced a crowd of old sweats as one could imagine. I was ... utterly disgusted with a system that could work so absurdly.'[35]

Across the gulf which etiquette imposed, misjudgements by officers are understandable. The other-ranks remained, as the more acute of officers saw, distant and unknowable. 'Did any of us know you?', asks Guy Chapman,

ever pierce your disguise of goose-turd green, penetrate your young skin and look through you to learn the secret which is the essential spirit, the talisman against the worst that fate can offer? No. That was yours. As you would have said: 'Gawd knows, but 'E won't split on a pal'. So you still remain a line of bowed heads, of humped shoulders sitting wearily in the rain by a roadside, waiting, hoping, waiting—but unknown.[36]

Other-ranks were equally emphatic that the officers did not, and could not, understand: 'as all those who served must realize, an officer, of no matter what rank, saw the war from an angle far remote from the viewpoint of Thomas Atkins ... they were only with us, not of us, and they cannot get inside our skins.'[37]

The scope for any officers to form a real personal bond with their men was limited not only by the system, but by the rapidity with which officers and men changed. The myth of the three-month life expectancy of subalterns is false.[38] Nevertheless, with sickness, leave, transfers, promotions, and training courses to add to casualties, changes could be extremely frequent. The 12th Battalion East Surrey Regiment, for example, had eight different

[34] Gibbons, *Roll On Next War*, pp. 71–2.
[35] E. N. Gladden, *Across the Piave* (1971), 95.
[36] Chapman, *Passionate Prodigality*, p. 60.
[37] A. Burrage, *War is War* (1930), 5.
[38] M. Middlebrook, *The Kaiser's Battle* (1978), 405–6.

commanding officers in the nine months from September 1916 to June 1917, involving twenty-two changes of command; B company of the same battalion had fifteen changes of company commander in two months. Not surprisingly,

it was about this period [February 1917] that an order came from Army H.Q. stating that the Army Commander had noticed with displeasure that men were often found to be ignorant of the very name of their officers. Nothing else was possible, when officers and men were shifted almost daily. Never mind that. Every man had to be instructed in the name of the Army Commander, the G.O.C. Division, his Brigadier-General, C.O., Adjutant, O.C. of his company, etc.[39]

Even in static line-holding operations, a normal feature was 'the continual drifting in and out of officers, the lack of any continuous contact'. As a result, 'those who commanded, company officers and platoon officers, did not know in 1918 the names or even the faces of those whom they had to lead'.[40] An other-rank in the 2nd Battalion Worcestershire Regiment who came out at this time, recalls that the officers commanding his sniper section 'never seemed to stay long and just came and went and I cannot remember their names, with the exception of our first, Captain Lightly, whose D.C.M. ribbon told us he had come up from the ranks. He was the one exception who had an influence on our section and treated us in a way different from all the others . . . he treated us like human beings.'[41]

The rank-and-file infantrymen turned over scarcely less rapidly. At the time of Third Ypres, 'the turnover of men in the infantry . . . was so rapid that the junior officers seldom had time to learn all their men's names. As I look back on my experiences, I see only a large mass of shapeless, nameless and faceless figures in the ranks.'[42] Moreover, even if from time to time officers and men were together long enough to begin to establish a relationship, the disciplinary system, with its constant denial of partnership and parade of a naked power relationship, sowed mistrust. A ranker wrote that

however well the system may have worked in old days, its present effect

---

[39] Aston and Duggan, *History of the 12th Bn.*, p. 82.
[40] R. H. Kiernan, *Little Brother Goes Soldiering* (1930), 15–16.
[41] F. A. J. Taylor, *Bottom of the Barrel* (1978), 64.
[42] W. Moore, *See How They Ran* (1970), 27.

is to take away almost every atom of liking between Officers and men
. . . ask the first hundred Tommies and N.C.O.s you meet casually in
the street, on buses, or on trains. If you get into their confidence and ask
for their candid opinion, you will be told that only a very small percentage of the Officers are loved by their men. Another small percentage are
tolerated, or if you prefer it, respected. A similar small number are
actively hated: but by far the largest proportion are feared. And there
you have it.[43]

This is the portrait painted by Frederic Manning in *The Middle
Parts of Fortune.* His 'Captain Malet' is a pre-war Territorial
officer, well-liked and admired, but, says 'Bourne', 'I begin to
look on all officers, N.C.O.s, the military police, and brass-hats,
as the natural enemies of deserving men like myself. Captain
Malet is not an exception, he comes down on us occasionally, and
disturbs the even tenor of our existence.'[44]

The need progressively to promote from the ranks, as the army
expanded and casualties thinned the numbers of public-school
officers, tended to exacerbate rather than to ameliorate the fail-
ings of the system. It came to embody the worst of both worlds.
It insisted on treating officers and other-ranks as creatures of a
different clay, and in a society where deference was still a powerful force that might not of itself have been as unacceptable as it
would be today. However, as the justification for this had first
been undermined by a rise in the social levels represented in the
ranks, so now it was demolished by a fall in the class origin of
officers. An infantry officer might be an ex-colliery surface
worker, educated at Market Street Elementary School to the age
of 12,[45] yet all the feudal trappings of the system were retained, to
the bitter resentment of many.

The French looked to the ranks for officers as a matter of
course. As a conscript army, drawing good men into the ranks,
they had always done so. Between 1904 and 1909, 59 per cent of
French second lieutenants commissioned were ex-NCOs,
whereas between 1906 and 1910, ex-NCOs had made up just 2.2
per cent of the British officers commissioned.[46] Yet the French
army did not trammel these officers about with a code of military

[43] C. E. Jacomb, *Torment* (1920), 234.
[44] F. Manning, *The Middle Parts of Fortune* (1977), 80.
[45] R. H. Haigh and P. W. Turner (eds.), *Not for Glory* (1969), 12.
[46] Porch, *The March to the Marne*, p. 79; Spiers, *Army and Society*, p. 4.

etiquette befitting an élite officer caste, and which, applied to ranker officers, would be merely absurd and provocative. The Germans went to the other extreme, but again matched appearance to substance. They retained the etiquette of caste, but kept also the actuality by promoting few new officers, and throwing a greater burden on the professional NCOs.[47]

No doubt there were good points in the British system overall. Spit and polish discipline, although often infuriating, must at times have provided a point of stability and reassurance in a chaotic world. Larger numbers of officers than in the German army at least meant that officers visibly shared the dangers of leading patrols which, on the other side of the wire, fell more often to the NCOs. The belief in keeping the men busy and treating them as if they were incapable of looking after themselves might lead to pointless fatigues, foot inspections, and bull, but meant also that great efforts were devoted to seeing that the men's comforts were looked after and recreations provided behind the lines. The Regular divisions were to take the lead in arranging divisional canteens, concert parties, and sports as early as the first autumn of the war, and this was one area where public-school officers, with their experience of arranging similar activities for the benefit of rather different groups of captive males, were well equipped to follow. These may seem small things in the context of a gargantuan conflict which daily tested men to the limits of endurance, but their significance behind the lines was, as we shall see, given surprising weight by observers at the time. The attitudes of the officers were to be one factor, though not the most significant, which contributed to their success. Still, great benefits would need to follow from these things if they were to redress the inheritance of disadvantage which the Regular army tradition in other respects bestowed.

---

[47] Middlebrook, *Kaiser's Battle*, p. 44; Simpson, 'The Officers', in Beckett and Simpson (eds.), *A Nation in Arms*, p. 87.

6

Life in the Line

Much can be understood about the nature of the British and Dominion soldiers' experience in the Great War by exploring the character and structure of the army of which they formed part. However, at least as much depended on the basic realities of the time and place in which they were called to serve.

As the fronts stabilized, the infantrymen's lives overseas assumed a pattern which applied more or less consistently to all theatres but was most developed on the Western Front. Broadly, once he had arrived with a front-line unit, the infantryman's life fell into five phases. An engaged brigade would normally have a part of its strength in the front line, a second part in close support, and a third at some distance, billeted in brigade reserve: the infantry of the brigade's four battalions, later three, would alternate through these three phases. The fourth phase came when the brigade as a whole moved into divisional reserve, for a division usually alternated brigades engaged as a brigade did battalions. The fifth phase was divisional rest, when the corps or army moved up a new division, allowing the relief of the old and its withdrawal, complete except sometimes for artillery, to a rest area.

Time in the front line and in close support was generally time spent in trenches. Brigade reserve and divisional reserve usually saw the men in billets, and divisional rest normally meant a move to a rest camp. Together, time spent in billets and rest camps generally constituted at least three-fifths of an infantryman's service with his unit on the Western Front. The 7th Battalion Royal Sussex Regiment, for example, formed part of the BEF from 1915 to 1918, and spent 42 per cent of this time in the front line or in support, 38 per cent in billeting areas, and 20 per cent in rest areas. The figures for the 16th Canadian Battalion were 34 per cent, 35 per cent, and 31 per cent respectively, and other battalions show similar proportions.[1] This split between time in the trenches and time out seems to have become quite quickly established in 1915, as the arrival of new troops allowed the crisis conditions previously prevailing to give way to a more systematized pattern, and remained very consistent until the climactic struggle of 1918 once more increased the proportion of trench time to more than half.

Time in the trenches was of course the hardest part of the infantryman's service, and the lot of infantrymen of all nations was here in many ways comparable. The same enemies recur in British and French troop journals: the mud, the rain, the cold, the shells, the lice, and the rats. This was the common environment.

There were congruities too in many areas which human agency had more power to influence. Food, for example, was central to a soldier's physical and mental well-being. A similar scale of rations prevailed in the British and French armies, yielding a virtually identical calorific value,[2] but in both armies complaint was frequent because problems of supply, particularly to the front line, made all ration scales largely notional. In practice, the British troops often subsisted largely on bully beef and bread or biscuits. The monotony and inadequacy of this diet was a frequent target of wit in the front-line journals throughout the war:

> On Monday we had bread and bully
> On Tuesday we'd bully and bread
> On Wednesday and Thursday we'd bully and toast
> Well that's only bully and bread
> So on Friday we called on the Major
> And asked him for a change so he said
> Alright, so on Saturday we got for a change
> Some bully without any bread.

The B.E.F. Times told the scarcely less tragic story of a Christmas repast:

> Sing a song of Christmas
> Pockets full of slush

---

[1] O. Rutter (ed.), *The History of the 7th (Service) Bn. The Royal Sussex Regiment 1914–1919* (1934), 278; Urquhart, *History of the 16th Bn.*, p. 416.
[2] *Statistics of the Military Effort*, p. 586.

> Four and twenty PBI
> A dixey full of 'mush'
> When the dixey opened
> The Tommies said 'Oh my!
> Its beef today by way of change'
> And then began to cry,

and *The Bankers' Draft* announced with lumbering irony that 'the quartermaster wishes to tender apologies for a certain sameness of rations lately. It is hoped to issue some bully beef and biscuits in the near future.'[3]

Beyond the humour there was often real resentment. In the 'Active Service Alphabet' of the 14th Battalion Argyll and Sutherland Highlanders, 'L' was 'for the liars who say we're well fed'.[4] Boils and ill-health from inadequate nutrition were reported as common.[5] The rations were often scarcely edible, for which the troops placed the blame squarely upon profiteering. One man remembers bully beef so full of impurities that it was not safe to eat it in the dark.[6] Another remembers turnip-tops in the plum and apple jam.[7] A third remembers a particular brand of the Maconochie-type tinned stews: 'the head of that firm should have been put up against the wall and shot for the way they sharked us troops'.[8]

Even so, the men were aggrieved that they did not get their full allotment. Conditions of cold and boredom alternated with hard physical work: 'a morbidity about food and drink possessed everyone'.[9] An abiding recollection for memoirists is their constant hunger.[10] The front-line soldier had no hesitation in attributing the shortfall to pilfering by the various base and transport units, through whose hands the supplies must pass. Army rations

---

[3] *The Swell*, 2 (Jan. 1916), 4; *B.E.F. Times*, 4/2 (Dec. 1917), 11; *The Bankers' Draft*, 1 (June 1916), 4. On French complaints, see Englander, 'The French Soldier', pp. 55–6.

[4] *The Dud*, 1 (Nov. 1916), 17.

[5] E. C. Corbett, *The Worcestershire Regt.: War Story of the 1/8th Territorial Bn.* (Worcester, 1921), 62–3; Black, *One Volunteer*, p. 99; Tucker, *Johnny Get Your Gun*, p. 176.

[6] Black, *One Volunteer*, pp. 102–3.

[7] T. P. Marks, *The Laughter Goes from Life* (1977), 27.

[8] Richards, *Old Soldiers*, p. 67.

[9] E. Hiscock, *The Bells of Hell Go Ting a Ling a Ling* (1976), 52.

[10] Gauld, *Truth from the Trenches*, pp. 82–3; E. Parker, *Into Battle* (1964), 40; Gray, *Confessions of a Private*, p. 4.

in the possession of French civilians seemed to confirm this; likewise the better diet enjoyed by those rear area troops with whom the infantry came into contact. Belief in such pilfering was therefore most widespread. *The Mudhook* commented:

> And that's the Army system
> It's good without a doubt
> For those who get the lion's share
> But Tommy does cop out.[11]

Most soldiers were not disposed to accept the matter so philosophically: 'discontent was rife. The troops knew they were not getting the quantity as authorized by army regulations.'[12] Not surprisingly, in 1917 food was reported to the War Cabinet as one of the principal causes of troop discontent.[13]

The medical services for the troops also came in for considerable criticism. The harshness of the MO and his too frequent resort to the No. 9 (laxative) pill, in default as it seemed of other medication unavailable to him, were two of the staples of humorous complaint in the trench journals. Perhaps too much should not be made of this, since the MO will always be one of the targets of the soldier's wit. But the hostility towards the Medical Corps (RAMC) was entirely undisguised. They were simply 'Rob All My Comrades' brigands, never seen 'nearer than 500 yards from the firing line'. Nothing aroused the front-line soldier's ire so much as to see their heroism praised in the home papers.[14]

The infantry had a hard life and the system did not make it easier. It was in the trenches that some of the most pernicious aspects of the Regular army outlook stood revealed. There was inevitably a large degree of compromise on 'bull', in recognition of the conditions, but still enough of the attitude persisted to cause outrage. One man recalls how, on the Somme, 'a group of staff officers appeared and we stood to attention. One of them asked our corp., "Why haven't these men shaved?" I could have shot him without compunction.'[15] This kind of thing seemed the

[11] *The Mudhook*, 7 (Sept. 1918), 17. Cf. *Stray Shots*, 9 (Feb. 1917), 7.
[12] H. Russell, *Slaves of the War Lords* (1928), 256. Cf. Smith, *Four Years*, p. 125.
[13] War Cabinet Minute 231, 12 Sept. 1917, CAB 23/4.
[14] *The Minden Magazine*, 5 (May 1916), 11; *The Gasper*, 21 (Sept. 1916), 8; *The Outpost*, 4/6 (Apr. 1917), 197–8; *The Listening Post*, 22 (Feb. 1917), 142.
[15] M. Middlebrook, *The First Day on the Somme* (1971), 248.

more unjust an imposition because the men were tired. With stand to, sentry duty, fatigues, carrying parties, inspections, and work on the trenches, they had comparatively little time to themselves. Some recreations were sporadically carried on, such as gambling, reading, and writing.[16] Collecting souvenirs was a hobby pursued with an obsessiveness which the troop journals satirized.[17] Mostly, however, the men were concerned to rest, 'squeezed up in muddy dugouts during the few hours in the daytime when they were not on duty and could get a sleep'.[18] *The Outpost* summed up the desire for a comfortable sleep with a cartoon of a soldier on sentry duty in the rain, captioned 'oh for the touch of a feather bed, and the sound of a spring-mattress'.[19]

On the German side, the sophistication, comfort, and security of dug-outs steadily improved, as the British troops well knew from the examples they found in captured trench lines.[20] They were inclined to blame the authorities for the fact that they lacked anything similar, and this neglect seemed the more uncaring because so much apparently futile effort was being directed elsewhere: 'it seemed to us that our superiors did not inwardly admit that comfort was desirable, or that anyone should seek to be in a dugout if the enemy were shelling the line'.[21]

In a sense, this suspicion was not entirely misguided, since official policy did hold that men should not be allowed to lapse into passive defence, and this could easily stray over into the belief that exposure to danger was necessary to maintain fighting spirit. An Australian officer, for example, recorded that 'it was well known and proved over and over again during the Somme fighting, that troops made accustomed to deep dugouts, immune from shell-fire, often lost their nerve in the open under heavy bombardment, and were tempted to cower in their shelters when they should have been manning their parapets'.[22] The subaltern and ranker who wrote the history of the 12th East Surreys gave it as their opinion that the authorities 'had not adopted this means

---

[16] J. Glubb, *Into Battle* (1978), 174; *Aussie*, 6 (Aug. 1918), 15; Graham, *Private in the Guards*, p. 190.

[17] *Aussie*, 7 (Sept. 1918), 6.

[18] Gauld, *Truth from the Trenches*, p. 31.

[19] *The Outpost*, 3/6 (Sept. 1916), 191.

[20] Ibid. 173–4.

[21] L. W. Griffith, *Up to Mametz* (1931), 126.

[22] Williams, *Gallant Company*, p. 167.

of minimizing losses' in order to discourage skulking and to maintain the offensive spirit.[23] The Germans evidently did not share this precept, which must have grown increasingly bizarre as shell-fire grew heavier. Instead, 'the enemy had realized more clearly than ourselves the value of the conservation of manpower'.[24] One can well understand why many men felt inclined to direct the 'offensive spirit' whipped up by their sufferings at their officers and Higher Command quite as much as at the Germans.

It should not be surprising either, especially when the relatively low level of training of officers and men is added to the equation, that the British were slower than the French or Germans to introduce a system of flexible defence. This became an increasingly common response to the growing weight of bombardments as the war progressed. By allowing forward trenches to be held lightly, it was designed to spare most of the troops in the line the trial of prolonged bombardment. British slowness to adopt this development was costly not just in lives and courage, but in the tonic to morale which a well-regulated defence, with its evidence of direction, support, and concern could provide.[25]

The British command's enthusiasm for frequent raids and artillery shoots, the 'active front' policy, was even more wearing to the troops. Their first concern was to survive, and where things were quiet there was an understandably strong temptation to adopt an attitude of 'live and let live' towards the enemy. There were limits to the extent to which such an approach could be explicitly admitted, but it is a mark of the latitude allowed by the censorship that it did appear in the troop journals. The magazine of the 56th London Division in November 1918 recorded 'the tacit law of this sector ever since the trenches were marked out': 'if you put down hurricane shoots upon our ration arrangements—as you can—we will leave talking of the place where your dump used to be—as we can'.[26] A cartoon in *The Brazier* depicted a Canadian, on digging operations, standing on a pile of earth between the trenches and addressing a German similarly intent upon improving his home: ' "say, Fritz, if you

[23] Aston and Duggan, *The History of the 12th Bn.*, p. 31.
[24] A. H. Ashcroft, *The History of the 7th South Staffordshire Regiment* (1920), 85.
[25] Edmonds, *History of the Great War*, 1917, i. 553–5.
[26] *The Dagger*, 1 (Nov. 1918), 13.

don't quit throwing your blooming earth over into our trench, there's going to be some trouble".'[27]

The officers of the battalion were the first threat to whatever peace had been achieved. The trench mortars are a frequent target of the troop journals' humorous complaints:

> Who is it when the 'stand to' is o'er
> Throws bombs at Fritz till he gets sore
> And throws at us a score or more
> The Trench Mortars.[28]

However, battalion officers at least shared to a degree the men's vulnerability and could often see the wisdom of accepting tacit truces in particular situations. Superior officers at brigade or higher were a different matter and would call for action in accordance with the 'active front' policy. An officer in the Rifle Brigade recalls such an occasion when a round of shelling was ordered:

the days of peace and quiet were ended, with no advantage to either side. The only result was that our ration parties had to go back and lug all the rations and stores and ammunition up on their backs through communication trenches for a mile or more. It certainly did not encourage the 'offensive spirit' amongst the troops, except against the idiots on the staff. This was the sort of thing that induced such a lot of bad feeling between the troops in the line and the staff behind it.[29]

Raids had the same effect. The British troops seem to have been aware that the Germans and the French made comparatively few raids, and to have felt that this made sound tactical sense: 'the sole chance of success lay in surprise attacks, carefully prepared on a foundation of definite knowledge of the ground and the enemy's dispositions ... I think everyone in the line realized this.'[30] On the British side, however,

to the end corps commanders persisted in ordering raids regardless of local conditions and with an arbitrary time limit—often 24 hours' notice—and usually with the condition of a great artillery programme. What commonly occurred was that the enemy, finding his wire being

[27] *The Brazier*, 2 (Mar. 1916), 8.
[28] *The Listening Post*, 18 (July 1916), 2. Cf. *The Whizz Bang*, 4 (Apr. 1916), 7; *The Mudhook*, 7 (Sept. 1918), 11; *The 5th Glo'ster Gazette*, 11 (Apr. 1916), 4.
[29] J. Nettleton, *The Anger of the Guns* (1979), 49.
[30] Kelly, *39 Months*, pp. 19, 40. On the French attitude of 'live and let live' see Edmonds, *History of the Great War*, 1916, i. 156.

ostentatiously shot to pieces, withdrew his posts to the flanks of the threatened trench: and when the forward troops (by means of an admirable system of light signals, much superior to our own) gave warning, down came a barrage of shells, trench-mortar bombs, and enfilade machine-gun fire on the gaps in the wire and the jumping off points of the raiders.[31]

There seems to have been a widely held view that British raids were on the whole 'ill prepared and seldom succeeded'.[32] Indeed, some men nourished the suspicion that they represented simply the rivalry of the sport-obsessed, upper-class staffs, who bet against each other with the lives of their men.[33]

But these raids did more than swell infantry hostility towards the staff. They also contributed to the attritional effect of trench warfare. As Lord Moran wrote, 'a man's courage is his capital, and he is always spending'.[34] The 'active front' policy forced him to spend at a prodigal rate. Testimony is unanimous as to the extreme unpopularity of these raids and their 'disastrous' effect on morale.[35] 'Peaceful penetration', the surprise and capture of German posts by rank-and-file Australians acting on their own initiative, became widespread in 1918 less from high morale than 'to avoid the necessity of undertaking formal raids'.[36]

Was there good in this system? Ashworth's *Trench Warfare* argues that it was precisely because of the 'active front' policy that the British did not follow the French into mutiny:

if, as appears from the French case, truces were allowed to endure and pervade trench war, all the while producing fellowship among enemies, and if raids were not systematically disrupting this process, then the unfettered growth of truces could well contribute to a comprehensive collapse of trench war, and an informal and general declaration of peace.

---

[31] Kelly, *39 Months*, p. 40.

[32] 'Random Reminiscences of an Ordinary Soldier in the Great War', *Army Quarterly*, 5 (1923), 298.

[33] Russell, *Slaves of the War Lords*, p. 97; F. C. Hitchcock, *Stand To* (1937), 229; D. W. J. Cuddeford, *And All For What?* (1933), 124.

[34] Moran, *Anatomy of Courage*, p. xvi.

[35] J. Milne, *Footprints of the 1/4th Leicestershire Regiment* (Leicester, 1935), 102–3; C. H. D. Ward, *The Welsh Regiment of Foot Guards 1915–1918* (1936), 72. Even the official report of the Kirke Committee, in 1932, concluded that raids had not had a beneficial effect upon morale—see Report of the Committee on the Lessons of the Great War, WO 32/3116, Appendix I, 15.

[36] Bean, *Official History*, vi. 41–2; Gammage, *Broken Years*, p. 153.

This, he says, is in part what the mutinies of 1917 represented:

to a degree, the French mutiny was nothing more than a dramatic demonstration of support for a policy of live and let live. As far as the Germans in the trenches knew, nothing had changed: tacit truces proceeded during the mutiny according to patterns established long before. The exchange of peace just went smoothly on.[37]

In fact, however, during May 1917 the French troops in the areas affected stood off at least thirty-nine German attacks, during June at least twenty-three, during July at least thirty-six.[38] This was hardly an exchange of peace. Moreover, one may wonder why, if the mutinies grew out of peaceful coexistence, they broke out on the most active front of the French army, the Chemin des Dames, instead of, for example, in the Vosges. Why also did they erupt after the failure of the offensive instead of before it began? And why, since 'exchange' presupposes mutuality, were the German divisions opposite not similarly affected?

Ashworth's study, written entirely from British sources, fails to understand the character of the French indiscipline and its views on combat are equally suspect. Its author does not entirely accept the staff notion of 'fighting spirit' as an abstract quality, primed by periodic doses of blood and shell-fire. Instead he postulates a motivation of personal vengeance, kept high by the loss of friends and comrades in raid and counter-raid.[39] However, the evidence suggests that in modern mass warfare most men do not fight for such reasons. Even if we characterize 'hate' in this way, still the study of American combat experience in the Second World War suggests that only a tiny portion of soldiers are thus motivated.[40] Moreover hate, as we have seen, was notably absent from the British troop journals and from the terms which the men habitually used to refer to their enemy. They fought not from hatred or vengeance, but from the more usual motives: because their living comrades expected it of them, or because they felt that it was a necessary war for their way of life.

Although superficially it is appealing to say that because an army does not make raids it cannot make offensives, because it does not make small attacks it cannot make big ones, it seems

[37] Ashworth, *Trench Warfare*, pp. 224–5.
[38] J. Terraine, *To Win a War* (1978), 26.
[39] Ashworth, *Trench Warfare*, pp. 190–1, 207–8.
[40] Stouffer (ed.), *The American Soldier*, ii. 109.

therefore that the connection is largely false. The willingness of troops to make an attack was not dependent upon keeping in practice; still less upon the frequent piling up of unnecessary casualties, which would be blamed on the staff as readily as upon the Germans. Instead, it depended upon their belief in the necessity and value of the risk they were being called upon to run, which was much more likely to be undercut than bolstered by a policy of raiding for raiding's sake.

If raids had always imposed a nagging doubt about the futility of sacrifices demanded, the later stages of the war saw these doubts raised on a far more significant scale. Third Ypres, or Passchendaele, seemed almost wilfully to test how far the men could be pushed before they would rebel. Douglas Jerrold, a junior officer in the 63rd Division, was to be a fierce post-war critic of the school of 'disenchantment' writing, but he himself recognized that this offensive, launched from the shell-raked Ypres Salient through the quagmire of Flanders, tried the spirit of the men severely:

the plain fact was that we were attempting an offensive under impossible conditions. The sacrifices exacted were obviously beyond any attainable reward. The trouble lay, in fact, just in that word 'obviously'. Not a song could be heard on the march anywhere on the Flanders front in October 1917. The morale of the troops was amazingly high. Everything they were asked to do was done to the utmost of their power, but they had seen too much to be in any doubt as to the outcome.[41]

Haig knew the importance of drawing German reserves and attention away from a French army whose sincere recovery he still doubted. He knew the urgency attached by the Admiralty to clearing the Belgian coast. However, as the commander of the Fifth Army commented,

our private soldiers knew nothing of the grave considerations which influenced Haig's judgement. They only knew that they were asked to fight under unprecedented conditions, with death above, around, below. At no time in the War was confidence in their leaders so difficult. It was little short of marvellous that men could stand such an intense strain.[42]

[41] D. Jerrold, *The Hawke Bn.* (1925), 168.
[42] H. Gough, *The Fifth Army* (Bath, 1968), 219.

Officers closer to their men knew just how difficult confidence could be:

it must be obvious that since there were many men of the highest intelligence gathered from out of civil occupations in which they had won the respect of their fellows, serving in the lower commands and ranks of a citizen army, a capacity for logical and hard thinking remained. As a Commander of one thousand men or more I found it frequently embarrassing when in chance conversation with a subaltern or sergeant to be asked to give reasons . . . 'Why do we always make our attacks in winter when any fool who knows anything about the front can see that they're bound to be a failure?' . . . 'What's the object of attacking Passchendaele? It only makes our position worse for the subsequent winter, and the position of the Germans better. Behind us there will be miles of land quite impassable except over tracks laid on sleepers which will be shelled to blazes day and night.'[43]

The overall picture had never looked blacker. On the one hand, there was the collapse of the Eastern Front, freeing a million Germans, perhaps more, to give them numerical superiority in the West, and a chance to crush the Allies before the Americans could intervene in force. On the other, the Western Allies seemed on the verge of prostration. Some men claim to have known of the French mutinies, and indeed it seems unlikely that some inkling of so vast a secret would not have passed between the common soldiers of the two nations.[44] At all events, French quiescence was discouraging, for the heart seemed to have gone out of that people's commitment. Even worse, Italy collapsed at the barren climax of the Passchendaele offensive, requiring emergency aid from her allies. Whilst the Allies seemed set on a course of slow disintegration, the Germans were apparently making steady progress: in 1915 they had knocked out Serbia, in 1916 Rumania, in 1917 Russia, and now, seemingly, Italy. British soldiers heard, or saw when they went on leave, that the food situation for their dependants was becoming more severe. Strikes multiplied, and with them the soldiers' sense of betrayal.[45] Mounting press criticism swelled the men's own doubts about

[43] G. S. Hutchison, *Warrior* (1932), 204–5.
[44] Tucker, *Johnny Get Your Gun*, p. 134; C. M. Slack, *Grandfather's Adventures in the Great War* (Ilfracombe, 1977), 153; Tilsley, *Other Ranks*, pp. 181, 227.
[45] T. Wilson, *The Myriad Forces of War: Britain and the Great War, 1914–1918* (Cambridge, 1986), 526–7; *The Outpost*, 5/1 (May 1917), 36; *The 5th Glo'ster Gazette*, 19 (June 1917), 121.

their High Command.[46] Yet the Allied governments spurned German initiatives for peace.

Within this depressing general situation, the conditions of the battle were of an unprecedented horror. Added to the mud, rain, and cold of a winter offensive, was the constant observation by the German guns on the high ground ringing Ypres. Bombardments were at their heaviest, having steadily increased for three years as the armies sought to pound their way out of the impasse, and not yet being limited by the restoration of semi-mobile warfare which was to follow. The most rudimentary protection could not be excavated in the waterlogged ground. A new and effective terror weapon made its appearance, as probably the most horrific of the war. According to a Canadian ranker,

the only time we were really worried by gas was when mustard gas first appeared on the scene in 1917. I heard of it when I came back from my first leave and was told at the same time that, as a result of it, the morale of the whole army was lower than a snake's belly. There seemed to be no answer to it. A sweating man, and when the guns were in action we were all sweating, broke out in horrible blisters. No one at the time knew what the final result might be.[47]

Gas shells had superseded the earlier reliance upon favourable winds and conditions. In all, it is not surprising that, according to analysis of the letters passing through the censorship, the experience of Third Ypres created 'a very striking difference' in morale between the troops engaged and those on quieter fronts.[48] Yet all remained docile, and obedient to the order to attack.

Scarcely less remarkable was their staunchness in the face of the German successes of spring 1918. When the Third Ypres battle was finally ended, the lack of appreciable gains seemed only to validate all doubts. The battle of Cambrai, which followed, having 'begun so brilliantly, had closed in defeat and nasty stories ran about of how it had been lost. And above all the German submarines were sinking the food ships and the ships

[46] Andrews, *Haunting Years*, p. 242; Blake (ed.), *Private Papers*, p. 274; Wilson, *Myriad Faces*, p. 547.

[47] Black, *One Volunteer*, p. 86.

[48] 'The British Armies in France as gathered from the censorship', CAB 24/36 G.T. 3044. On Third Ypres as the grimmest battle of the war, see Andrews, *Haunting Years*, pp. 241–2; Nettleton, *Anger of the Guns*, p. 121; V. F. Eberle, *My Sapper Venture* (1973), 134.

full of munitions, and unless this drain was stopped, the war would certainly be lost.'[49] The government, nervous of Haig's willingness to expend lives for no apparent gain, was starving the army of replacements, forcing the break-up between January and March 1918 of one in four of all infantry battalions and a shrinking of brigades.[50] The Regular army mentality, with its respect for tradition and consequent determination to preserve the most senior battalions, ruled out any such simple method of reduction as the dissolution of the weakest or worst battalion in each brigade. Instead, battalions were shuffled between brigades. It was an 'astonishing and demoralizing exercise . . . during which the roads of France were filled with British units seeking their new "homes", and during which an esprit de corps built up in years of common experience was thrown away'.[51]

German numbers were, to the contrary, increasing: 'it seemed as though reserves were giving out and all the time men knew that crowded troop trains were moving across Germany from the East to the West, and that in a few weeks the storm would burst'.[52] Worse, this blocking of reinforcements looked like a betrayal by the very regime which men were being called upon to defend:

we read into this fiddling about with battalion and brigade establishments a message from the government—it is like a sentence of death. It means that no more men and guns are being sent out to help us, and that each day, while Jerry masses ever more men and guns on the Western Front, we will grow ever weaker from the normal wastage of war. And when, in a little while, his big offensive comes, he will swallow Haig's armies at a gulp. Haig and his armies have been betrayed from the beginning, and this last treachery will be the end.[53]

The French had their difficulties in maintaining unit strengths, but there had never been any question of the front-line soldiers being wilfully starved of support. Men might well ask why they should fight on for a government willing thus to abandon them. Others might wonder what it said about the degree of confidence reposed in the army's leaders.

[49] Burton, *Silent Division*, pp. 253–4.
[50] Edmonds, *History of the Great War*, 1918, i. 13, 50–3, and 1918, ii. 470.
[51] J. Terraine, *Impacts of War 1914 and 1918* (1970), 142–3.
[52] Burton, *Silent Division*, p. 262.
[53] Croney, *Soldier's Luck*, p. 212.

Then, on top of the slow demoralization, there came the smashing German successes of the spring. Now, not only were all gains liquidated on the Somme, and the Salient drawn tighter than ever around Ypres, but this was achieved in weeks where the original advances had cost months of British effort and hundreds of thousands dead. Not only was the slim evidence of Allied progress towards victory wiped out, but also the Germans had demonstrated their own superiority as a fighting force: 'it became obvious to even the most simple that our generalship was at fault and the morale of the troops . . . fell to a low point'.[54] Even if defeat could be averted, the path to victory seemed endless.

And yet there was no collapse. Confused by a belated shift in defensive tactics, disorganized by the shuffling of battalions to create the new three-battalion brigades, confronted by overwhelming numbers, by masterfully co-ordinated barrages, and by revolutionary infiltration tactics, the British troops yet offered dogged resistance and ultimately halted the onset.[55] There was nothing like the Italian débâcle at Caporetto the previous autumn in the face of an infinitely weaker Austro-German offensive. Indeed, a few months later, the British and Dominion armies were able to shift over to the offensive and claim the largest bag of prisoners and guns in the continuous advance, vigorously pressed, which finally forced Germany to yield. Conditions had tested the British and Dominion armies severely, but they had weathered every test.

[54] G. Brenan, *A Life of One's Own* (1975), 221.
[55] Edmonds, *History of the Great War*, 1918, ii. 483–4.

7

Behind the Lines

Leave

The spirit of the men, often tried to the limit during spells in the line, had somehow to be restored during their time away from the trenches if the mood of strain and frustration was to be prevented from steadily building up to a point where it would threaten the willingness of the army to obey orders. Leave alone could not do the job. The scarcity of leave was one of the foremost grievances of the French mutineers,[1] but it was scarcer still for the British. In June/July 1917, more than 107,000 British soldiers had had no leave for eighteen months, and 403,000 no leave for twelve.[2] Leave was humorously defined as 'a pleasant but impossible theory, a foolish dream, a wild exaggerated imagining, the product of an over-hopeful brain'.[3] The British front-line soldier could hope for ten days leave, or fourteen from November 1917, in perhaps fifteen months. The *poilu*, in the wake of Pétain's reforms, enjoyed seven days leave, and later ten, at intervals of only four months. Frozen at a single moment, the difference was reflected in the fact that at 15 January 1918, 350,000 French soldiers were on leave as against just 80,000 British.[4]

Small wonder, then, that a 'Simplified French Dictionary' produced by the Royal Naval Division included, 'Permission—leave. An institution common in the Army of Our Ally.' This was 'the old grouse of our leave compared with the Frenchman'.[5] The men, Haig warned, 'are aware that the French soldiers get very much more': to many it seemed that unlike the *poilus*, or yet the Germans, 'it is only the English "Tommy" who is considered

---

[1] Pedroncini, *Les Mutineries*, pp. 108–9, 127, 142, 144, 234.
[2] Englander and Osborne, 'Jack, Tommy and Henry Dubb', p. 601.
[3] *The Mudhook*, 3 (Jan. 1918), 4.
[4] Edmonds, *History of the Great War*, 1917, i. 554, and 1918, i. 39.
[5] *The Mudhook*, 8 (Oct. 1918), 13; *The Outpost*, 5/6 (Oct. 1917), 188.

unworthy of any concessions or chance of having human sympathy from his own people to hearten him up for the struggle. The bitterness is accentuated by the fact that Officers, on the other hand, do get leave at reasonable intervals.'[6]

The much greater frequency of officer leave, in fact, created 'a very definite and serious current of discontent and dissatisfaction'.[7] The same grievance was to be the prime cause of the mutiny of a Portuguese battalion in 1918.[8] Equally infuriating, the rear area troops once more fared better than the men who bore the brunt of the struggle. Troop journals appealed repeatedly for a fairer distribution of leave.[9]

The Dominion troops suffered in many ways worst of all, because home was so far away. Generally 'Blighty leave' was the most that could be hoped for, and this would inevitably be a rather rootless affair. Yet the longing for leave does not seem to have been appreciably diminished.[10]

In fact it would be hard to overstate the eagerness with which a spell of leave was awaited by troops of every nationality. For all its disorientations, leave offered a chance to see loved ones, a release from discipline, and an intense interval of pleasure. Men waited 'with enduring hope for the next leave, as for a reincarnation'.[11]

However, for all the importance of the leave question as an issue, the direct effect upon the morale of the army of this spasmodic contact with the Home Front appears to have been limited and ambiguous. On the one hand, as we have seen, leave was likely to disturb the soldiers by bringing home to them both the hardships of their families and the gulf in spirit between the Home Front and the front line. On the other, leave might, at least, by renewing soldiers' contacts with the people and things they loved, remind them of what they were fighting for. But much could happen to morale in a matter of weeks, and a less than annual contact with home was scarcely to be relied upon as

---

[6] Edmonds, *History of the Great War*, 1918, i. 39; Jacomb, *Torment*, p. 252.

[7] Brown, *Tommy Goes to War*, pp. 232–3.

[8] Blake (ed.), *Private Papers*, p. 302.

[9] *The Very Light*, 1 (Mar. 1917), 7; *6th K.S.L.I. News*, 1 (Aug. 1917), 20; *The Brazier*, 1 (Feb. 1916), 5; *The 5th Glo'ster Gazette*, 16 (Dec. 1916), 18.

[10] *Aussie*, 5 (June 1918), 2.

[11] *The Outpost*, 4/6 (Apr. 1917), 209. Cf. *The Listening Post*, 32 (Dec. 1918), 25.

the regular tonic to morale which the routine of repeated trench
tours demanded.[12]

The Civilian World behind the Lines

Closer at hand and much more regularly visited were the rest
areas behind the lines. Edmund Blunden was one among many
who recorded the pleasure and relief of moving out of the line
into the countryside behind:

> O how comely it was and how reviving
> When with clay and death no longer striving
> Down firm roads we came to houses
> With women chattering and green grass thriving.[13]

Billets themselves may often have been of a very poor standard,
but at least soldiers were brought once more into contact with a
world outside the war, and given a brief opportunity to sample its
pleasures before another looming spell which could extinguish
them for ever.

Greatly appreciated were the village *estaminets*, where wine,
beer, or egg and chips could be had, and which served as a
substitute for the pubs at home. The troop journals hymned their
delights.[14] It is hard to credit Sassoon's estimate that his own
battalion was spending £500 a week in the *estaminets* of one village
during rest, but it gives an indication of his own view of their
popularity.[15]

Drink was of course the most obvious of the *estaminets'* attrac-
tions. Home Front homilies against alcohol were much resented
because it was seen as a vital necessity. *Aussie* ran a poem in June
1918 entitled 'In Billets':

> You say we're mad when we strike the beer!
> But if you'd stood in shivering fear
> With the boys who bring the wounded back
> Cross no-man's land where there ain't no track

[12] On the disorientating effects of leave, see R. Holmes, *Firing Line* (1987), 90–2.
[13] E. Blunden, *Undertones of War* (1965), 220.
[14] *Posh Stew*, 1 (Jan. 1917), 3.
[15] S. Sassoon, *The Complete Memoirs of George Sherston* (1972), 626.

You'd read no psalms to the men that fight!
You'd take to drink to forget the sight
Of torn out limbs and sightless eyes
Or the passing of a pal that dies.[16]

Estaminets offered also the prospect of flirtation with French
girls. For men starved not just of sex but contact with women and
with all things beautiful and civilized, this was an irresistible
enticement. The journals recognized that the soldier was easy
prey for the unscrupulous, but still indulged themselves in praise
of the more attractive of the local women. A large part of the
chaffing in their columns dealt with men lucky enough to have
formed some relationship with local girls. Stories and cartoons
depicted pursuits of French girls, humorous or otherwise.

For all this interest, however, memoirists maintain that
brothels played no significant part in most infantrymen's lives.
They were principally for the base depots: 'we front line men
either have the money and not the opportunity, or the opportunity and not the money, or both and not the inclination'.[17] Of
course one would not expect memoirists of the period to say
otherwise, whatever the truth. The troop journals, not surprisingly, have nothing to say on the subject, but the large number of
memoirists who record visiting a 'red lamp' 'for a look' does give
pause for doubt. More tangibly, there is no gainsaying the figures
for hospital admissions for venereal disease. These reached a
peak in 1918, with some 60,000 British and Dominion soldiers
receiving treatment, or thirty-two out of every 1,000 men on the
ration strength of the forces under Haig.[18] The front-line men
were certainly represented in this total, but there is perhaps some
truth in what the memoirists say about the disproportion of rear
area troops and the reticence of many men. Opportunities were
certainly limited, with most troops billeted away from the big
towns. Contemporary morality and attachment to loved ones
were certainly important. In addition, fear of venereal disease
seems to have been widespread, and the army, anxious to
minimize the flow of men to hospital, took full advantage.
According to a private in the 1st Essex, venereal cases in his

[16] *Aussie* 5 (June 1918), 16.
[17] T. S. Hope, *The Winding Road Unfolds* (1937), 147.
[18] T. J. Mitchell and G. M. Smith, *Medical Services: Casualties and Medical Statistics of the Great War* (1931), 164, 174.

battalion were classified 'sick through negligence' and 'not only is
a man's pay stopped, but also the allotment he makes to his
mother. There is no hiding his shame.'[19] The 'red lamps' are
remembered as sordidly practical and peopled by unattractive
women, unlikely to appeal to the hunger for the aesthetic felt by
many men.[20] Finally, men were short of money and time, for if
the dream of rest saw men enjoying the pleasures of the world
outside the war, the reality was often very different.

Negative Features

For pay, the essential prerequisite for many pleasures, British
infantrymen fared not so badly as the French, but the contrast
with the rear area troops was marked and bitterly resented. *The
5th Glo'ster Gazette* declared that 'the status of the infantryman is
a sad blot on our Nation's history': 'why', it wanted to know,
'pay the infantry less than anyone else'.[21] A current verse ran:

> Providence made men
> Bees make honey
> The Shropshires [or Glo'sters, or any infantry]
> do the work
> The RE get the money.[22]

The Dominion troops too, the 'fuckin' five bobbers', brought
home to the lowly Tommy, with his shilling a day, his relative
poverty, while at the same time intensifying this by driving up
prices behind the lines: 'the English infantryman was very conscious of the disparity between the pay of the Imperials and the
Colonials'.[23] Recalls one machine gunner, 'my saddest memory of
the war is my continual state of poverty'.[24]

    Rest, as well, was lacking. Endless fatigues devoured much of
the soldier's time out of the line: 'in support, or further back in
reserve, men would get warned for duty under some casual

[19] Croney, *Soldier's Luck*, p. 66.
[20] M. Gibbon, *Inglorious Soldier* (1968), 204; H. E. L. Mellersh, *Schoolboy into
War*, pp. 148–9; Tucker, *Johnny Get Your Gun*, p. 29; Andrews, *Haunting Years*,
p. 217.
[21] *The 5th Glo'ster Gazette*, 19 (June 1917), 21.
[22] Ibid. 15 (Oct. 1916), 8; *The Dud*, 2 (July 1916), 15.
[23] Aston and Duggan, *History of the 12th Bn.*, p. 100. Cf. Tucker, *Johnny Get Your
Gun*, p. 109.
[24] G. Coppard, *With a Machine Gun to Cambrai* (1980), 77.

cigarette-smoking sapper sometimes almost before they had got
their packs off'.[25] As *The Gasper*'s 'Cockney Critic' commented,

it's a wonder to me Tommy don't get fed up. 'E goes ter the trenches,
risks 'is precious life, puts up barbed wire, mends parapets, digs saps,
does engineers' work, and comes out for a Rest, with a big R. They puts
'im on fatigue dooty unloadin' railway trucks, carryin' up stores and all
sorts o' jobs that them transport chaps, Ally Sloper's Cavalry, signed on
ter do. 'Stead o' which one of these chaps just bosses the job and watches
Tommy work ... Restin'? There ain't no bloomin' rest fer 'im
anywhere.[26]

To a degree, this was inevitable. As the army of an ally, the
British forces could not, like the Germans, impress French and
Belgian labour. They had no over-age Territorials on hand to
employ, like the French, for digging and carrying. The Labour
Corps had, by the end of 1917, grown to a strength of over
300,000 men, but of these very few were available for work in the
forward areas, the majority being occupied to the rear in jobs
which, in the French zones, were performed by civilians. Indeed,
prior to the German offensive in March 1918, just 1,714 men out
of this large total were working on defences.[27] The bulk of the
labouring and carrying tasks fell upon the infantry and were
bitterly resented by men desperate for rest.[28]

Exigencies notwithstanding, there was probably also an element of policy in keeping the troops always busy. This was part
of the old Regular army code, well expressed now by an officer in
the Highland Light Infantry: 'the rest was certainly more mental
than physical ... However it at least kept them employed, and if
they had had too much time on their hands they would only have
got into mischief with the French people.'[29] Certainly army fatigues were a byword for bad organization and lackadaisical
working methods.[30] They seemed to be undertaken less from

[25] W. G. Hall, *The Green Triangle, Being the History of the 2/5th Bn., The Sherwood Foresters (Notts. and Derby Regt.) in the Great War 1914–1918* (Letchworth, 1920), 90.

[26] *The Gasper*, 19 (June 1916), 4.

[27] Edmonds, *History of the Great War*, 1918, i. 39–40.

[28] Gray, *Confessions of a Private*, pp. 104–15; Russell, *Slaves of the War Lords*, p. 124; Aston and Duggan, *History of the 12th Bn.*, p. 71; Gauld, *Truth from the Trenches*, p. 41; C. O. G. Douie, *The Weary Road* (1929), 110.

[29] Cuddeford, *And All For What?*, p. 78.

[30] *The 5th Glo'ster Gazette*, 6 (Sept. 1915), 4; *The Forty-Niner*, 4 (Jan. 1915), 24–5; Gray, *Confessions of a Private*, p. 114; 'Random Reminiscences', *Army Quarterly*, 5 (1923), 298.

necessity than because 'the sight of a man resting is as hateful to
the sight of a Brigadier as a vulgar picture postcard from Margate
is hateful to the sight of a refined maiden lady'.[31]

On top of all this, there was the eternal 'bull'. The shortest
respite would see a frenzy of polishing as troops were brought
back 'up to the mark'.[32] This was often bitterly resented by men
weary almost to death from their time in the line. It was hard to
accept that 'it was discipline to make a man polish his boots and
buttons on the Somme, where, in the driest parts, the mud was
never less than a foot deep and rain or snow fell almost without
ceasing'.[33]

But most time-consuming of all was training. Unit War Diaries
show the exhaustiveness and repetitiveness of training programmes, which generally occupied at least every morning, with
afternoons increasingly as the war went on set aside for other
activities. *The 5th Glo'ster Gazette* as usual put the troops' complaints in ironic form, asking in a mock examination paper, 'if
parading at 4 a.m. with field operations ensuing until 9 a.m.
comes under the heading of "rest", describe your ideas as to how
a busy day should be spent'.[34]

Undercut on all sides, the very name of 'rest' became a joke:
'the words "Divisional Rest" were the signal for a huge and
sardonic guffaw'.[35] The journals defined it as

a refined form of punishment to troops. A certain cure for men tired of
being 'up the line'. A short term used to express endless parades, ceaseless polishings, burnishings and 'inspections';

a period of torture for infantry during which they are . . . assiduously
instructed in the art of cleaning buttons and shining mess-tins, saluting
by number and by request, and such intricate knowledge as the correct
manner of pointing the toe in the 'slow march'. After a couple of weeks
of rest they are generally quite willing to return to the trenches.[36]

An 'Etymological Review' explained how 'rest' 'came to mean
labour in its most intense form', whilst another paper carried a
cartoon of a soldier toiling under an immense burden, with the

[31] Burrage, *War is War*, p. 72.
[32] Priestley, *Margin Released*, pp. 134–7.
[33] Gauld, *Truth from the Trenches*, p. 31.
[34] *The 5th Glo'ster Gazette*, 13 (July 1916), 1.
[35] Jacomb, *Torment*, p. 116.
[36] *The Mudhook*, 3 (Jan. 1918), 4; *The Listening Post*, 28 (Sept. 1917), 192.

caption: '6 days shalt thou labour, and the "rest" of the time carry heavy weights'.[37] More baldly, *The Trench Echo* asked: 'can't a more appropriate name be found for Rest Camp? Its present one is a delusion and a snare.'

The crowded activity of British (and to a lesser extent of Dominion) rest periods made them very different from those enjoyed by, for example, French troops. The relative immunity of the French from 'bull' and fatigues gave them opportunity for genuine physical recovery and for more sophisticated training.[38] Given the danger of *le cafard*, can it be said that this was to be preferred? Pétain's action in the wake of the French mutinies suggests that it was. Rather than step up the work demanded of the troops on rest, he laid down that the troops should enjoy three or four days of *repos absolu* at the start of each rest period.[39] During this time there was to be no training, and training would be only gradually reintroduced in the days following. If boredom was a problem, it was a mistake to imagine that onerous, unpopular, and unfulfilling activity was the answer, for men who were mentally and physically exhausted. Even as a distraction, only the most patronizing view of the private soldier's mental capacities could justify a belief that minds were prevented from turning to 'mischief' by kit-cleaning, mechanical labouring tasks, and constantly repetitive training. Few things, in fact, could have been better calculated to provoke 'mischievous' thoughts: tiredness was 'quite a big factor in lowering the morale. There was so little rest even when out on "rest".'[40]

This was dangerous because morale had particularly to be nourished during time out of the line. Not only did men have to be restored for a further spell in the trenches, but the period of preparation for return was the time at which the risk of mass indiscipline was greatest. It was among troops on rest or reserve that the French mutinies broke out.[41] The constraining presence

[37] *New Year Souvenir of the Welsh Division* (Jan. 1917), 61; *The Bankers' Draft*, 2 (July 1915), 12; *The Trench Echo*, 4 (Dec. 1917), 16; *The Dud* (Argyll and Sutherland), 1 (Nov. 1916), 9.

[38] J. Terraine (ed.), *General Jack's Diary* (1964), 193–4; Feilding, *War Letters*, pp. 284–5. For all that they were fewer, the French troops still resented the parades to which they were subjected. See Englander, 'The French Soldier', p. 55.

[39] Pedroncini, *Les Mutineries*, pp. 237–9.

[40] Groom, *Poor Bloody Infantry*, p. 58. Cf. Edmonds, *History of the Great War*, 1918, i. 40–1.

[41] Pedroncini, *Les Mutineries*, p. 90.

of the enemy opposite was removed; access to drink and facility of assembly, planning, and action all improved. However, it seemed significant to many observers that the best as well as the worst features of Regular army paternalism stood revealed behind the lines, for it was this tradition that underlay the remarkable growth in leisure facilities which came to play an important part in the pattern of life in the active war theatres.

8

Leisure

Canteens

After an uncertain start, the British authorities throughout the war and in every war theatre made progressively greater efforts to improve periods of rest and reserve, within the constraints set by fatigues, bull, and training. In this army, so rapidly expanded, 'at heart most of the brigade and divisional commanders were regimental officers. Whatever their deficiencies in the sphere of tactics may have been, the best of them understood and insisted on the highest possible standards of unit administration'.[1] The troop journals made frequent kicks at the inadequacy of divisional showers and laundries, and the ubiquity of lice, but never in a form that suggests that they did not accept these as inevitable features of the situation. Otherwise, the men were adequately clad and shod, and complaints were rare. This is a very significant fact, but it is perhaps scarcely more than other armies achieved, in the German case in the face of much greater difficulties arising from the Blockade. The French troops may have fared marginally worse in the matter of, for example, laundry arrangements, but they did not mutiny on account of poor unit administration.[2] What may, however, have been peculiar to the British was the extent to which many officers devoted effort to supplying more than these basic material wants to their men.

In this direction the Regular Divisions often led the way. It was, for example, from the 4th Division that the 51st Division copied in early 1916 such institutions as the divisional canteen. When a colonel on the staff of the 51st was moved to the 17th in the autumn of 1916, he in turn repeated the process by raising a loan in the No. 1 Mess to start a canteen.[3] The canteen was

---

[1] H. Essame, *The Battle for Europe, 1918* (1972), 111–12.
[2] Englander, 'The French Soldier', p. 58; Pedroncini, *Les Mutineries*, p. 311.
[3] W. N. Nicholson, *Behind the Lines* (1939), 206, 253.

nothing new in the army, having long been used as a means of
eking out the soldier's meagre pay, keeping him in bounds and
under control, and binding the unit together by stimulating off-
duty socializing among the men whilst showing evidence of
paternal care by the officers. Now new divisions were moved to
adopt the institution, not only by the example of the Regulars,
but also by the exorbitant prices being charged by *estaminets*.[4]
The divisional canteen spread to all types of division, including
those serving in war theatres other than France or Flanders.[5]

The normal stock of these canteens seems to have included
items such as tobacco, beer, soft drinks, books and newspapers,
candles, tinned goods, biscuits, and chocolates.[6] After the German retreat in spring 1917 had drawn a large part of the British
army deep into the devastated area, where civilian provision was
often not available for troops on rest or reserve, some canteens
responded by expanding their stock. The canteens of the 36th
Division, for example, then began to supply fruit, vegetables,
eggs, bread, cakes, and even fish, all of this organized by the
division's Q staff.[7]

Divisional canteens were the most highly organized, but battalions too might have their own canteens, with officers again
putting up the capital and providing administrative support. The
1/4th West Riding Battalion, for example, had a canteen started
by their transport officer which, until the winter of 1917/18, also
accompanied them into the line.[8] The 16th Canadian Scottish
record some accounts for their own canteen, which show that
between June 1916 and June 1918 it took $11,200 in the wet
canteen and $65,000 in the dry canteen, yielding a total profit of

[4] Edmonds, *History of the Great War*, 1916, i. 134; J. Ewing, *The History of the 9th (Scottish) Division 1914–1919* (1921), 416.
[5] H. R. Sandilands, *The 23rd Division 1914–1919* (Edinburgh, 1925), 132; F. P. Gibbon, *The 42nd (East Lancashire) Division 1914–1918* (1920), 69; H. Stewart, *The New Zealand Division 1916–1919* (New Zealand, 1921), 142; Bean, *Official History*, v. 20; A. B. Scott and P. M. Brumwell, *The History of the 12th (Eastern) Division in the Great War* (1923), 257.
[6] Nicholson, *Behind the Lines*, p. 257.
[7] C. Falls, *The History of the 36th (Ulster) Division* (Belfast, 1922). Cf. Gibbon, *42nd Division*, p. 69; F. W. Bewsher, *The History of the 51st (Highland) Division, 1914–1918* (Edinburgh, 1921), 269.
[8] P. G. Bales, *The History of the 1/4th Battalion Duke of Wellington's (West Riding) Regiment 1914–1919* (Halifax, 1920), 312–13.

$7,000, which was used to buy sports equipment, concert party properties, and extra food for free distribution.[9]

The work of the canteens was supplemented by civilian organizations like the YMCA, the Church Army, and the Dominion Comforts Funds, which the army allowed to set up facilities just behind the front. The Church Army established more than 800 canteens and recreation rooms on the Western Front and in Italy, whilst the YMCA had ten in the Ypres Salient alone in the later years of the war, turning over in March 1918 some 260,000 francs.[10] Well might *Aussie*, for example, pay tribute to 'what our Aussie YMCA does for us'.[11]

Among other services, the YMCA canteens distributed free magazines to the troops. *The Forty Niner* recorded in January 1915 that one canteen near the battalion had passed on over 500 lb. of such material in eighteen days in 1915.[12] The YMCA also had libraries in its recreation huts,[13] and a number of battalions maintained their own unit libraries.[14] In addition, the Camps Library Organization provided libraries for training and rest camps if requested by the camp commanders, the normal rate being one book to every six men. The army authorities co-operated fully, Haig himself appealing to the public for books.[15]

Excursions

More surprising perhaps is the army's involvement in organizing seaside excursions for men newly returned from the trenches. The destination might now be Dunkirk or Boulogne instead of Dunoon or Brighton, and travel might be by army lorry rather than by bus or train, but it was still a bizarre reproduction of peacetime pleasures and a telling illustration of the efforts of many officers to keep their men amused and contented. The

[9] Urquhart, *History of the 16th Battalion*, p. 224.
[10] Edmonds, *History of the Great War*, 1916, i. 139–41.
[11] *Aussie*, 5 (June 1918), 12. Cf. *The Brazier*, 4 (July 1916), 7; *M&D*, 2 (1917), 10.
[12] *The Forty Niner*, 4 (Jan. 1915), 27.
[13] *Aussie*, 5 (June 1918), 12; Burton, *Silent Division*, pp. 183–4; Gladden, *Ypres*, p. 131.
[14] *The Outpost*, 6/1 (Nov. 1917), 16; *The Linseed Lance*, 1/6 (May 1917), 78; Bales, *History of the 1/4th Battalion*, p. 314.
[15] T. W. Koch, *Books in Camp, Trench and Hospital* (1917), 21.

effort was perhaps more appreciated than the event, though any change was welcome. An officer in the 2nd Royal Fusiliers (an ex-Regular battalion) recorded one such trip in 1917 for a raiding party he had led the previous day:

two lorries were put at our disposal and Benson and I took the holidaymakers for a ride northwards to Dunkirk. We amused ourselves by studying the countryside and . . . the sight of the anglers sitting on the canal bank and watching their upturned umbrellas which served as floats gave rise to much hilarity. At last the lorries stopped in sight of the sand dunes and the sea, and here the drivers asked me for further instructions. Looking seaward I noticed the bleak stretches of sand . . . I decided to put it to the vote—sea bathing or a drink at the estaminet which happened to be just opposite the spot where the lorries had halted. The poll was unanimous, and so we paid for drinks all round and returned.[16]

Such trips are also recorded for other infantry units of all types.[17] One man remembers also longer seaside holidays for a week with extra pay, given in mid-1917 to those with the longest overseas service.[18]

Trips were also laid on to divisional horse shows. These do not seem to have been particularly popular. The lorries provided appeared to one private as 'one of those official arrangements to ensure that there was a sufficient sprinkling of "other ranks" at the essentially aristocratic amusement'.[19] Similarly, the Canadian Scottish visited horse shows 'more, it is suspected, for the sake of getting a day off from the war than from any vital interest in the exhibits'.[20] Since these exhibits tended to comprise officers' show jumping contests and turn-out competitions for every form of military limber, spiced up with mule races and wrestling on horseback, this is not altogether surprising. Nevertheless, horse shows seem to have been common on all fronts and they did at least help in 'alleviating the monotony of life . . . and eliminating the *cafard*'.[21]

[16] Parker, *Into Battle*, p. 80.
[17] War Diary of the 7th Battalion East Kent Regiment, WO 95/2049, 2 Sept. 1917; Gibbons, *Roll On Next War*, p. 85; W. J. Harvey, *The Red and White Diamond* (Melbourne, 1920), 208.
[18] Tucker, *Johnny Get Your Gun*, p. 160.
[19] Gladden, *Across the Piave*, p. 145.
[20] Urquhart, *History of the 16th Bn.*, p. 221.
[21] Villari, *The Macedonian Campaign*, p. 77. On the ubiquity of horse shows see Nicholson, *Behind the Lines*, p. 145.

The cousin of the horse show was the race meeting. This proved more popular with the rank and file, not least because it allowed them to indulge the passion for gambling which seemed to have been stimulated by war to the highest degree.[22] *Aussie* in August 1918 recorded one such event, for which bookmakers were registered with a supervisory committee:

a Digger dearly loves a horse-race . . . Randwick or Flemington have never attracted a more eager and interested crowd. Every Aussie from miles around turned up per every conceivable method of locomotion . . . It was a bright and joyous 'day out' and a welcome relief to the monotony of broken houses, shell holes, wire, general untidiness and Fritz.[23]

A lieutenant in the 1/23rd Londons attended a similar event and reflected afterwards 'what better tonic than that, for a division of Londoners with their Sandown, Kempton and Hurst Parks and, of course, Epsom Downs'.[24] In Palestine in particular, where the mounted divisions were a large and active part of the army, 'these race meetings became a prominent and well-liked feature of military life . . . whenever formations were resting'.[25]

Sport

As at home, football surpassed even race meetings in popularity, with other sport also attracting much enthusiasm. General Jack did not exaggerate when he wrote that 'no British troops ever travel without footballs or the energy to kick them'.[26] Soccer went with the various expeditionary forces to every fighting front. There was 'many a hard game' played in Macedonia.[27] At Gallipoli, although no part of the peninsula was safe from Turkish shell-fire, a Corps Tournament was organized and

---

[22] Graham, *Private in the Guards*, p. 190; Burton, *Silent Division*, pp. 190–1; Black, *One Volunteer*, p. 71.
[23] *Aussie*, 6 (Aug. 1918), 16.
[24] Middlebrook, *Kaiser's Battle*, p. 360.
[25] A. J. Hill, *Chauvel of the Light Horse* (Melbourne, 1978), 100–1.
[26] J. Terraine (ed.), *General Jack's Diary* (1964), 227.
[27] C. Wheeler, *Memorial Record of the 7th (Service) Bn. Ox. and Bucks. Light Infantry* (Oxford, 1921), 50. Cf. *Middlesex Yeomanry Magazine*, 2 (Oct. 1917), 8–9.

played out.[28] Even in Mesopotamia, 'Platoon, Company and Battalion football matches were played, ten minutes each way, at 110 degrees in the shade, just as the sun was setting',[29] and in Palestine, 'in spite of the unfavourable conditions (and less propitious circumstances could hardly be imagined!) football loomed large in the activities of the Kensingtons when the sun had passed its zenith'.[30] In France, 'socker [sic] football was as much a fetish in the Expeditionary Force as it is at home'.[31] An other-rank in the 1/4th (Dundee) Battalion Black Watch remembered how 'most of our men were playing football within half an hour of finishing a heavy march after a fortnight in the trenches'.[32] Astonishing as such enthusiasm among men so weary sounds, it echoes the account of a Durham miner who recalled how, before the war, the local lads worked ten hours a day in the pits, and then gathered on the village green to play a hard game of football without flinching.[33] As the historian of the 18th Division observed, 'our armies on the Western Front, no matter how much they were overworked, always raised a bit of spare energy for games'.[34]

No opportunity was missed. The 2/5th Battalion Notts. and Derby Regiment enjoyed a spell in Brigade Reserve in June 1917, and 'the ubiquitous football made its appearance and assumed its old-time place as first favourite among the men, even though the time was high summer'.[35] Longer spells of divisional rest saw a similar outburst. According to one troop journal, 'any time you like to look round after the soldier is "at rest" you will see small knots of warriors kicking the leather spheroid about'.[36]

This last observation was made not of a city battalion, but of the 5th (Cinque Ports) Battalion Royal Sussex Regiment. The

---

[28] R. R. Thompson, *The Fifty-Second (Lowland) Division 1914–1918* (Glasgow, 1923), 156.

[29] L. R. Missen, *The History of the 7th (Service) Bn. Prince of Wales's (North Staffs.) Regt. 1914–1919* (Cambridge, 1920), 67.

[30] O. F. Bailey and H. M. Hollier, *The Kensingtons, 13th London Regiment* (1936), 272.

[31] Corbett, *War Story of the 1/8th Bn.*, p. 123.

[32] Andrews, *Haunting Years*, p. 143.

[33] W. J. Baker, 'The Making of a Working Class Football Culture in Victorian England', *Journal of Social History*, 13 (1979), 246.

[34] G. H. F. Nichols, *The 18th Division in the Great War* (Edinburgh, 1922), 189.

[35] Hall, *The Green Triangle*, pp. 89–90.

[36] *The Cinque Ports Gazette*, 1 (May 1916), 8.

ubiquity of army sport is a forceful reminder of the common culture shared by the great majority of British troops, even those from the more rural areas. For the 6th (Banff and Donside) Gordon Highlanders, out at rest in 1916, 'football was, as usual, the favourite game'.[37] The pages of the *5th Glo'ster Gazette* reveal the enthusiasm for the game in this country battalion.[38] Inter-battalion soccer competitions were also played out in Divisions like the 36th (Ulster) and the 38th (Welsh).[39]

The Dominion troops at least matched this enthusiasm for sport. Among the Canadians, 'the moment our men get out of the trenches they begin to play baseball, football, cricket, etc.'. Inter-brigade baseball in the summer of 1917 'attracted as much interest as any league match in Canada'.[40] Among the New Zealanders, 'most of our men would sell their souls for football'.[41] And for the Australians, in the winter of 1917/18, 'football competitions were the supreme interest behind the Messines front . . . "The battalions are just like a lot of Oxford colleges in the October term (says an Australian diarist)—more keen on their football for the moment than on anything else in the world"'.[42] Australians at Gallipoli had played cricket on Shell Green, on the eve of the evacuation, 'to give an appearance of normality'.[43] It is not surprising to find that the troop journals, British and Dominion alike, reflected this interest by allotting extensive coverage to reports and results of inter- and intra-battalion matches of all kinds.

Much of the activity was spontaneous and unorganized. Official reaction to the soldiers' enthusiasm for sport had at first been sometimes negative. In July 1915 Haig, then in command of First Army, noted an increase in the number of cases of men asleep on sentry duty, and commented in his diary that 'men should rest during the day when they know they will be on sentry duty at night. Instead of resting they run about and play football.'[44] As

[37] D. Mackenzie, *The 6th Gordons in France and Flanders* (Aberdeen, 1922), 79.

[38] *The 5th Glo'ster Gazette, passim*. On the rural character of the 5th Gloucesters see Green, *British Army*, p. 41.

[39] Falls, *History of the 36th Division*, pp. 135–7; A. B. Beauman, *With the 38th in France and Italy* (Lichfield, 1919), 12, 39.

[40] Dawson, *Living Bayonets*, p. 129; Urquhart, *History of the 16th Bn.*, p. 221.

[41] C. H. Weston, *Three Years with the New Zealanders* (1918), 252.

[42] Bean, *Official History*, v. 20.

[43] Smith, *The Anzacs*, p. 138.

[44] Terraine (ed.), *General Jack's Diary*, p. 91.

the war dragged on, however, officers at all levels came to recognize the value of sport, and began actively to promote it. Gough, as GOC Fifth Army, ordered in August 1916 the establishment of football grounds in each brigade area.[45] At divisional level, the assistant adjutant and quarter-master general of the 36th Division issued, in August 1917, a directive on winter comforts for the men:

it is not at present possible to judge to what extent the ground will be suitable for football in the winter months. If it is suitable the men themselves may be relied upon to play, and no doubt the game will be properly organized by officers and a liberal supply of footballs maintained . . . If, however, football and hockey are not possible later on, it should always be possible by means of a little clearing of debris to provide good handball alleys in each village. This is a very popular game with Irishmen and there is no better form of exercise.[46]

Divisional commanders increasingly encouraged the organization of football competitions among the units under their command, the champions being presented by these surrogates of royalty with a championship cup. Divisional pioneers were set to work clearing and laying out sports fields. By 1917, the facilities available could be impressive. The divisional area taken over by the 1st Canadian Division in June of that year, when it relieved the 3rd Canadian Division in the line, contained nine baseball fields, one indoor field, three football fields, three tennis courts, one basketball square, and two boxing platforms.[47]

Sport overspilled the designated grounds, and divisional orders had to remind officers and men of the interests of the French farmer, whose land was thus taken over.[48] Battalions had company and platoon competitions, matches between officers and sergeants, and ordinary 'kickabouts' as a feature of training. Increasingly, it became the norm for formal military training, on rest, to end at lunchtime, with the afternoons given over to sport. A man of the 20th Battalion London Regiment, returning to his

[45] War Diary, 5th Army A and Q Staff, WO 95/523, Aug. 1916, ref. Q 673/26 Schedule 3.

[46] War Diary, 36th Division A and Q Staff, WO 95/2493, Aug. 1917, Appendix 21.

[47] War Diary, 1st Canadian Division A and Q Staff, WO 95/3731, June 1917, Appendix E.

[48] War Diary, 4th Division A and Q Staff, WO 95/1449, Routine Orders, 18 Apr. 1915; War Diary, 5th Division A and Q Staff, WO 95/1517, 'Extracts from Routine Orders, Etc.', p. 9.

unit in the autumn of 1916 after six months absence, noted that 'we have longer spells in the trenches, but our "rest" days are far better. In the morning we have parades, but our afternoons are devoted to sport, such as football and company running.'[49]

Competitive matches between units could attract large crowds. 1,500 attended a match between officers of two Highland Light Infantry battalions; 1,500 again a match between the 14th Battalion Royal Irish Rifles and the 11th Battalion Royal Inniskilling Fusiliers; 2–3,000 a match between the 6th Battalion Connaught Rangers and a Northern Irish battalion (played 'in a spirit of friendliness which, so far as I am aware, seems unattainable on Ireland's native soil'); 2,500 the inter-battalion final of the 48th Division's Fanshawe Cup.[50]

Compulsory attendance was rare. Norman Gladden, in the 11th Battalion Northumberland Fusiliers, remembers, in 1918,

a compulsory parade to watch our platoon play Number 7 at soccer . . . Compulsory sport was extremely unpopular even with addicts, of whom we had plenty, for the company's sporting record was an excellent one, but this was the only time I experienced anything of this sort in the army. No doubt the imposition on this occasion was the outcome of someone's bad temper.[51]

For great numbers of men, attendance at a big match was welcome, not least as a reminder of home. Buses were laid on to take men from the 17th Battalion Highland Light Infantry to the semi-final of their Divisional Cup competition. According to the battalion magazine, 'travelling by "Motor" in the early hours of a Saturday afternoon to a football match is one of the nearest approaches we have had to the old days before the war'.[52] It was a glimpse of their *Scotia irridenta*, a reminder of the way of life for which they were fighting.

Support for the battalion team was also valuable in symbolizing and reinforcing unit *esprit de corps*. In the AIF, sport

did much to keep the competitive spirit at a high pitch and develop the unit esprit-de-corps; competitions were followed with the keenest interest by the soldier 'sports'. Every unit had its team, and the esprit de

[49] *Invicta Gazette*, 10 (Apr. 1917), 17.
[50] *The Outpost*, 3/2 (May 1916), 59; *The Incinerator*, 1 (May 1916), 11; Feilding, *War Letters*, pp. 169–70; *The 5th Glo'ster Gazette*, 10 (Mar. 1916), 3.
[51] Gladden, *Across the Piave*, p. 73.
[52] *The Outpost*, 4/2 (Dec. 1916), 105.

corps which animated every section of the army was reflected in these competitions. Battalions carried their colour to the field of contest, marched to conquest to the music of their bands, and strove to retain their reputation by every form of demonstration.[53]

In the British units, as local character came to be swamped by the flood of conscript replacements, sport sometimes had to help create *esprit de corps* before it could reflect it. *The Outpost* exhorted: 'lately as a Battalion it has been our good fortune to "play". With what zest did we cheer "ours" in all the events! May we now in the great game be able to say with the same zest: "Good old Umpteenth".'[54]

Officer involvement in sport did something to break down the dehumanizing barriers of military protocol. Among the Australians, it is not to be wondered at that 'matches between the officers and NCOs provided keen enjoyment for the troops, who relished the privilege when "barracking" of calling the officers by their Christian names or nicknames. Even the acting CO was not exempt from the popular practice . . . the Diggers employed all their powers of humour in supporting both sides.'[55] Similarly the Canadians held a baseball competition in the summer of 1917, and

the supporters of the different teams . . . shouted such witticisms and jeering remarks at the players—irrespective of rank—as bewildered the British officers . . . It was bad enough to hear a group of privates tell a non-commissioned officer who was pitching that he had 'a glass eye', but it seemed to them as if discipline had completely broken down when a crowd of all ranks kept yelling in chorus at the batting of the Brigadier-General, 'He swings like a gate, the blighter—he-swings-like-a-gate'.[56]

For once, however, the Canadians painted the British as worse than they actually were. The sports field was privileged ground, and the spectacle of the officers, few of whom perhaps had played the Association game at school, irresistibly funny. Games between officers and sergeants were treated as farcical entertainments, staged for the pleasure of the other-ranks. In a Belfast

[53] E. Wren, *Randwick to Hargicourt: the History of the 3rd Bn. A.I.F.* (Sydney, 1935), 270; Harvey, *The Red and White Diamond*, p. 201.

[54] *The Outpost*, 5/5 (Sept. 1917), 157.

[55] Harvey, *The Red and White Diamond*, pp. 116–17. Cf. Wren, *Randwick to Hargicourt*, p. 270.

[56] Urquhart, *History of the 16th Bn.*, p. 221.

battalion in 1915, 'several of these matches were played, their principal object being to amuse the men. At any rate, so it always proved.' Because the officers were more familiar with Rugby, 'the unconventional methods of the latter provided huge amusement to the men, and every opportunity to develop their irony and chaff'. In May 1916, however, 'the sergeants turned up smiling comfortably, and the men bordered the touch-line in readiness to criticize sarcastically without fear or favour', but the officers won: 'nobody can explain it . . . the men are uncommunicative on the subject, but dark hints seem to suggest that they resent being deprived of what was to have been their best alternative to a visit to the Belfast pantomime'.[57] In the 17th Battalion Highland Light Infantry, more happily, a match between officers and sergeants 'afforded much amusement to the spectators. The antics of the Officers were funnier than anything yet seen—which is saying much.'[58] In sports of all kinds, 'officers descended from their giddy altitudes of discipline and became almost chummy. They held the tape for you in the different heats, fielded the cricket ball or loaned you their shorts and sweaters, and you rubbed "flashes" with them in the crowd without having to salute and look as though you realized the enormity of your offence.'[59] It was a welcome reassertion of human relationships in an army which did so much to set up a barrier between officers and men.

Sport allowed above all a brief mental escape from stress and horror: the longer the War continued the more obvious it became that if 'rest' periods were to do any good to the men at all they must be periods of mental as well as physical rest, and games of all sorts provided the required relaxation more than anything else. On coming out of the trenches, weary, muddy, possibly hungry, and almost certainly wet through, the men's first moments of freedom were spent in a game of football.[60]

Such moments of relief were a vital part of adjustment to Western Front conditions. *The Outpost* remembered the shock of the first encounter: 'nothing we had ever seen or heard of could prepare us for that terrible initiation period, when we

[57] *The Incinerator*, 1 (May 1916), 11.

[58] *The Outpost*, 4/2 (Dec. 1916), 102.

[59] Ibid. 5/2 (June 1917), 46.

[60] F. C. Grimwade, *War History of the 4th Bn. The London Regt. (Royal Fusiliers) 1914–1919* (1922), 293.

encountered more difficulties and hardships than we had ever "dreamt of in our philosophy"'. Now, though,

we are settling down to the life. The conditions at first were inclined to take our breath away, and we couldn't find any time to devote to the social side of our life. But now that we have had time to adapt ourselves to the new conditions, social activities are springing up everywhere. Of course we have never been without our happy evenings in billet or dug-out when we 'sing a song or tell a story', but now we are getting right into the swing of things and are blossoming forth, with football matches and full-fledged concerts . . . There is no doubt about it, life out here is pretty much what we make it, and we, who always make the best of everything, never let the thought of war interfere with our enjoyment.[61]

No less important, such entertainments were a relief from boredom, and boredom was the inescapable condition of army life, for all its activity, in every war theatre. It was perhaps worst in the alien and sparsely settled terrain of Mesopotamia, the Macedonian hills, or southern Palestine. On the Salonika Front, for example, the inhabitants had been banished from a wide sector behind the line so that the troops 'practically never saw a civilian face for months on end—sometimes for 6 months, they went, without quitting for a minute their own little khaki world'.[62] Similarly, during the long deadlock before Gaza, on the fringe of Palestine, the line was stranded in the desert, 'seemingly isolated' with 'no local inhabitants still in the rear tending estaminets'.[63] But, however envious the troops on other fronts, even in France, according to the magazine of the 5th Glo'sters, 'if we were asked what were our feelings about the War most of us would probably say we were bored to tears'.[64] The experience of the 44th Battalion CEF was not untypical:

does the reader weary of the endless repetition— 'up the line' and 'out', march and working party, casualty and reinforcement—in this chronicle? Let him judge, then, of the unutterable monotony that weighs the souls of men whose lives are bound in the narrow routine of war. 'Up the line'—days in cramped trenches are punctuated by shells, bullets, bombs, the issue of rations, comrades killed and wounded; nights are hours of ceaseless work and tense watching. 'Out on rest'—a

[61] *The Outpost*, 2/6 (Feb. 1916), 178.
[62] F. Tuohy, *The Crater of Mars* (1929), 218–19.
[63] E. Blackwell and E. C. Axe, *Romford to Beirut* (Clacton on Sea, 1928), 87–8.
[64] *The 5th Glo'ster Gazette*, 22 (Mar. 1918), 5.

succession of working, carrying, training. And always over all—rats, vermin, gas, the irk of discipline, the haze of uncertainty, the sense of utter futility, the knowledge that each moment of life is enslaved to other men in some remote headquarters.

In this context, 'the best of all antidotes . . . prove to be games. Sports break the deadening inertia, introduce to the men a new interest in which they revel—and are utilized, more and more, as a definite part of the day's programs.'[65]

Sports were an activity for segregated males, uniquely well-adapted to be translated to the war fronts, and to do something to avert the terrible monotony of the soldiers' lives. They were particularly valuable once the German retreat of early 1917 drew much of the army forward into 'the Teuton-made veldt'. Divisional staffs responded with intensified programmes of sports, and also of concerts. Battalions followed suit. Rest in 'Annihilation Waste', *The Outpost* admitted, was 'not like old times': the friendly villages and farms were gone, 'but still, resting isn't fighting, and there is always a great deal to be thankful for in this life. Games have not lost their zest, nor concerts their charm, and it is wonderful how happy we can be when we try.'[66] For a battalion of the 5th Division, with fine weather for sports, the divisional concert troupe close at hand, divisional baths and a canteen, 'it is doubtful whether there was any special desire to get back to a French village as excursions to Arras were very few both as to occasions and numbers'.[67]

Army sport discharged in military life many of the social functions which had been optimistically identified in a civilian context by the middle-class advocates of proletarian sport, and which in practice sport did achieve according to historians of the period. It brought together officers and other-ranks in a friendly spirit just as at home it provided 'practical exercises in class collaboration' to mitigate antagonism;[68] it solved the 'problem' of proletarian leisure by engaging the military proletarian in a pursuit, hopefully self-improving and propagandizing for the ideals of the

[65] E. S. Russenholt, *Six Thousand Canadian Men* (Winnipeg, 1932), 103–4.
[66] *The Outpost*, 4/6 (Apr. 1917), 196.
[67] J. E. B. Fairclough, *The First Birmingham Bn. in the Great War 1914–1919* (Birmingham, 1923), 106–7.
[68] V. G. Kiernan, 'Conscription and Society in Europe before the War of 1914–1918', in M. R. D. Foot (ed.), *War and Society* (1973), 146.

status quo, but at all events diverting and preoccupying; it functioned as compensation and pleasure to improve his mood. But it
operated also in ways which its advocates less clearly foresaw.
These ways, though less directly a means of social control, were
none the less important, for they satisfied needs which the soldier
himself felt, and so reduced in some measure dissatisfaction with
his unhappy lot. As in civilian life, sport provided an affirmation
of community, an area of some autonomy away from the rigid
obedience of the work-place, an opportunity for a sort of
creativity, and a displacement of real anxiety by play stress,
yielding escape and excitement innocent of fear.[69] There was
much more than just nostalgia or boredom to the soldier's
enthusiasm for football. Only thus is the avidity with which it
was pursued by men weary to exhaustion explicable.

Army Concert Parties

Army concert parties performed the same sorts of functions as
sports. They enjoyed also a similar ubiquity. They featured on
the Salonika, Palestine, and Western Fronts, and in
Mesopotamia there were at least battalion concert parties.[70]
Again, there had been some initial resistance. In the Salonika
force, for example, the authorities had only in the winter of 1917
begun actively to encourage 'sane and healthy amusement': the
collapse of Russia seemed to have set the stage for an interminable war, whilst the shipping shortage severed ties with home.
Before this, amusements for the troops had been regarded in
official circles as a 'luxury', and one which reflected badly on the
seriousness with which the force was setting about its task: 'OCs
of units or concert parties had to proceed warily . . . like the
worship of the early Christians, the early development of our
theatres proceeded slowly and quietly'.[71]

Perhaps the force of this hostility owed something to the special sensitivity about popular jibes at the inactivity of the

---

[69] R. McKibbin, 'Work and Hobbies in Britain 1880–1950', in J. M. Winter (ed.),
The Working Class in Modern British History: Essays in Honour of Henry Pelling (Cambridge, 1983), 127–46.

[70] See Appendix B.

[71] H. C. Owen, *Salonica and After* (1919), 118–20.

'gardeners' of Salonika, enjoying a pleasant 'holiday' in the south of Europe, but feelings of similar sort existed also in some units in France. There, some disapproved of such 'luxuries' as out of keeping with a serious national effort; others maintained that, 'such trifles made the men "soft" and unfitted them for hard trench warfare conditions; adding as an afterthought, that discontent would quickly spread if the luxury supply was not kept up'; others again simply protested that it 'wasn't war'.[72]

In some cases, therefore, the groups which eventually became official brigade or divisional concert parties had first evolved in YMCA huts or 'almost spontaneously' in the open at rest.[73] In other cases, battalion officers had been the first to recognize the utility of concert parties and had formed their own, from which the best performers were subsequently taken when brigade or divisional parties were formed.[74]

Once the idea took hold, the authorities put considerable effort into supporting it. Members of the troupes were usually exempted from all but light duties, becoming virtually full-time entertainers.[75] Pioneers were set to constructing theatres or converting barns. Divisional funds or sums subscribed by the officers were used to provide the capital for costumes, lights, and properties.

At divisional level, the Regular Divisions seem to have led the way. 'The Follies' of the 4th Division and 'The Fancies' of the 6th 'were the forerunners of the Divisional theatrical troupes which subsequently became universal'.[76] Different dates are given for their formation, but certainly 'The Fancies' were in existence by February 1915 and 'The Follies' as early as Decem-

[72] Nicholson, *Behind the Lines*, p. 249.

[73] Anon., *History of the 10th (Service) Bn. The East Yorks. Regt. (Hull Commercials)* (1937), 73, 130; R. O. Russell, *History of the 11th (Lewisham) Bn. The Queen's Own Royal West Kent Regt.* (1934), 176; Burton, *Silent Division*, pp. 183–4; Russenholt, *Six Thousand Canadian Men*, p. 56.

[74] W. E. Grey, *The 2nd City of London Regt. (Royal Fusiliers) in the Great War 1914–1919* (1929), 221; T. Chalmers, *An Epic of Glasgow: The History of the 15th Bn. The Highland Light Infantry* (Glasgow, 1934), 54; R. Hodder-Williams, *Princess Patricia's Canadian Light Infantry 1914–1919*, i (1923), 140; T. Ternan, *The Story of the Tyneside Scottish* (Newcastle, 1920), 139–40.

[75] S. Gillon, *The Story of the 29th Division* (1925), 102; A. H. Maude, *The 47th (London) Division 1914–1919* (1922), 221; Aston and Duggan, *History of the 12th Bn.*, pp. 64–6; W. C. C. Weetman, *The Sherwood Foresters in the Great War 1914–1919: 1/8 Bn.* (Nottingham, 1920), 162.

[76] T. O. Marden, *A Short History of the 6th Division* (1920), 11–12.

ber 1914.[77] Sometimes the dissemination of the idea can be
directly traced. A party from the 48th Division saw the 4th
Division 'Follies' in late 1915: 'on the way home many of us,
talking over the matter, came to the conclusion that what the 4th
Division have accomplished we of the 48th Division could surely
emulate'. Sure enough, the next issue of the battalion journal
recorded the first performance of the 48th (South Midland) Division concert party, financed by the Deputy Lord Mayor of
Birmingham and another local worthy.[78] Similarly, the 51st Division copied its concert party from the 4th ('who were, perhaps
justifiably, but amazingly conceited about their administrative
excellence'), and in turn provided the model for the 17th when
one of its staff officers transferred.[79]

Like sports, the concert parties were not confined to any one
section of the army. All four Scottish Divisions supported an
official troupe, as did the single Ulster, both the Welsh, at least
one of the two Southern Irish, the single New Zealand, and the
four Canadian Divisions.[80] Among the Australians, by late 1917,

every Division now had its concert party, almost every Brigade had its
entertainers, while even the Battalions were beginning to organize
troupes which were to be set apart to do nothing more than keep up the
spirits of the war-weary men—a task which was difficult enough and
important enough to justify all the efforts that were bent to it.[81]

By the end of 1916 most divisions had formed an official concert party, and by the latter part of 1917 they were practically
universal. Brigade and battalion concert parties were not superseded but supplemented. Field Ambulances, RE and ASC companies also had their troupes which the infantryman might visit
or which might tour to him. Given this profusion, there were
often concert parties resident in the rest camps and reserve billets
performing every night. Otherwise, they might tour to the camps
and villages, or the troops might travel to nearby theatres on foot
or in lorries provided by the authorities.

There were five theatres in the rest area taken over by the 3rd
Canadian Division in January 1918; even when it moved back

---

[77] See Appendix B.
[78] *The 5th Glo'ster Gazette*, 8 (Dec. 1915), 14, and 9 (Feb. 1916), 7.
[79] Nicholson, *Behind the Lines*, pp. 206, 253.
[80] See Appendix B.
[81] Harvey, *The Red and White Diamond*, p. 202.

into the line, there were three in its new area.[82] A machine-gunner, on rest near Arras in August 1917, found that

within five minutes walk of our Camp no less than four large concert halls had now been erected, and every night Concert Parties, belonging to the various Divisions stationed on the Arras front gave first-rate concerts, to which all troops were admitted for the sum of half a franc. These concerts were greatly appreciated by our soldiers, especially after a long dreary spell of duty in the 'trenches'.[83]

Similarly, in December of the same year, the lee of Vimy Ridge seemed to one private in the London Rifle Brigade like 'a kind of suburb of London . . . On the right were the 62nd Divisional concert party, then an infantry camp, then the Bow Bells [56th Divisional concert party], and so on right down the Lens road.'[84] Even in Palestine, the magazine of one of the signals units of the 52nd Division noted in March 1918, 'recently we have had the pleasure of witnessing performances by several good concert parties—The Jinks—The Balloonatics—The Tangerines and the concert party of the Light Railway. Why not one of our own?'[85]

Most of the concert parties charged a small fee for admission to theatre performances (as opposed to the open-air shows often given on tour). It was only a matter of a franc or so, but, given the infantryman's poverty, free trips were sometimes provided out of battalion funds, and this sufficiently often for there to be reduced rates offered for block bookings.[86]

Men took advantage of the variety of productions available. Many ordinary soldiers remember visiting a number of different brigade and divisional troupes in the course of their service.[87] Smaller shows, too, were enjoyed beyond the precincts of their unit. A pantomime put on by the 85th Field Ambulance, where establishment strength was less than 250 men, attracted an aggre-

[82] War Diary, 3rd Canadian Division A and Q Staff, WO 95/3842, Jan. 1918, Appendix A, 2, and Feb. 1918, Appendix A, 4.

[83] A. Russell, *With the Machine Gun Corps* (1923), 135.

[84] Smith, *Four Years*, p. 297.

[85] *White and Blue*, 1 (Mar. 1918), 5.

[86] Grimwade, *War History of the 4th Bn.*, p. 223; Harvey, *The Red and White Diamond*, p. 204; War Diary, 4th Division A and Q Staff, WO 95/1449, Routine Orders, 5 Aug. 1915.

[87] A. S. Dolden, *Cannon Fodder* (Poole, 1980), 122, 157; E. Morrow, *Iron in the Fire* (Sydney, 1934), 182–3, 237; Gladden, *Ypres*, pp. 103, 154, 160–1; W. J. Wood, *With the 5th Glo'sters at Home and Overseas* (1925), 28, 58, 93, 100; A. H. Davis, *Extracts from the Diaries of a Tommy* (1932), 108, 148, 182, 190, 194.

gate audience of about 35–40,000, and this on a front where 'few units of any importance had not made some sort of attempt to amuse themselves, and one found concert parties and theatres all over the country'.[88]

The frequency with which men could get to shows is impossible to calculate with any degree of accuracy. As some indication, 'The Goods' of the 58th Division gave about 250 shows in their first year of existence.[89] Divisional theatres seem to have ranged in capacity from about 400 to 800 seats.[90] They are recalled as 'packed', 'packed every night', 'packed every evening': 'they had unbounded popularity; the houses were invariably packed to overflow, the applause was vociferous, the laughter deafening. If it was medicine as I believed it to be, then it was swallowed in great gulps.'[91] If packed they were, then an average house might be about 600. Touring performances might have greater or smaller audiences according to local conditions. They might play to a battalion billeted in a village or, as 'The Goods' did at Achiet in 1917, to 4–5,000 men in the natural amphitheatre formed by a crater.[92] Probably outdoor audiences were on the whole the larger, so an extension of the figure of 600 would not be imprudent. The result would be, very tentatively, an aggregate audience for the year of around 150,000, or about eight times the entire complement of the division. Then there might also be concert parties for any of the three brigades, the twelve battalions, the three field ambulances, the artillery, transport, and engineers.

Even when formally constituted concert parties did not exist in the unit itself, or in nearby units, still no period of rest or reserve

[88] Anon., *Aladdin in Macedonia*, p. xii; Owen, *Salonica and After*, p. 118.

[89] Anon., *A Souvenir of 'The Goods' Divisional Concert Party*, CUL War Collection, 30, gives the figure of 250 performances. Internal evidence shows that this souvenir must have been produced just prior to the staging of the 1917 Christmas pantomime, and the troupe was formed in Dec. 1916: Grimwade, *War History of the 4th Bn.*, p. 236.

[90] War Diary, 56th Division A and Q Staff, WO 95/2936, Jan. 1918, Appendix A; Gillon, *Story of the 29th Division*, p. 108; Scott and Brumwell, *History of the 12th Division*, pp. 88, 257–8; Nicholson, *Behind the Lines*, pp. 253–4; Cutlack (ed.), *War Letters of General Monash*, pp. 161–2.

[91] H. A. Foley (ed.), *Scrap Book of the 7th Bn. Somerset Light Infantry* (Aylesbury, 1932), 72; Eberle, *My Sapper Venture*, p. 75; G. Dugdale, *Langemarck and Cambrai* (Shrewsbury, 1932), 62; Nicholson, *Behind the Lines*, p. 256.

[92] C. A. C. Keeson, *The History and Records of Queen Victoria's Rifles 1792–1922* (1923), 295–6.

was without its *ad hoc* concerts, at which soldiers would perform, singing, reciting, conjuring, doing comedy or ventriloquy. In addition to these concerts, whether arranged by the unit Entertainments Committee, by the OC Entertainments, or improvised by the rank and file in billets or *estaminets*, YMCA huts and tents also saw the production of such entertainments.[93]

From divisional troupe to impromptu concert, all reveal a large debt to music hall. Often they included specific borrowings. The programme of 'The Curios' of the 48th Division in June 1917 included

> Ri-ti-ti-ti . . . A Coster Number
> Music Hall Singers Burlesqued
> Motoring . . . Mr Harry Tate's Great Sketch.[94]

'Motoring', in fact, was a particular favourite. It featured also in the shows put on by 'The Crumps' of the 41st Division, or 'The Tonics' of the 92nd Brigade.[95] 'The Cheerios' of the 2/6th Battalion King's Liverpool Regiment sang songs made famous by Albert Chevalier.[96] Concerts included the songs of Harry Wheldon, George Robey, or Harry Lauder, or 'the usual comic songs about mother-in-law and fat ladies bathing at the seaside'.[97] Entertainments of every type featured also the sentimental songs which were the other face of the halls.[98]

The style of performance too was unmistakably that of music hall. There were ensemble sketches, but they fitted into a general format which was a succession of 'turns'. A performance of the 29th Division's 'Diamond Troupe' in September 1917 featured a trick cyclist, a Chaplin mimic, a 'girl' vocalist, a 'Zummerzet yokel' describing his love affairs, and a 'tall, droll-faced Jock' who 'played the simpleton sublimely'.[99] The theatres themselves

---

[93] *The Sling*, 1 (Jan. 1917), 25; F. E. Noakes, *The Distant Drum* (Tunbridge Wells, 1952), 114.

[94] *The 5th Glo'ster Gazette*, 19 (June 1917), 18.

[95] Aston and Duggan, *History of the 12th Bn.*, pp. 64–6; Anon., *History of the 10th (Service) Bn. The East Yorkshire Regt.*, p. 134.

[96] C. E. Wurtzburg, *The History of the 2/6th (Rifle) Bn. 'The King's' (Liverpool Regiment) 1914–1919* (Aldershot, 1920), 250.

[97] *N.Y.D.*, 4 (Dec. 1916), 3; D. Sutherland, *War Diary of the 5th Seaforth Highlanders* (1920), 39, 44; D. Boyd, *Salute of Guns* (1930), 274; *The Sling*, 2 (Oct. 1917), 7; P. Gosse, *Memoirs of a Camp Follower* (1950), 30.

[98] Anon., *Souvenir of 'The Goods'*, p. 3; *The Outpost*, 4/2 (Dec. 1916), 88.

[99] Gillon, *Story of the 29th Division*, p. 108. Cf. *The Outpost*, 4/2 (Dec. 1916), 88.

were 'Empires', 'Coliseums', or 'Hippodromes', like those at home.[100] Even many of the performers were music hall professionals in peacetime.[101]

The tone of the performances also matched that of music hall, which was characterized by 'fatalism, political scepticism, the evasion of tragedy or anger, and a stance of comic stoicism'.[102] Just as music hall tended 'to laugh at misfortune rather than give it the bitter articulation of the broadsides',[103] so the concert party troupes presented the soldier's plight in comic fashion. The 5th Division, like many divisions, was aggrieved at being put in twice on the Somme: when it came out for its spell of rest, its troupe, 'The Whizz Bangs', had a song for it to the tune of Robey's 'Another Little Drink':

There was a famous div went to take a certain farm
They put the wind up Fritz and caused him great alarm
But the Corps Commander said,
When he heard what they had done,
Well! another little stunt wouldn't do 'em any harm.[104]

This sort of topicality was easiest for battalion rhymesters, in touch with specific grievances. A battalion of the 20th Londons had such a man, a machine-gunner called Walkey, 'always ready with some topical parody on passing events'. On their first spell in the line some men, overcome by hunger, ate their iron rations and were punished with a heavy dose of pack drill, which some still had not completed when they arrived back in billets at the end of the tour:

[100] J. H. Boraston and C. E. O. Bax, *The 8th Division in War 1914–1918* (1926), 60; V. E. Inglefield, *History of the 20th (Light) Division* (1921), 120; Feilding, *War Letters*, p. 207.
[101] Aston and Duggan, *History of the 12th Bn.*, pp. 64–6; Fairclough, *1st Birmingham Bn.*, p. 41; Russell, *History of the 11th (Lewisham) Bn.*, p. 98; Grey, *2nd City of London Regt.*, pp. 90–1; Maude, *The 47th Division*, pp. 223–4; Anon., *Souvenir of 'The Goods'*, pp. 15, 25; Tucker, *Johnny Get Your Gun*, p. 137; *The Direct Hit*, 3 (Dec. 1916), 9–10.
[102] G. Stedman Jones, 'Working Class Culture and Working Class Politics in London, 1879–1900: Notes on the Remaking of a Working Class', *Journal of Social History*, 7 (1974), 478–9.
[103] P. Summerfield, 'The Effingham Arms and the Empire: Deliberate Selection in the Evolution of the Music Hall in London', in Yeo and Yeo (eds.), *Popular Culture and Class Conflict 1590–1914*, p. 233.
[104] Fairclough, *1st Birmingham Bn.*, p. 72.

imagine, therefore, their joy when, at the battalion concert held the next night, Walkey recited this effort:

> Where's your Iron, where's your Iron
> Where's your Iron Ration?
> It's not for use, that's no excuse;
> Your iron rations you must produce.
> It's only meant for ornament,
> You must be in the fashion,
> But you'll get it hot if you haven't got
> Your Iron, Iron Ration.

After a typical army 'rest', Walkey came up with:

> Hullo! hullo! when's the next parade?
> Can't we have a minute to ourselves?
> Five, nine, three: another after tea:
> Oh! oh! oh! they've done us properly.

> Hullo! hullo! what's their dirty game,
> Working us at ninety in the shade?
> It wasn't the tale they told when we enlisted,
> Now it's all parade, parade.

He was killed at Loos, but 'other comedians arose to take Walkey's place'.[105] In fact, according to the historians of soldiers' songs in the First World War, most units had at least one such competent parodist producing topical ditties.[106] The *Invicta Gazette* paid tribute to their value: 'long live the men who have the happy knack of turning out these impromptu parodies . . . for they play a tremendous part in keeping up the men's spirits in the trenches, much more so than most people imagine. May they flourish and continue their versifying till the end of the chapter.'[107]

More generalized grievances were also dealt with in this way. There were jabs at the Home Front, at the support troops, at the scarcity of leave and of real rest, and at the endlessness of the war. Even the fear of being swallowed up by the bottomless mud was turned into a joke. The story was told of a man finding a service cap lying on the surface of the mud. Picking it up, he found a man immersed up to his neck underneath. The finder earnestly enquired of the man thus buried whether he was all

[105] *Invicta Gazette*, 6 (Dec. 1916), 16.
[106] J. Brophy and E. Partridge, *The Long Trail* (1965), 15.
[107] *Invicta Gazette*, 6 (Dec. 1916), 16.

right, and received the reply that he was indeed fine, but a little concerned about the driver of the motor bus on which he was riding.[108]

The commonest target of humour was authority, in whatever guise. A private in the 11th Battalion Northumberland Fusiliers remembers how 'The Dumps' of the 23rd Division, by 'a mixture of bawdy and pointed allusions to our betters combined to keep the audience literally doubled up with laughter. Had we been students of psychology I feel sure we should have seen this entertainment as an excellent means to releasing those tensions by which we are all inevitably troubled.'[109] Someone evidently less appreciative of this brand of humour none the less bore witness to its prominence: 'we went to a concert last night and strange to relate not one of the "funny merchants" tried to pull a gag at the expense of the officers. They had real wit instead.'[110] For battalion concert parties and concerts, the story was the same: 'any crudely written sketches that ribbed authority were certain favourites'.[111] Officers were sent up, and the pleasure was all the greater for the victims' presence. Beyond pleasure, the value of the occasion was also increased. Officer attendance, and often participation, gave their implicit sanction to the proceedings. They accepted the comic strictures offered from the stage; they did not stand on their dignity; they were 'alright' at bottom, simply men doing their job. Blunden remembered such a concert:

innocent activities like the famous Sergeant-Major's drainage improvements at Roussel Farm, needed but to be mentioned—a magnificent and general laugh at once burst forth, echoing through the rafters. The Medical Officer's simple remedies were sufficiently ridiculed, and he himself, battering away at the piano and roaring out in a most parching voice 'The Battle Cry of Freedom', was declared on all sides to be 'a cure'.[112]

Unit cohesion was fostered in this way, but at the same time

---

[108] *The Outpost*, 4/2 (Dec. 1916), 89; 'Private 940', *On the Remainder of Our Front* (1917), 86. The story had several variants, see A. F. Barnes, *Story of the 2/5th Bn. Gloucs. Regt.* (Gloucester, 1930), 69; *Aussie*, 1 (Jan. 1918), 2; *The London Scottish Regimental Gazette*, 231 (Mar. 1915), 63.
[109] Gladden, *Ypres*, p. 154.
[110] *Iodine Chronicle*, 15 (Easter 1918), 3.
[111] Hiscock, *Bells of Hell*, pp. 40–1.
[112] E. Blunden, *Undertones of War* (1965), 146.

the shows acted also more directly to promote *esprit de corps*. The single element of the music halls which was not translated to the Western Front was their ebullient jingoism. The soldier had no time for such sentiments. Any officer rash enough to attempt the delivery of a patriotic recitation at a battalion concert was doomed to ignominious failure.[113] As for the permanent troupes, 'they know what we like best . . . they do not put patriotic stuff over'.[114] Yet the soldier did not entirely forsake the self-congratulatory songs of the halls: he simply narrowed the orbit of his approval. There might be things wrong at home, rotten apples in the barrel, but if he could no longer hymn 'Britannia', he could at least sing the praises of 'The 29th' or 'The RND'. Divisional songs delivered by the troupes could be as tub-thumping as any music hall anthem:

> With a roll of drum, the division came
> Hotfoot to the battle's blast;
> When the good Red Sign swings into the line,
> Oh! There they'll fight to the last.

In the 29th Division, this 'took the division by storm'.[115] The troop journals too, though shunning jingo poems or any heroic depiction of the soldier in general, were not at all averse to hymning 'The DLI', 'The King's', and so on.[116]

Whatever the mood, communal, comic, or sentimental, concerts and concert parties allowed a brief moment away from the depressing realities of active service life: 'all thoughts of War vanish when listening to their songs and jokes'.[117] In Salonika, 'by make-believe we made of our valley some semblance of the world we had left. Canteens and concerts, games and horse shows, took us away from the war that was just round the corner.'[118] Entertainments acted to dissipate boredom and anxiety, but also, at a deeper level, to assuage the men's craving for the brightness and pleasure of civilian life. It was this fact that struck Sassoon when he reflected on the paucity of entertainments for

---

[113] J. C. Dunn (ed.), *The War the Infantry Knew 1914–1919* (1938), 189–90.
[114] Morrow, *Iron in the Fire*, p. 105. ·
[115] Gillon, *Story of the 29th Division*, p. 263.
[116] *The Whizz Bang*, 7 (Aug. 1916), 7; *The Swell*, 2 (Jan. 1916), 4.
[117] *The Mudlark*, 3 (June 1916), 12.
[118] S. Casson, *Steady Drummer* (1935), 149.

the troops. The men had good reason for feeling fed up, he thought:

'Of course they have! That is why we are so grateful to them and so proud of them', reply the people at home. What else do they get, besides this vague gratitude? Company football matches, beer in the canteens, and one mail in three weeks.

I felt all this very strongly a few evenings ago when a Concert Party gave an entertainment to the troops. It wasn't much; a canvas awning; a few footlights; two blue-chinned actors in soft, felt hats—one of them jangling ragtime tunes on a worn-out upright; three women in short silk skirts singing the old, old soppy popular songs; and all of them doing their best with their little repertoire.

They were unconscious, it seemed to me, of the intense impact on their audience—that dim brown moonlit mass of men. Row beyond row, I watched those soldiers, listening so quietly, chins propped on hands, to the songs which epitomized their 'Blighty hunger', their longing for the gaiety and sentiment of life.[119]

Such civilian troupes were very rarely seen by the front-line soldiers, but the army troupes might also in some degree appease the men's 'Blighty hunger'. Their shows were a reminder of peacetime pleasures, and an embodiment of the England with which the troops identified: 'to many thousands of men they were the one link with the gaieties and the comparatively carefree existence they knew before the war'.[120] They aimed 'to keep the morale going, to carry the little touch of Blighty that makes the world go round, into the dreary places'.[121] They sent the soldiers away 'with our heads full of the tuneful songs and happy jests. And so to bed, feeling that we had caught a glimpse—even if only a faint one—of a happier "Blighty" life.'[122] Above all, they were a reminder of what men were fighting to preserve, a promise of a happier future, and as such a counsel against despair. One ranker recalls how

we issued forth from the wooden hall into the sweet light of the moon feeling a renewed interest in life in that we had enjoyed ourselves thoroughly. Such little pleasures sufficed to remove the cobwebs from our souls and to stimulate the hope that, after all, life might prove

[119] Sassoon, *The Complete Memoirs of George Sherston*, p. 605.
[120] Owen, *Salonica and After*, p. 122.
[121] Anon., *Souvenir of 'The Goods'*, p. 31.
[122] Fairclough, *1st Birmingham Bn.*, p. 51.

something more than a barren wilderness, and that we might scrape through to happier things.[123]

Even their posters were a touch of 'Blighty'. At Estaires in July 1915, the Indian and 8th Divisions had music halls and 'each division advertised its programme on walls and shop windows, just like the Halls at home. The Meerut Division had the whole town billed.'[124] All over the British sector of the Zone of the Armies, the posters throughout the war 'stood out boldly, a splash of cheerful colour against the ruins'.[125] In Arras in the summer of 1917

here and there the shattered walls of the houses proclaimed the fact in gigantic letters that the 'Jocks' or the 'Follies' or the 'Spades' or the 61st Divisional Cinema would be pleased to entertain all who came to February Circus, to the Canal Basin, or to the Old Theatre at 6.30 p.m. for the nominal charge of half a franc . . . Arras was looking up.[126]

Even in Palestine this glimpse of Blighty life could be seen.[127]

Posters were not above exploiting the appeal of the concert party 'girls'. One for 'The Goods' showed a dainty, alluring flapper parting the curtains to reveal a heart-shaped face and a long, bestockinged leg.[128] Curiously, these female impersonators seem to have generated considerable sexual excitement. According to one ranker, 'judging from the way [the men] sat and goggled at the drag on stage it was obvious that they were indulging in delightful fantasies that brought to them substantial memories of the girls they had left behind them in London, Manchester, Glasgow, wherever'.[129] An officer described the same phenomenon: 'each man in the audience dwelt upon the plaits, golden curls and rouged faces, upon the eyes made large, liquid and living . . . Each herded man in the audience was fascinated, filled with longing, stirred by lust which made him shout or grin or hide his facial feelings according to the experiences, or lack, of his body.'[130] Often, it seems, the female imper-

[123] Gauld, *Truth from the Trenches*, p. 195.
[124] Dunn (ed.), *The War the Infantry Knew*, p. 138.
[125] Anon., *Souvenir of 'The Goods'*, p. 6.
[126] Gauld, *Truth from the Trenches*, p. 175.
[127] *Lines*, 1 (Nov. 1917), 5.
[128] Anon., *Souvenir of 'The Goods'*, p. 6.
[129] Hiscock, *Bells of Hell*, p. 42.
[130] H. Williamson, *The Golden Virgin* (1957), 121.

sonator did not attempt to caricature the part but, like the impersonator in the 4th Division concert party, 'did his best to put himself forward as a natural female and not to guy the part'.[131] A good impersonator called forth 'an upsurge of amorous feeling'.[132] It might be very far from the real thing, but 'how the sex-starved troops loved it'.[133] The realism of the concert party 'girl' is a subject which crops up again and again in the troop journals and in survivors' memoirs. 'It all seems to show that English beauty is essentially masculine', suggests one.[134] More probably, judging from photographs, it shows the intensity of the desire to believe.

But why was there this desire? The Zone of the Armies was not without real women, in the shops and *estaminets*, on the farms and in the hospitals. It is true that, especially after spring 1917, some troops might go weeks without seeing these, but it seems likely that the appeal of the concert party 'girls' owed as much to their emphasis upon glamour as to the sheer fewness of females. Peasant girls, working hard at practical tasks with their menfolk away, were often the reverse of 'feminine' in the restricted sense of the age:

> Women of shattered Picardy,
> Why are your boots so flat and vast?

queried *Aussie*.[135] 'The French girl as imagined at home', chic and glamorous, was contrasted with the French girl 'as she is', dowdy and frumpish.[136] The trappings of elegance and luxury were the negation of war and squalor and, as such, a potent fetish of peace. The female impersonators therefore took care over the fripperies, having lingerie sent out, or going on special leave to London or Paris to select the items themselves.[137] On stage they sang the sentimental songs which represented the greatest frippery of all, asserting the idealized stereotype of soft and vulnerable romantic femininity.

[131] B. Latham, *A Territorial Soldier's War* (Aldershot, 1967), 23.
[132] Gladden, *Ypres*, pp. 160–1.
[133] Groom, *Poor Bloody Infantry*, p. 63.
[134] Owen, *Salonica and After*, p. 121.
[135] *Aussie*, 4 (Apr. 1918), 15.
[136] *The Outpost*, 4/2 (Dec. 1916), 136.
[137] Smith, *Four Years*, p. 345; Cutlack (ed.), *War Letters of General Monash*, p. 251; A. Rule, *Students under Arms* (Aberdeen, 1934), 149.

Alongside them, however, the concert parties gave vent also to the earthier side of the soldier's longings. The divisional concert parties were held to a standard of propriety; the brigade and battalion troupes much less so. Many of these could be outrageously broad:

the divisional concert party are billeted in the village and the brigade pierrots are in tents along with the rest of us. Consequently, there is no lack of entertainment; they play to full houses every night. The divy concert party give a most delightful performance in a huge barn, but as one man's meat is another man's poison, those who require poisoning assemble in a vacant hangar where the brigade pierrots dish it up hot and strong. It was rumoured that the old Brig. threatened to send them all up into the line if they did not rein themselves in; the Follies, in Paris, is a church convention in comparison.[138]

Here, female impersonators might be more akin to pantomime dames, 'with rather broad views about ladies' behaviour and ladies' underclothes'.[139] Concert audiences might be regaled with songs which were frankly and unashamedly obscene, alongside songs of the purest sentiment. It was the variety of the halls, given a special intensity by the sense of privation which affected 'more or less consciously all these segregated males, so that they swung between the extremes of a sticky sentimentalism and a rank obscenity, the same mind warping as it were both ways in an attempt to throw off the obsession'.[140]

The concert parties seem, in this as in other aspects, to have very successfully matched their appeal to the taste of the troops. They were no doubt helped to achieve this by the fact that, aside from the usual officer leader of the troupe, the performers were almost invariably other-ranks. There was inevitably a certain amount of censorship by the officer managers, but the structure of the entertainments as, very often, a series of 'turns', left considerable autonomy to the performer. In the 'Diamond Troupe' of the 29th Division, for example, the shows were first produced, in 1917, by Major Gillam: 'the custom at this time was for each performer to choose and rehearse his own turns and submit them

---

[138] E. J. Rule, *Jacka's Mob* (Sydney, 1933), 266. Cf. Gibbon, *Inglorious Soldier*, p. 184; J. C. V. Durell, *Whizzbangs and Woodbines* (1918), 69; Gillon, *Story of the 29th Division*, p. 102; Chalmers, *Epic of Glasgow*, p. 54.

[139] Gibbons, *Roll On Next War*, p. 62.

[140] Manning, *Middle Parts of Fortune*, p. 50.

to the manager for his final approval but concerted numbers were always drilled and rehearsed by the management, in order that lighting, costumes, music and action should all combine properly'. Later, Gillam left the division and a Colonel Wright took over as manager: 'the programmes were now most carefully thought out with the purpose of giving variety between each turn, at the same time allowing each player the proper time in which to dress'.[141] Neither regime sounds to have been concerned principally with the content of performance, but rather with production values. One should not, however, deny the office managers, as producers, their share in the success of the concert parties. An Australian corporal, writing home in the summer of 1917, paid tribute to 'the wonderful understanding which has been put into the building of the programmes'.[142]

They certainly achieved their desired effect. 'Concert party night', recalls a London rifleman, 'was one of the highlights of our rest periods. The troupe did a wonderful job. Their work was of immeasurable value in raising morale, and one could almost forget that the few days of safety would soon be over.'[143] Blunden's poem 'At Senlis Once' recalls concert party night as the crown of the men's pleasures at rest

> How they crowded the barn with lusty laughter
> Hailed the pierrots and shook each shadowy rafter
> Even could ridicule their own sufferings
> Sang as though nothing but joy came after.[144]

It is not surprising that these entertainments were felt greatly to enhance the recuperative value of a rest period. 'Field theatres', said *Aussie*, 'are something more than a luxury—they are a necessity.'[145] General Monash considered them 'of incalculable value to the troops'.[146] An Italian liaison officer with the British Salonika force was so impressed by their tonic effect that he undertook, successfully, a campaign to have them copied by his own country's contingent there: 'officers attached to the postal censorship assured me that these performances produced

[141] Gillon, *Story of the 29th Division*, pp. 104–5.
[142] Morrow, *Iron in the Fire*, p. 105.
[143] Groom, *Poor Bloody Infantry*, p. 63.
[144] Blunden, *Undertones of War*, p. 220.
[145] *Aussie*, 3 (Mar. 1918), 4–5.
[146] Cutlack (ed.), *War Letters of General Monash*, p. 215.

extraordinarily good results, as appeared from the soldiers' letters, the general tone of which showed a marked improvement since the introduction of theatres'.[147] Officers on the Western Front were reaching the same conclusion. *Hints on Training*, issued by XVIII Corps in May 1918, positively recommended the running of divisional theatres.[148]

The concert parties reinforced the soldiers' habit of attempting to defuse the horrors of their situation through humour. A ranker in the 12th Battalion Rifle Brigade remembered the performances of 'The Very Lights' for his division on rest from Passchendaele, and in particular a song called 'Living in the Trenches': 'it always used to bring the house down. It was so typical of what we had to go through, but somehow making a joke of it when you knew you had to go back to it made it all just bearable.'[149] It was in many ways a familiar solution, put over in a long-accustomed way. As poverty, drink, or marital strife were subjects for humour in the pre-war music hall, so now, with a bolder leap, mud, lice, army discipline, and the war itself were dealt with in similar fashion. According to R. H. Mottram, 'that is how audiences composed of people who spent their holidays at Blackpool, Southend or Dunoon resisted war conditions by sheer detraction. They just wouldn't admit what they really felt, for they were being killed in the intervals of such foolery.'[150]

Above all, entertainments offset the bad features of 'rest'. Max Plowman noted of his battalion:

the men are 'fed up', and small wonder. Who wouldn't be, on finding himself after those unspeakable trenches, condemned to ceaseless parades, shut up in this village with no time or scope for any kind of decent recreation or enjoyment? What wonder that they grumble and fill their letters with hopes of leave? It's not discipline, it's change these men need.

If ever I have a company of my own, I know of some essentials to that contentment which is the foundation of all good discipline. A battalion on rest wants a company canteen, a reading- and writing-room with games, inter-platoon and inter-company football matches every free

[147] Villari, *The Macedonian Campaign*, p. 78.
[148] *Hints on Training Issued by XVIII Corps* (1918), 6.
[149] Macdonald, *They Called It Passchendaele*, p. 152.
[150] Mottram, *The 20th Century*, pp. 49–51.

Saturday, musical instruments, a gramophone—anything; and company concerts at least once a week.[151]

The army decreed that men could not be spared the 'petty militarism and worrying restlessness' which 'set them grumbling',[152] but the bad effects could at least be counteracted. A sergeant in the 13th Battalion Rifle Brigade recorded the irritation with which the men, hoping for 'a period of rest and relaxation', received the resumption on 'rest' of

the eternal 'training for the Attack', which seemed to us rather an unnecessary occupation for troops who had recently been Over the Top three times in three weeks. However, things were not so bad on the whole, for the play spirit was encouraged in every way by Colonel Stewart and the other officers and there was a programme of concerts, football and sports.[153]

As *The Outpost* noted, the soldier 'gets wind of a rest and looks forward to a long loaf; but during his 'rest' he is turned out to dig trenches and roads in the area he has just left'. All this might try the spirit of the weary men back from the line but happily it was not the only feature of 'rest' and 'what with Company Concerts, rugger and soccer matches and water to wash in, we are really enjoying ourselves'.[154]

Cinemas

One element of troop entertainments remains to be examined. In addition to a divisional concert party, many divisions had also a cinema. Appendix A lists some twenty-eight (out of seventy-four) British and Dominion divisions on active war fronts known to have had a divisional cinema, but this is by no means an exhaustive count. Some were bought from divisional funds, generated by running other activities such as canteens or concert parties. Others were supplied by the YMCA, Comforts Funds, and the Expeditionary Force Canteens organization. Some of these could tour. The mobile cinema supplied to the XVIII Corps by the

---

[151] M. Plowman, *A Subaltern on the Somme* (1927), 200.
[152] Blunden, *Undertones of War*, pp. 39–40.
[153] Rowlands, *For the Duration*, p. 100.
[154] *The Outpost*, 3/1 (Mar. 1916), 1, 16.

Expeditionary Force Canteens organization, for example, 'is transported in its own lorry from which current is also supplied, and it can be set up in any suitable building in an hour or so'.[155] In addition, some brigades had their own equipment.[156] The whole added up to a substantial organization. In the Fourth Army, for example, eleven divisions strong in April 1917, there were at that period some twenty-five cinemas attracting at least 40,000 soldiers a week.[157]

Cinema seems to have made less impact on the troops than concert parties. The only figure mentioned in troop journals or in memoirs was Chaplin:

> They say as Charlie Chaplin ain't
> A doing of his bit
> Yet all the same with all the boys
> He sure has made a hit;
> He licks the Western cowboy and
> His Broncho-busting trick—
> Of all the reels upon the film
> Old Charlie is the pick.[158]

One officer wrote to his wife in April 1917

last night I went to the Divisional cinema, which is in a restored barn among the ruins of Ervillers. Charlie Chaplin was there, figuratively, and at his best. I confess I am getting to appreciate him; and if you could see how the soldiers love him you would like him too. When his image appears upon the screen they welcome it with such shouts of approval that it might be the living Charlie. The men all flock to these shows, and hundreds are turned away nightly.[159]

Chaplin mimics featured in the concert parties and Chaplin caricatures in the troop journals.[160] Of course, his vogue was

[155] War Diary, XVIII Corps A and Q Staff, WO 95/954, Routine Orders 15 June 1918, 2.
[156] I. A. Mack, *Letters from France* (Liverpool, 1932), 78; C. E. Carrington, *The War Record of the 1/5th Bn. the Royal Warwickshire Regiment* (Birmingham, 1922), 17.
[157] War Diary, XVIII Corps A and Q Staff, WO 95/954, 'A and Q Notes, 11 Apr. 1917', n. 592.
[158] *N.Y.D.*, 3 (Aug. 1916), 6. Cf. D. W. McCaffrey (ed.), *Focus on Chaplin* (1971), 18.
[159] Feilding, *War Letters*, p. 223.
[160] Gillon, *Story of the 29th Division*, p. 108; *Lines*, 1 (Nov. 1917), 10–11; *The Mudlark*, 3 (June 1916), 14; *Aussie*, 3 (Mar. 1918), 4; *The Whizz Bang*, 1 (Jan. 1916), 7.

world-wide, but still it is interesting to see him so well-remembered, when no other cinema performer seems to have made any impact at all. One reason, perhaps, was the special fitness of his humour to the war. In a sense, the whole conflict was like a giant Chaplin gag:

men had been taught to believe that the whole object of life was to reach out to beauty and love, and that mankind in its progress to perfection had killed the beast instinct . . . all poetry, all art, all religion had preached this gospel and this promise. Now that ideal had broken like a china vase dashed to hard ground. The contrast between That and This was devastating. It was in an enormous world-shaking way like a highly dignified man . . . suddenly slipping on a piece of orange peel and sitting all of a heap with silk hat flying in a filthy gutter.[161]

At a more immediate level, active service life constantly pointed up such contrasts between aspiration and reality. Some Canadian artillerymen, watching the flight of two officers pursued by bursting shells, were doubled up with laughter:

I have often wondered about that event. There was really nothing funny about it. The Germans were trying to kill two of our men and we laughed as if we were watching a funny movie. Perhaps the word movie is the key. The great comic of those days and for long after was Charlie Chaplin. Some critic has said that the basis of Chaplin's humour was the sudden collapse of a great and overwhelming cardboard dignity. We all knew that the gulf between the ranks, though necessary, was arbitrary and in a sense a sham. The collapse of that cardboard dignity may have been the reason for our mirth.[162]

The brutality of much early Chaplin humour also matched the laughter to which front-line conditions could drive a man as the only relief for stress.

This might apply to many other film comedians. Early silent film humour was necessarily crudely physical. But as early as 1915, Chaplin stood out from his rivals in beginning to temper the brutal anarchy of slapstick with sentiment and pathos. Like Dan Leno, 'he was defiant, jaunty and sorrowful, and the screen comedian's instinctive search for a persona was directly inspired by Leno as well as by the music hall. In fact the Bioscope once called Chaplin "the Dan Leno of the screen".' He drew exten-

---

[161] Gibbs, *Realities of War*, p. 92. Cf. Panichas (ed.), *Promise of Greatness*, p. 41.
[162] Black, *One Volunteer*, pp. 76–7.

sively for material upon the music hall routines which he had himself performed with Karno's troupe, or which he had seen others perform.[163] As a consummate artist he appealed to men of all nations, but it is easy to see that for the British, it required no imaginative leap to appreciate his brand of humour.

Overall, though, the handicaps under which cinema laboured seem to have limited its appeal. Fighting soldiers, unable to get to divisional headquarters, could always run their own troupe or improvise a concert: cinemas were beyond their means, and screenings could not be improvised. Few cinemas were equipped to tour extensively: they could hardly give an impromptu performance from the back of a lorry as some concert parties did. Precipitated into an environment which designers could never have envisaged, primitive cinema equipment was prone to breakdowns in the hands of its inexperienced operators.[164] Cinema shows were not topical, nor tailored for an army audience by fellow soldiers. The enthusiasm with which concert party performers were received is universally remembered, but film screenings engaged the emotions rather less. The men kept up a 'running commentary' of criticism:

they spot the weak points at the films to which we all went. A couple embracing with a baby clutched in the woman's arms, 'What a 'ope the kid's got'. Again, a lady inspects the new butler with the aid of her lorgnette; that evening she creeps to the study to steal, minus the spy glass and peeps through the curtains. 'Oi, mun, she can see orl right without her b— — glasses.'[165]

Sometimes advantage might be taken of the darkness for a different sort of criticism: 'somewhat illuminating remarks were frequently shouted out with reference to the conduct of the War, particularly if staff officers were present in the audience'.[166] By the time of the Second World War, the balance would have changed, but for the moment the advantage lay with the concert parties and they did a great work in keeping up morale.

---

[163] R. Sobel and D. Francis, *Chaplin: Genesis of a Clown* (1977), 170–4, 179–98.
[164] Hall, *The Green Triangle*, p. 94; Bailey and Hollier, *The Kensingtons*, p. 58.
[165] F. Delamain (ed.), *Going Across* (Newport, 1952), 94, 127. Cf. H. Sulzbach, *With the German Guns* (1973), 123, 146.
[166] Smith, *Four Years*, p. 335.

9

Continuity in the Soldiers' Lives

Continuity of Enthusiasms

Taken together, the range of recreations available for the soldier on rest was widely recognized to be an important factor in morale. In the opinion of one regimental officer, who wrote perceptively of the experience of his battalion,

a very careful study of men exposed to the conditions of static warfare is ... essential to an understanding of the British soldier in France and Flanders. It may be stated at once that apparently trivial ancillary services ... grew to be of supreme importance. I do not believe that sufficient attention has been paid to this fact, although such services formed often for long periods the sole recreative interest of the fighting Divisions. I refer to Divisional Concert Parties, Race Meetings, Horse Shows, Football Matches, Boxing Tournaments and suchlike.[1]

In the French and German armies, senior officers were undoubtedly aware of the importance of such facilities. A relationship was considered by them to exist between high morale and the availability of such recreations during 'rest'. Particular efforts were made to lay on concerts and plays for the German troops in training for the great offensive of March 1918.[2] On the French side, the participation of the 5th Division in the mutinies of 1917 was the object of special attention. It was advanced as proof of the Command's belief in a subversive conspiracy at the root of the crisis: discontent, so ran the argument, could not have come to a head without such outside influence because 'cette division a été l'objet de grands prévenances: elle a eu droit au repos à des représentations théâtrales par des troupes profession-

---

[1] Hutchison, *Warrior*, pp. 172–3. Cf. Sandilands, *The 23rd Division*, p. 132.
[2] E. F. W. Lunderdorff, *My War Memories* (1919), 389–90; Middlebrook, *Kaiser's Battle*, p. 62.

elles, à des suppléments sérieux de nourriture à la création d'équipes sportives, notamment de football'.[3]

Yet, notwithstanding the faith here expressed, the British troops enjoyed organized recreations on a scale greater than in either of these armies, or among the Italians. 'Equipes sportives' would not have rendered any British division so singular a focus of attention. The French troops put on concerts, but the elaborate structure of permanent soldier troupes, with custom-built theatres, costumes, lights, and all the theatrical paraphernalia, was not matched. 'Le Théâtre aux Armées' was a civilian organization, which 'ne jouait que trop rarement devant des troupes vraiment combattantes; son répertoire leur était peu approprié, mais il comportait heureusement toujours quelques rôles de femmes, vraies ou tout au moins demi-actrices'.[4] A British officer with the Italians, considering the causes of the Caporetto débâcle, felt that one factor was 'their failure to make adequate provision for the amusement and relaxation of the troops when in rest, such as the YMCA and various concert parties provided for British troops, to combat inevitable war-weariness'.[5] On the German side too, 'the French civilians of the areas occupied by the enemy have repeatedly expressed their astonishment at the number of entertainments provided for our troops compared with those arranged by the Germans, and they believe that this accounts to a large extent for our moral [sic] outlasting that of the enemy'.[6]

The faith of French and German commanders, and the initial scepticism of the British authorities, suggests that the explanation for this difference cannot be traced to the attitudes of the Higher Command. As a British regimental officer commented, 'during the Great War organized Entertainment flourished rather upon its own initiative than due to the ordination of the General Staff'.[7] Attitudes at lower levels were probably more significant. The development of recreations in the British army, as has been shown, owed much to the lead given by the Regulars, which in turn built upon the traditions of the peacetime army.

[3] Pedroncini, *Les Mutineries*, pp. 122–3.
[4] Meyer, *La Vie quotidienne*, pp. 347–9.
[5] Dalton, *With British Guns*, p. 142. Cf. R. Seth, *Caporetto, The Scapegoat Battle* (1965), 195.
[6] Ashcroft, *History of the 7th South Staffs. Regt.*, pp. 145–6.
[7] Hutchison, *Warrior*, p. 173.

These traditions had evolved in response to the social character of the peacetime army and the isolation of garrison life overseas. They allowed the officers to indulge their taste for sport and theatricals, and their conviction that the men should not be left to their own devices. As a result, the pre-war army offered a very wide range of recreational facilities.[8] There might be resistance to the idea of transferring this structure of recreations to a war sector: such diversions had no place in the sweeping war of movement and swift decision envisaged on the pattern of 1859–71. As the reality of static warfare dawned, however, the groundwork was there for a response which would help men to meet the challenge. *Notes for Young Officers*, issued in 1917, articulated the old philosophy: 'an officer must not think that his duties end with the dismissal of his platoon after the parade. The life of an average private soldier is a dull one, the class from which he comes has not much time for amusement, and it is his officers who have to teach him to amuse himself in the right way.'[9]

The Territorials had not been slow to follow the model set, because the idea of soldiers organizing entertainments was for them also not unfamiliar. Territorial soldiering had, for many, been conceived chiefly in terms of pleasurable recreation. In order to attract recruits, the Volunteers (as they had been until 1907) 'found themselves offering a kind of package deal, providing an institution within which a man could pursue any number of leisure activities'.[10]

The experience of Regulars and Territorials alike was very different from that of the conscript French army. In France, for a brief period from about 1902, the social role of the army had been stressed, with officers encouraged to wean their men from local bars by active promotion of regimental canteens, libraries, plays, officer lectures, and so forth. Such a change was 'nothing short of revolutionary', but already by 1909 a reaction had set in: these activities, it was felt, interfered too much with the intensive military training essential to a short service force.[11]

Yet the differences between the British and other armies in respect of entertainments were not simply a matter of specific

[8] Skelley, *Victorian Army*, pp. 160–4; Spiers, *Army and Society*, pp. 63–4.
[9] *Notes for Young Officers* (1917), 68.
[10] Cunningham, *The Volunteer Force*, pp. 110–19, 153.
[11] Porch, *March to the Marne*, pp. 119–21, 126–32, 185, 202–3.

institutional background. The same contrast can, for example, be observed between the British and German fleets. At the German bases, little was done to alleviate boredom,

yet at Scapa Flow, an even bleaker and less populated location, the British navy managed to conduct under similiar conditions of preparedness such sports as football, boxing, racing and rowing. Moreover, all large British vessels were equipped with reading and billiard rooms, and the crews were urged to pursue such varied activities as painting, theatricals, and movies.

This was only one small element in the total picture of German naval morale, but it was important enough to be recognized by the authorities. Admiral Scheer, in his report on the 1917 mutiny, recommended that along with improved rations increased effort be made to organize sports for the men.[12]

British officers, in army and navy alike, did not need such injunctions from above. The traditions of peacetime were not swamped by the influx of wartime officers in large part because the newcomers shared enthusiasms which, as we shall see, were general. The public-school officers 'organized games for the men and took part themselves, because that was the public school recipe for usefully occupying young males in their spare time'.[13] But, at the opposite end of the scale too, organizing a game of football would not be strange to working-class officers promoted from the ranks.

Music hall too had become a culture of all classes: it was partly the creation of this 'second audience' for music hall that had influenced the subsequent development of the original working-class modes.[14] Even battalion commanders might, in concerts, perform 'a realistic impersonation of George Robey' or sing 'in an authentic Cockney accent—with all the appropriate capers too— My Old Dutch or We Knocked 'em in the Old Kent Road and other coster songs of Albert Chevalier'.[15] Consequently, concert parties found their organizers, and their protectors at brigade or division, among officer enthusiasts and believers in the peacetime role of the halls. Potentially, the barrier of caste which inhibited

[12] D. Horn, *Mutiny on the High Seas* (1973), 26.
[13] J. Keegan, *The Face of Battle* (1976), 274.
[14] Stedman Jones, 'Working Class Culture and Working Class Politics', pp. 494–6.
[15] Noakes, *Distant Drum*, p. 65; A. F. Behrend, *As from Kemmel Hill* (1963), 146.

German officers from concerning themselves too closely with the welfare of other-ranks dogged the British also. The national obsessions, however, overrode caste.

All the efforts of British and Dominion regimental officers would have been useless or even counter-productive had there not existed a genuine and passionate enthusiasm for sports and music hall among the rank and file. To appreciate the value of recreations to the troops, it is necessary to realize the omnipresence and influence that sports and music hall had achieved for a generation before 1914, and the extent to which this carried over to the Zone of the Armies. It then becomes apparent that their replication in the active war zones did not only represent the transfer of convenient social institutions which performed the functions described in the previous chapter. It also signified a more general application of value systems deriving from civilian life, which brought subtle benefits for morale.

Music Hall

Looking first at music hall, this 'appealed to all sectors of the working class from the casual labourer to the highly paid artisan. Its importance as a social and cultural institution in proletarian districts was second only to that of the pub.'[16] Its cultural influence spread far beyond its London centre. In the North-East, the history of the industrial folk song showed the influence of music hall progressively supplanting that of the heirs of the radical tradition.[17] In the slums of Manchester, music hall songs which 'gained anything more than an ephemeral vogue . . . were thumped out on pub pianos and bawled in chorus with a devastating regularity. Folk songs were entirely unknown.'[18] At the opposite extreme of economic life, Kenneth Grahame in rural Sussex watched an attempt to revive the old mummers: 'hardly any of the good old "St George and the Dragon" left. Instead, cheap comic songs from the London music halls.'[19]

Throughout the country, a profusion of provincial halls existed

---

[16] Stedman Jones, 'Working Class Culture and Working Class Politics', pp. 478–9.
[17] A. L. Lloyd, *Folk Song in England* (St. Albans, 1975), 371, 375, 391–2.
[18] Roberts, *Classic Slum*, p. 119.
[19] R. Pearsall, *Edwardian Life and Leisure* (Newton Abbot, 1973), 127.

to disseminate the new culture. As J. A. Hobson wrote in 1901, 'the art of the music hall is the only "popular" art of the present day: its words and melodies pass by quick magic from the Empire or the Alhambra over the length and breadth of the land, re-echoed in a thousand provincial halls, clubs, and drinking saloons, until the remotest village is familiar with air and senti-ment'.[20] It may be true that in the case of jingoism, working-class resistance to the concept was sufficient to prevent its sincere adoption.[21] But in most cases, the songs and sentiments thus communicated were not so clearly the children of theatre managers and theatrical convention, nor so opposed to work-ing-class experience and outlook. They 'linked their lyrics to reality'.[22] They had an appeal which enabled music hall entertainments to invade the working men's clubs, often against the resistance of the club committees, and to edge out political and educational activities, as well as the older forms of entertainment.[23]

Some historians have argued that music hall's influence was on the wane by 1914.[24] Certainly in the war years civilian music hall moved towards a fatuous jingoism which, as has been seen, angered many soldiers, whose shows developed in the opposite direction. But this constituted more a divergent development of the tradition than its repudiation by one section. Soldiers remained firmly rooted in music hall culture. Their antiheroic songs were not so much a radical new departure, as a response to wartime conditions based upon the popular culture in which they were steeped. Many of the songs of music hall were themselves 'self mocking and humorously defeatist'.[25] The Boer War had seen an equivalent development of this tradition. The antiheroic sentiments of one troop song at Blickfontein, for example, would be hard to beat:

---

[20] J. A. Hobson, *The Psychology of Jingoism* (1901), 3–4.
[21] R. Price, *An Imperial War and the British Working Class* (1972), 238–9, 241.
[22] Roberts, *Classic Slum*, p. 119.
[23] T. G. Ashplant, 'London Working Men's Clubs 1875–1914', in E. Yeo and S. Yeo (eds.), *Popular Culture and Class Conflict 1590–1914* (Brighton, 1981), 249–51, 260–2.
[24] L. Senelick, 'Politics as Entertainment: Victorian Music Hall Songs', *Victorian Studies*, 19 (1975/6), 179–80.
[25] Summerfield, 'The Effingham Arms and the Empire', p. 235.

> Hiding in the ammunition van,
> Midst the shot and shell I've been,
> While my comrades fought as comrades ought,
> I was nowhere to be seen.
> Ta ra ra.
>
> Hiding in the ammunition van,
> Listening to the din and strife,
> When the fight was o'er out once more,
> And that's how I saved my life.[26]

Now the antiheroic songs appeared once again too swiftly to be the product of any autonomous trench culture. The song,

> Send out my mother,
> My sister and my brother,
> But for Gawd's sake don't send me,

was already popular in September 1914, and the refrain, so often recalled in survivors' memoirs,

> Are we downhearted?
> No!
> Then you damn soon will be!,

was being delivered by men already enlisted to new recruits early in 1915 before either had even seen the front.[27]

Similarly, the troop journals drew upon a well-established vein of humour. *The Times Literary Supplement* noted late in 1916 that 'the British soldier . . . who never thinks of himself as a "Tommy" and rather resents the affixing of such a journalistic label, has not succeeded in doffing his individuality, and it follows that his humour—as revealed in his trench journals—is not essentially different from the humour of the home keeping crowd'.[28] Again, if one compares an earlier adaptation of 'the humour of the home keeping crowd', the Ladysmith siege newspapers of the Boer War edited by the professional correspondents immured there, there is a remarkable congruity with the troop journals of the Great War. There is the same self-mocking assumption of antiheroic stance: 'Lost, a Pluck. Finder will be suitably rewarded upon returning same to Excavation No.

---

[26] C. R. Innes, *With Paget's Horse to the Front* (1901), 97–8.
[27] Terraine, *Impacts of War*, p. 73; *The Red Feather*, 2 (Feb. 1915), 34.
[28] *The Times Literary Supplement*, 12 Oct. 1916, 481–2.

401, River Bank.' There is the same humorous treatment of the horrors like shell-fire, drawing upon the characteristic 'comic stoicism' of the halls: 'Try Joubert's Hair Curlers. Hundreds of testimonials from the manager of the Royal Hotel, Mr Carter, prominent surgeons and others.' There is the same scepticism about politicians, freely expressed in the halls, but now given added weight by specific bitter experience: 'a shell from Long Tom burst in the War Office this afternoon . . . Unfortunately the Ordnance Committee were not sitting. A splinter broke into the Foreign Office and disturbed the siesta of the Prime Minister.'[29]

Continuity of attitude may be a difficult thing to pin down, but there are sufficient explicit references to music hall to suggest that it did retain a strong influence with the troops, and that many of the parallels between civilian and military outlook can be attributed in some measure to its continuing hold. For example, Stephen Graham wrote that 'though we possessed many splendid old national songs, you'd listen in vain to hear one sung by soldiers. Or if the old airs were sung, they were merely the accompaniment of modern words or parodies. The imitation of music hall humour and music hall singing was most widespread. In fact they had the culture of the music hall.'[30] Similarly, the historians of the songs and slang of the British army in the First World War noted 'the predominant singing of music hall songs, old and new, not otherwise connected with the army or the War'.[31] The publicity given to the soldiers' own creations, by shows like *Oh What a Lovely War*, has built up rather a distorted impression of what the British soldier of the Great War sang.

Outcrops of this underlying culture were everywhere in evidence. This was an army in which a rum ration might be greeted with Robey's 'Another Little Drink'; in which reveille might be the occasion to sing Harry Lauder's chorus,

> It's far too early in the morning for to waken me,
> For such a thing as early rising I can't see,
> And I may say that with my health it never did agree—
> Rising early in the morning;

[29] *The Ladysmith Lyre*, 5 Dec. 1899.
[30] Graham, *Private in the Guards*, pp. 196–7.
[31] Brophy and Partridge, *The Long Trail*, p. 24. Cf. Aston and Duggan, *History of the 12th Bn.*, pp. 99–100.

and in which a battalion might be played out of bed every day at rest to the tunes of 'It's Nice to Get Up in the Morning', 'Never Let Your Braces Dangle', and 'He's a Cousin of Mine'.[32] Music hall tunes were hammered out on innumerable machine guns.[33] The Queen's Westminster Rifles topped even that: 'up at Ypres we used to sing and whistle the Policeman's Holiday at stand to, and fire our rifles—crack!—crack! to emphasize the last two notes'.[34] In soldiers' slang a 'Harry Tate' was a plate, or an RE8 aeroplane, a 'Harry Randle' a handle, a 'Wilkie Bard' a playing card.[35] 'The Bing Boys' were the Third Army on the Western Front, the Indian mountain batteries in Palestine.[36] The infantry themselves, of course, were 'Fred Karno's army'.[37] Music hall associations were always ready to hand. A man with a crumpled face might trigger a memory of 'the comedian Billy Merson who was famous for that music hall song, Alphonso the Toreador', or a sergeant might have a manner 'so cheerful and boisterous it reminded me of that famous sketch, "Saturday to Monday" '.[38]

The banter of a marching column might be set around the comic songs of the halls, 'Kitty, Kitty' or 'Give Me the Switch, Miss, for Ipswich, It's the Ipswich Switch which I require',[39] and the banter itself might owe much to music hall. Ford Madox Ford tries to give some flavour of it when he has 'Tietjens', exasperated at the ragtime aspect of his men, burst out:

'For God's sake put your beastly hats straight! . . . Your hats all at sixes and sevens give me the pip!' . . . And the whispers of the men went down the little line: 'You 'eer the officer . . . Gives 'im the pip, we do! . . . goin' for a wawk in the pawk wiv our gels, we are . . .' They glanced nevertheless aside and upwards at each other's tin-hat rims and said: 'Shove 'im a shade forward 'Orace . . . You tighten your martingale,

[32] H. E. Harvey, *Battle Line Narratives* (1928), 132; Rutter, *History of the 7th Bn.*, p. 138; Burrage, *War is War*, p. 105.

[33] L. Housman (ed.), *War Letters of Fallen Englishmen* (1930), 210; N. Fraser-Tytler, *Field Guns in France* (1929), 59; Haslam, *Cannon Fodder*, p. 175; Rowlands, *For the Duration*, p. 48; Burrage, *War is War*, p. 79; Tucker, *Johnny Get Your Gun*, p. 49.

[34] Housman (ed.), *War Letters*, p. 210.

[35] Brophy and Partridge, *Long Trail*, pp. 131, 204.

[36] Coppard, *With a Machine Gun*, p. 130; Hutchison, *Warrior*, p. 82; Black, *Red Dust*, p. 270; F. Reid, *The Fighting Cameliers* (Sydney, 1934), 28.

[37] Brophy and Partridge, *Long Trail*, p. 33.

[38] Hiscock, *Bells of Hell*, p. 54; A. Fennah, *Retaliation* (1935), 68.

[39] A. French, *Gone for a Soldier* (Kineton, 1972), 68–9.

'Erb!' They were gaily rueful and impenitently profane: they had had 36 hours of let off. A fellow louder-than-hummed:

> As I wawk erlong ther Bor dee belong
> Wiv an independent air . . .
> W'ere's me swagger kine, you fellers!

It seems entirely appropriate that the company should contain two music hall comedians; that Tietjens should promise, moved by a sudden impulse of feeling, 'I'll give every one of you a ticket for Drury Lane next Boxing Day'; and that his offer should be answered, 'polyphonically and low', with a mixture of humour and theatrical knowledge, 'Mike it the old Shoreditch Empire, sir, 'n we'll thank you!', 'I never keered for the Lane meself! Give me the old Balham for Boxing Day', and so on.[40]

The troop journals too were studded with this reference. *The Whizz Bang* featured caricatures of Will Evans and Little Tich, 'seen at the halls'; of George Robey and Alfred Lester, 'the Bing Boys'.[41] The Kaiser and the Crown Prince were presented in Harry Tate's 'Motoring' sketch as the would-be motorists who cannot get going.[42] A dug-out was 'like Dan Leno's house: if you think you will sit in your dining room there you are; if you wish for your bedroom, there you still are'.[43] Burlington Bertie was depicted joining the sappers; Gilbert the Filbert surfaced in France as Daniel the Spaniel.[44] And prominent place was given to the Christmas greetings sent by music hall's stars: 'now, as ever, they speak across the footlights in the same spirit that has moved so many of us to laughter and tenderness'.[45]

The forms of humour, in many cases, adopted the features of music hall. 'Songs and their singers' were suggested, pantomime parts allocated to members of the unit, 'pantomime posters brought up to date'.[46] Answering a charge, or sick parade, or 'a Heinie overhead' were presented as dramatized comic sketches,

[40] F. M. Ford, *The Bodley Head Ford Madox Ford*, iv (1963), 344–6.
[41] *The Whizz Bang*, 1 (Jan. 1916), 9, and 7 (July 1916), 11.
[42] *The Invicta Gazette*, 9 (Mar. 1917), 9.
[43] *The Linseed Lance*, 1/5 (Jan. 1917), 61.
[44] *Akakar Magazine*, 5 (Apr. 1918), 10; *The Leadswinger*, 3 (Oct. 1915), 20.
[45] *Akakar Magazine*, 2 (Dec. 1917), 8. Cf. *The Switchboard*, 5 (Dec. 1916), 3; *The 20th Gazette*, 7 (Dec. 1915), 32–3.
[46] *The Mudhook*, 2 (Nov. 1917), 13; *The Open Exhaust*, 2 (Feb. 1916), 3; *The Invicta Gazette*, 6 (Dec. 1916), 16–17; *The Standard of C Company*, 1 (July 1917), 7; *The Sphinx*, 6 (Dec. 1915), 24.

perhaps even with stage directions.[47] But the most popular of all the devices of humour was the presentation of life on the Western Front as a comic variety bill. The 6th Battalion Duke of Cornwall's Light Infantry depicted one of their moves up to the line in this way, with its

> beauty chorus of Sanitary men . . . The irresistible 'Duckboard Dance' in which the entire company will join, accompanied by Gus Gong the handbell artiste (Daily Telegraph: 'A scream from start to finish. Even the audience fell over themselves') . . . The Aeroplane Guard, an arresting piece by Stan Still, the noted siffleur. The whole finishing with the laughable harlequinade 'Busses' (the audience will do well to wait).[48]

For all the anger that its fatuous jingoism aroused, the domestic music hall remained overwhelmingly popular as a resort for soldiers on leave. A favourite form of humour in the troop journals contrasted the dream of leave with the rude awakening, and part and parcel of the dream were 'the Pav and the Palace, the Gaiety, all', or the vexed problem of 'whether I should go to the Hippodrome once, or twice, during my short stay'.[49] The return home when victory has finally been won was fondly imagined: the first night would be taken up with a civic reception, but 'next night we shall have the stalls and dress circle of the Alhambra reserved for us'.[50] Sadly, reality was not always so kind. *The Outpost* depicted a soldier in full kit, just arrived from the front, standing despondently outside a music hall with a 'No Bookings for the Next Fortnight' sign up: 'And they promised me a good time', runs the caption.[51]

Even to the Dominion troops, the motifs of music hall were to some extent familiar. Forty-two per cent of the men of the CEF were, after all, British born, and a lesser proportion of the Australians and New Zealanders.[52] The great stars of the halls

---

[47] *The Cinque Ports Gazette*, 1 (May 1916), 4; *The Bairns Gazette*, 1 (May 1917), 4; *M & D*, 4, 11.

[48] *The Red Feather*, 6 (Dec. 1915), 126. Cf. *The Minden Magazine*, 2 (Dec. 1915), back cover; *6th K.S.L.I. News*, 1 (Aug. 1917), 21.

[49] *A.O.C. Workshops Gazette*, 4 (Mar. 1916), 7; *Stray Shots*, 8 (Aug. 1916), 6; *The Packing Note*, 1 (Jan. 1916), 7.

[50] *The Outpost*, 5/4 (Aug. 1917), 131.

[51] Ibid. 6/3 (Jan. 1918), 76.

[52] E. H. Armstrong, *The Crisis of Quebec 1914–18* (New York, 1937), 248. For the Australians and New Zealanders, see Ch. 10.

toured: Lauder was in Australia when war broke out.[53] Consequently, there was some familiarity with their stage personae. The 91st Battalion Canadian Militia were 'the "Harry Lauders" . . . from the jaunty bonnet and feather worn by them'. Lauder himself found Australians and Canadians familiar with him and his songs when he entertained the troops in France.[54] Familiarity with music hall was to be increased by the Dominion troops' resort to London on leave, by their attendance at British army shows in France, and by the fact that their own concert parties drew heavily upon British material. The 'C2s' of the Canadian 2nd Division, for example, included Lancashire and Yorkshire character bits in their programmes, whilst in the concert party of the 5th Canadian Field Ambulance

Bob Ferris was the star comedian and this America-born Lancashire lad from the Canadian army did much to brighten the war with his droll dialogue monologues and his songs, 'I'm Not So Young As I Used To Be', 'Try a Little Piece of My Wife's Cake', 'That Was Me Last Night in Poper-in-jee', 'I Was Standing on the Corner of the Street', etc.[55]

Aussie, with its bent towards 'Australianism', complained about the shortage of specifically Australian material in the programmes of the concert parties of the AIF.[56]

Behind the surface of music hall was a value system, which seems in several respects to have been robust and appropriate enough to carry over to active service conditions, not just in the context of the concert party shows but more generally. According to some historians, music hall attitudes reflected a genuine shift in working-class aspirations and beliefs, following from the apparently diminishing prospect of any real change in the capitalist ordering of society.[57] Others argue rather that it was the 'instigator and not the receptor of popular opinion'; that the evolution of music hall culture was less a spontaneous response to audience demand, than a product of specific local government and

[53] H. Lauder, *A Minstrel in France* (1918), 19–21; D. Farson, *Marie Lloyd and Music Hall* (1972), 77.
[54] Urquhart, *History of the 16th Bn.*, p. 16; Lauder, *A Minstrel in France*, pp. 177, 285–6.
[55] Noyes, *Stretcher Bearers*, p. 203.
[56] *Aussie*, 3 (Mar. 1918), 4–5, and 5 (June 1918), 16.
[57] Stedman Jones, 'Working Class Culture and Working Class Politics', pp. 460–508; M. Vicinus, *The Industrial Muse: A Study of 19th Century British Working Class Literature* (1974), esp. 191.

managerial initiatives, often in conflict with this demand; but that the attitudes 'absorbed by audiences under the influence of camaraderie, chorus-singing and spirits, both high and alcoholic', whilst 'no doubt superficial', 'continued over the course of decades to grow into a creed'.[58] The truth must lie somewhere between these interpretations. The influence of licensing and theatre management on the evolution of music hall is hardly to be denied; yet the businessmen of popular entertainment, by definition, could not dare to run their vast theatres in total opposition to popular taste. But whether in origin creator or reflector, the important feature is that music hall had, before the First World War, become a powerful vehicle for the attitudes of the new culture.

Cheerfulness, for example, was a constant music hall theme. Typically, music hall 'bade you be of good cheer and Micawber-like wait for something to turn up'.[59] Song titles told their own story:

almost every lion comique sang not only his drinking songs, but also verses exhorting the listeners to cheerful loyalty and hard work. Among the best remembered were 'Be Happy-go-lucky, Never Say Die', 'Work, Boys, Work And Be Contented', 'Try to be Happy and Gay, My Boys', and 'Act on the Square, Boys, Act on the Square'.[60]

One of the favourites was Mark Sheridan's 'Here We Are Again':

> Here we are! Here we are! Here we are again!!!
> We're fit and well and feeling right as rain
> Never mind the weather, now then altogether!
> Hullo! Hullo! Here we are again!

Now, to soldiers coming out of the line weary and decimated, a song like this was a reminder to reflect upon their manifest good fortune in being alive:

> We are marching back from the battle,
> Where we've all left mates behind,
> And our officers are gloomy,
> And the N.C.O.'s are kind,—

---

[58] Senelick, 'Politics as Entertainment', pp. 150, 155–6; Summerfield, 'The Effingham Arms and the Empire', pp. 209–40.

[59] Pope, *Carriages at Eleven*, p. 212.

[60] Vicinus, *The Industrial Muse*, pp. 259–60.

When a jew's harp breaks the silence,
Purring out an old refrain;
And we thunder through the village
Roaring 'Here we are again'.[61]

Similarly, the ideal of humour in adversity found constant expression in the troop journals. *The Mudhook* had a cartoon of two soldiers contemplating a colossal dud the size of a cart: 'Bill (out since Mons, to one of the new draft): "There my lad, now you understand why we 'as ter wear our tin 'ats".' *The 5th Glo'ster Gazette* pictured two men meeting chest-deep in a flooded trench: 'Bong jour Alf! Have you changed your socks today? If not, why not?"[62] The device of the comic music hall bill, itself a sort of invocation of music hall values, was used to take the sting out of quite serious grievances. The much put upon private soldier became

Thomas Atkins
With his famous song
Yes Sir! Yes Sir! Three bags full.[63]

Similarly the 5th Battalion Gloucestershire Regiment presented their own unhappy experience on the Somme in the same way:

The G.O.C. Presents His World Renowned Troupe of
Variety Artistes
THE 48TH DIVISION
Over Fifteen Thousand Performers
Stupendous Attraction.

The ASC would give a recitation, 'How I won the Battle of Pozieres, a tale of London Gallantry', with, as an encore, 'Life on Six Bob a Day'. The infantry would also feature 'highly trained strong men; great feats in walking, weight lifting, etc. etc. etc.'. The entire troupe, it was promised, would perform three times every battle.[64] The grievances aired here, the neglect of the county regiments for the London Territorials, the privileges of the ASC, the sorry lot of the infantry, and the over-use of the 48th Division, were all bitterly felt as comments elsewhere in the

[61] *The Outpost*, 4/6 (Apr. 1917), 210.
[62] *The Mudhook*, 9 (Dec. 1918), 6; *The 5th Glo'ster Gazette*, 18 (Apr. 1917), 21.
[63] *The Kemmel Times*, i. 1 (July 1916), front cover.
[64] *The 5th Glo'ster Gazette*, 15 (Oct. 1916), 8.

battalion's magazine reveal, but there was evidently some relief to
be had in applying the allusions and associations of music hall to
unhappy events. Less darkly, many other, more personalized,
mock music hall bills gently chaffed members of the unit producing the journal.

Another parallel with music hall lay in the concentration of the
troop journals upon the intervals of pleasure in the soldier's life.
Just as the 'culture of consolation' at home dwelt upon a glass of
'glorious English beer' or a hearty meal of 'boiled beef and car-
rots',[65] so the troop journals hymned the pleasures of rum, wine,
tobacco, the mail, or leave. One feature of this attitude was the
great popularity which Omar Khayyam enjoyed among the
troops. Quotations from him, or imitations of his style, were a
very common feature of the troop journals.[66] He crops up with
the same frequency in survivors' memoirs, and the basis of this
popularity was the poet's 'nihilistic philosophy', his presentation
of the viewpoint that 'I don't know why I came. I don't know
where or when I'm going. I like the flesh pots of Egypt and while
I'm here I'm going to enjoy myself as much as I can.' This was
'the only way to look at things'.[67] In escape from the awfulness of
conditions, from the heavy-handed provocations of the authorities, says the 'Rubaiyat of a Digger',

> 'How sweet the issue rum!'—think some
> Others—'How great the Blighty leave to come!'
> Ah. Seize each present joy and blow the rest
> With too-long waiting, our Desires grow numb.
>
> Oh, leave the Heads to wrangle and to roar
> And fly with me to Madame's open door
> There 'twixt red wine and Babette's dancing eyes
> Forget we are the helpless tools of War.[68]

The French journals too dwelt on material conditions, but they
dealt also more seriously with the war itself. In the British and
Dominion journals, 'the war, except as a subject for jokes, was

---

[65] Stedman Jones, 'Working Class Culture and Working Class Politics', pp. 490–3.
[66] *The Outpost*, 4/6 (Apr. 1917), 222; *The Moonraker*, 3 (Dec. 1917), 26; *New Church Times*, 1/1 (Apr. 1916), 7; *The Leadswinger*, 1/6 (Dec. 1915), 12; *New Year Souvenir of the Welsh Division* (Jan. 1918), 25–7.
[67] Bowra, *Memories*, p. 87; G. E. M. Eyre, *Somme Harvest* (1938), 207–8.
[68] *Aussie*, 8 (Oct. 1918), 16.

almost ignored'.[69] Undoubtedly there was a difference of national style here, but such exclusive concern with trivialities perhaps owed something also to the British and Dominion troops' sublime confidence, rarely shaken, in the ultimate success of their cause. The chauvinism which made them contemptuous of the contributions of their allies, was at the same time a great military asset. As a private in the Kensingtons recorded, 'I do not think it occurred to any of us that we could ever be defeated, so great was our pride and faith in the British Empire with all its great traditions'.[70] A Dane serving in Canadian ranks noted this peculiarity of his fellows in May 1918, at the crisis of Allied fortunes:

things have been looking pretty serious for our cause several times during my stay here, and I have shown my comrades my map and explained to them the narrowness of the strip of land we are still holding near Amiens. What are the chances of the Germans cutting through our communication lines with the French armies here? Wouldn't that finish us off for good? The boys listened to me and laughed: 'Rot, my lad— don't you know England wins all her wars?' England has not been conquered for close upon a thousand years now. England rules the waves and half the world—but the British soldier of the line has not yet grasped the fact that this time the Empire is fighting for her very life.[71]

Similarly in the AIF, 'few Australians at any time imagined being beaten', whilst in the BEF, according to an American who served in British ranks, 'for Tommy it is never "Who is going to win?", but always "How long will it take?" '.[72]

This simple-minded faith in British arms and the British Empire, coupled with a humorous contempt for things foreign, was one of the dominant strains in music hall culture, and the underlying faith survived now even when the accompanying jingoism was lost. It rested on strong historical foundations of economic success and a record of military victory, but it was music hall and the popular press that made it a living creed. Blunders and absurdities along the way were to be expected from

[69] Audoin-Rouzeau, *Les Combattants*, pp. 73–82; L. P. Yates Smith, 'They Laughed at War', *Defence* (Jan. 1940), 13–14.
[70] Tucker, *Johnny Get Your Gun*, p. 179.
[71] T. Dinesen, *Merry Hell! A Dane with the Canadians* (1929), 170.
[72] Gammage, *Broken Years*, p. 217; A. G. Empey, *From the Fire Step* (1917), 131, 134.

the officer class comically but affectionately depicted in the halls, but ultimate defeat was almost impossible to conceive. The morale of such troops would be very hard to break.

Kipling and the Soldiers

If music hall provided many men with national stereotypes, there was also a more detailed stereotype of the soldier which seems to have been very widely known to both British and Dominion troops. The first edition of *The Pow Wow*, in November 1914, ran a humorous article, 'A Grouser's Grouse', complaining that the infantry training was hopelessly at fault in that 'it omits all mention of the fact that the first duty of a soldier is to "grouse". When we become trained soldiers we must have reduced grousing to a fine art; otherwise we might as well never have been vaccinated or "measured" for our uniforms.'[73] Officers and other-ranks alike expected grousing and it was tolerated, or even actively encouraged, by the troop journals. Partly this was because it 'has always been the unquestioned privilege of the British Army . . . and we like to keep up the old traditions', but above all it was because of the widely held conviction that 'grousing clears the air like a summer storm without doing any harm'.[74] *The Vic's Patrol* contrasted the pessimist with the grouser who 'makes derogatory remarks about being "a — pack mule", and then cheerfully carries another load'. According to *The Stand Easy*, 'the army grouser is proverbial . . . he grumbles with a smile on his lips and a joke at the end of his tongue'. *The Snapper* summed up the licence to which the soldier was entitled, and the good which was felt to follow:

> Don't be afraid to grouse and growl
> When working—'tis your right,
> And the finest set of grousers
> Are the best men in a fight.[75]

The belief in the positive value of such grousing was in fact very common, forming a minor variant of the general belief in the

[73] *The Pow Wow*, 1 (Nov. 1914), 4.
[74] V. G. Seligman, *The Salonika Sideshow* (1919), 79.
[75] *The Vic's Patrol*, 1 (June 1916), 6–7; *The Stand Easy*, 3 (Oct. 1916), 49; quoted in *The Vic's Patrol*, 2 (July 1916), 16.

sovereign power of humour and the unique aptitude of the British for employing this. Grousing was 'recognized as harmless'; it served as 'a moral No. 9 [laxative], so to speak'; it was the British soldier's 'privilege, and even though he may be suffering under an injustice, his grouse is seldom very serious':

> Grouse, do I? Well, why grudge a soul its salve,
> Engines would burst without their safety valve.[76]

Furious at being paraded unnecessarily, 'you light another cigarette and start to pack up. Your anger and annoyance has gone—no, not gone, but changed (in that way, wonderful way, patent to the British army in particular and to the British in general) from big words to small jokes.'[77] 'A healthy soldier', in fact, 'always grouses': when he stopped was the time to worry.[78]

To a large extent, this comic pessimism was perhaps a natural outgrowth of the 'culture of consolation' which found expression in the halls. However, Major-General George Younghusband, observing the phenomenon, offered a more specific explanation. At the time of the Boer War, he expressed the surprise he and his brother officers felt in witnessing the change that had come over the private soldier: 'my early recollections of the British soldier are of a bluff, rather surly person, never the least jocose or light hearted, except perhaps when he had too much beer. He was brave always, but with a sullen, stubborn bravery.' The modern soldier, quite different in behaviour, had, he concluded, invented himself on the pattern of Kipling's stories.[79]

We may doubt the extent to which Kipling worked the change alone. Rather, Kipling drew upon the culture of the halls, and so embodied in his writings an impression, however stylized, of the new spirit of the working class. From the stages of the various 'Empires' and 'Palaces' which he enthusiastically attended, 'Kipling took the style of speech and preoccupations, and developed them in numerous poems and songs'.[80] He wrote 'in the

---

[76] Graham, *Private in the Guards*, pp. 7–8; *The Third Battalion Magazine*, 1 (Aug. 1918), 2; *The Outpost*, 3/1 (Mar. 1916), 16; *The Vic's Patrol*, 2 (July 1916), 11.

[77] *Invicta Gazette*, 3 (Sept. 1916), 4.

[78] Mackenzie, *The 6th Gordons*, p. 18. Cf. W. R. Dent, *Show Me Death* (1930), 325; Black, *One Volunteer*, pp. 77–8.

[79] G. Younghusband, *A Soldier's Memories* (1917), 187.

[80] Summerfield, 'The Effingham Arms and the Empire', p. 233.

language of the people and with the rhythm of the music hall'.[81]
His style reflected so closely that of the halls that 'it would seem
likely there are parallels and even cross fertilizations between his
art and theirs'.[82] His message, too, carried echoes of the music
hall. On the one hand *Barrack Room Ballads* illustrated 'like . . .
the London music hall songs they echo . . . the determined
hilarity in which the strain and despair find release'; on the other,
his prose stories of 'Mulvaney', 'Ortheris', and 'Learoyd' depicted 'the sort of collective griping and irreverence that sustained
the Soldiers Three in their hard life'.[83]

These two collections were the basis of Kipling's popularity,
which was immense. *Barrack Room Ballads* had been 'for a generation the most popular and widely selling of all volumes of
English verse'.[84] Through recitation of his work on the music hall
stage, their author had become 'one of the first great poets for
centuries whose work became known, on a large scale, to those
who could scarcely read, or did not do so at all'.[85] For many of the
temporary soldiers of the Great War, given the social apartness of
the old Regular army, Kipling's soldier must have been the only
soldier they knew. Certainly a ready degree of familiarity is indi-
cated by Kipling's popularity at the front. Paul Fussell is misled
by his study of a cultural élite in suggesting that the troops
spurned Kipling for Conrad or Hardy.[86] Conrad might find
readers 'among what Russian revolutionary soldiers and work-
men call indiscriminately "the bourgeois" but not among the
rank and file'.[87] Neither he nor Hardy featured anywhere in a list
of the most popular authors in hospital libraries: Kipling came
behind only Nat Gould and Jack London.[88] At the front, Kipling
recitations were given at unit concerts.[89] He was the most quoted
and most imitated author in the trench journals: 'they say that Mr
Rudyard Kipling has ceased to be the soldier's poet. But he is

[81] P. Mason, *Kipling: The Glass, the Shadow and the Fire* (1975), 73.
[82] C. MacInnes, 'Kipling and the Music Hall', in J. Gross (ed.), *Kipling: The Man, his Work and his World* (1972), 59.
[83] A. Wilson, *The Strange Ride of Rudyard Kipling* (1977), 145, 147.
[84] J. I. M. Stewart, *Rudyard Kipling* (1966), 73.
[85] MacInnes, 'Kipling and the Music Hall', p. 60.
[86] P. Fussell, *The Great War and Modern Memory* (1975), 163.
[87] Graham, *Private in the Guards*, p. 195.
[88] Koch, *Books in Camp, Trench and Hospital*, p. 13.
[89] *The Listening Post*, 5 (Oct. 1915), 19; *The 5th Glo'ster Gazette*, 15 (Oct. 1916), 5; *Invicta Gazette*, 6 (Dec. 1916), 17.

parodied much more often than any other author, and even when an original stave is said and sung, the Kiplingesque anapaests go by in column of route.'[90] References to his work were legion, and almost invariably they approved or endorsed his sentiments. He was as well-known to the Dominion forces as to the British. *The Canadian 20th Gazette* could speak of a soldier as 'of the Mulvaney–Ortheris–Learoyd type', and expect to be understood.[91]

What music hall created, then, Kipling adapted and gave specific application to the army, and the resulting depiction, hailed for its veracity, was known to millions who had few enough other models to serve them upon their sudden induction into khaki.

Sport

Sport was at least the equal of music hall in popularity in both Britain and the Dominions. Football, cricket, and to a lesser extent rugby, initially codified and to a considerable extent spread by public-school enthusiasts, were increasingly crowding out other traditional sports.[92] Even among groups as self-contained and resistant to outside influence as the mining communities of South Northumberland, these games and the ethics with which their public-school apostles attempted to imbue them, were winning for themselves a place. Historically, miners' sport, whether bowling, pedestrianism, or rowing, had served as 'a vehicle for miners to express their individuality and physical prowess', a focus of community, and an arena for gambling. Playing to win, and to win money at that, was its key. By the late 1880s, football and amateur sport were beginning to break into this closed world:

the emergence of amateur sport signified the introduction of an ideology antithetical to that espoused by the majority of miners. Underlying amateurism was the idea of playing the game for the game's sake, a

---

[90] *Times Literary Supplement*, 12 Oct. 1916, 482.

[91] *20th Gazette*, 2/2 (July 1916), 13.

[92] J. Walvin, *The People's Game: A Social History of British Football* (1975), 45–8; T. Mason, *Association Football and English Society 1863–1915* (Sussex, 1980), 21–4; P. Bailey, *Leisure and Class in Victorian England* (1978), 137–9; J. Lowerson and J. Myerscough, *Time to Spare in Victorian England* (Sussex 1977), 121–3.

rejection of money prizes, the idea of building character, and the demonstration of desirable behaviour on the playing field. Throughout the 1890s, amateur sport was the exception rather than the rule in the coalfield, but its very existence signified the introduction of a value system corrosive of traditional mining community values.[93]

The working class was of course not a passive recipient, and the games spread the faster as they were subtly adapted to fit the needs of their widening constituency. Within football, the emphasis on competition steadily grew, and games became an affirmation of fierce community loyalties. In consequence football, with professional clubs at the apex and an immense under-pinning of amateur enthusiasm, enjoyed 'phenomenal growth . . . among all working class groups'.[94] Something of the 'sporting ethos' survived. The Sheffield *Football World*, for example, could recognize that a team's first aim was to win, but still advocate alongside this that it should give its opponent 'the fairest of fair play'.[95]

In the Dominions, greater working-class leisure and prosperity, the universal availability of space, and, except in parts of Canada, more favourable climates, had given sport a prominence perhaps even greater than in Britain. In Australia, sport was 'the national obsession': sporting heroes were national heroes, for their prowess at once gave expression to an emergent nationalism with few opportunities to feature on the world stage, and laid to rest disquieting pseudo-scientific theories about the 'degeneration of the race' outside northern climes.[96] In New Zealand too there was 'probably far more actual playing of games . . . than almost anywhere else. It is only recently that there has even been a suggestion of any very serious development of professionalism in sport with the consequent degradation of fine games to gladiatorial exhibitions before crowds of non-players.'[97]

As in Britain, the equivalents of the public schools had played an important part in spreading the cult, and with it the code of

[93] A. Metcalfe, 'Organized Sport in the Mining Communities of South Northumberland 1880–1889', *Victorian Studies*, 25 (1982), 492–5.
[94] Metcalfe, 'Organised Sport in the Mining Communities', p. 494.
[95] Mason, *Association Football*, p. 256.
[96] G. P. Cuttriss, *Over the Top with the 3rd Australian Division* (1918), 109; R. Ward, *The History of Australia: The Twentieth Century 1901–1975* (1978), 27, 66, 90.
[97] Burton, *The Silent Division*, pp. 123–4.

sportsmanship.[98] In public and state schools alike, schoolbooks and journals deluged the pupils with propaganda about the specificity to the British race of the sporting virtues such as cheerfulness, lack of rancour, manliness, and self-control.[99] In Canada, when the author of 'Play up and Play the Game' visited in 1923, he was gratified by the popular response to his verses, but 'as for "Play up and play the Game" it's a kind of Frankenstein monster that I created thirty years ago and now I find falling on my neck at every street corner! In vain do I explain what is poetry: they roar for "Play up"; they put it on their flags and on their war memorials, and their tombstones; it's their national anthem.'[100]

The activities of the soldiers overseas showed that their enthusiasm for sport had survived the transference intact. This enthusiasm in itself distinguished them from the men of other armies. The passion for sport was, for example, something as yet relatively little-known to the French: 'French people, I found, could not understand the reason why the English spent so much of their life on football. They wondered why our soldiers played so much instead of practising warfare.'[101] In France 'it was not until the Twenties that modern sport became an integral element in popular culture'. The First World War was its great missionary period:

football and rugby teams were popularized through makeshift battalion teams, and peasants from the remoter provinces soon picked up some of the new interests of their urban companions in the trenches . . . From about a thousand clubs in 1920, the Federation Française de Football (F.F.F.) almost quadrupled in size within the next five years.[102]

The Outpost described a match between its own battalion team and an eleven representative of a French division. It was

not exactly a proper test for the Battalion . . . The goalkeeper was not tested, the French players never being able to control the ball suffi-

[98] I. Turner, 'The Emergence of Aussie Rules', in Cashman and McKernan (eds.), *Sport in History*, pp. 264–5; W. F. Mandle, 'Games People Played', *Historical Studies*, 15 (1973), 511–35; D. Leinster-Mackay and G. Hancock, 'Godliness, Manliness and Good Learning: Victorian Virtues and West Australian Exemplars 1891–1911', *Melbourne Studies in Education* (Melbourne, 1979), pp. 141–54.
[99] Firth, 'Social Values in the New South Wales Primary School', pp. 123–59; Malone, 'The New Zealand School and the Imperial Ideology', pp. 3–12.
[100] P. Howarth, *Play Up and Play the Game* (1973), 1.
[101] B. Willey, *Spots of Time* (1965), 136.
[102] R. Holt, *Sport and Society in Modern France* (1981), 70, 215.

ciently to bring it near enough to the goal mouth to cause any anxiety in that quarter. The French players were fast enough and would no doubt make good footballers if they had more practice with British teams.[103]

The French, then, were only setting out on a path already well trodden by British popular culture. Their organization of sports, apart from being less widespread than in the British army, could also not draw upon the established cultural background of sporting values, from which sport among the British troops drew much of its force.

Sport in the British and Dominion forces betrayed many traces of the sportsmanship idea which survived from civilian life. Football matches were described as 'very sporting', or 'played in the usual good sporting spirit'.[104] Bad sportsmanship was loudly disapproved. The cry 'H.L.I.', for example, originating in pre-war competition, would be raised against any team indulging in time-wasting to safeguard a lead.[105] 'Playing the game' was much harped upon by the troop journals. The Navy was playing it, the strikers were not, but above all it must be played by the soldier, for

> Right is bound to win in time
> If you play the game right through.[106]

The Listening Post protested at the frequency of such admonitions, but at the same time implicitly accepted their worth, adding to them its own:

> From the day you first don khaki,
> And you lose your blooming name,
> There's a little song they sing you
> Whistle, dance it: 'Play the game'
> Play the game, play the game,
> From reveille until lights out it's the same
>
> .   .   .   .   .   .
>
> When someone big has blundered,
> And they want to fix the blame,

[103] *The Outpost*, 5/1 (May 1917), 26.

[104] *The Outpost*, 3/4 (July 1916), 122; *The 5th Glo'ster Gazette*, 10 (Mar. 1916), 5; *The Incinerator*, 2 (June 1916), 36; *Illustrated 718*, 2 (Jan. 1917), 38.

[105] Rule, *Students under Arms*, pp. 184–5; G. S. Hutchison, *Footslogger* (1931), 249.

[106] *The Gasper*, 18 (June 1916), 7, and 21 (Sept. 1916), 4; *The Outpost*, 5/5 (Sept. 1917), 157, and 1/1 (Feb. 1915), 8; *Illustrated 718*, 4 (Apr. 1917), 80.

While they cast about for victims,
They keep yelling, 'Play the game'.
Play the game, play the game,
While the German staff are laughing. My! it's
tame.

But Tommy he must stick it—
There is nothing else to do;
Be it open ground or thicket,
It's up to me and you;
We must keep the line from breaking,
Though the trees and rocks are quaking,
And the earth with gunfire shaking
'Play the game'.[107]

Many among the rank and file used the phrase unself-consciously. They might jib at its glib facility in the mouth of a young officer. A private in the 1/4th Black Watch remembered one such occasion: 'there was a youngster who, when our trench was being assailed by whizz-bangs . . . walked white faced among us and said; "Now boys, play up and play the game". An old NCO said: "Excuse me, sir, this isn't a cricket match. It's a bloody war".' Still the same memoirist could record that 'when a man lay dying in the trench he would say to his own familiar friend: "You'll tell the girl I played the game, won't you? Tell her not to forget me".'[108]

The attachment to the sportsmanship ethic also found less tragic expression in what Fussell terms 'the British Phlegm style' of private soldiers' letters and diaries, by which horror and danger were understated to a degree at times almost ludicrous. Similarly, the French troops noted, and sometimes imitated, 'la forme favorite de l'humour britannique, "l'understatement" '.[109]

Perhaps the most bizarre manifestations of the sportsmanship ethic were the occasions when British soldiers went into the attack kicking footballs. This seems to have been an action approved of by many of their fellow soldiers, and not simply by the home press.[110] It showed a proper lightheartedness; it was

---

[107] *The Listening Post*, 31 (July 1918), 14.
[108] Andrews, *Haunting Years*, pp. 143, 287.
[109] Fussell, *Great War and Modern Memory*, p. 181; Meyer, *La Vie quotidienne*, p. 173.
[110] *Dead Horse Corner Gazette*, 2 (Dec. 1915), 21; Williams, *Comrades of the*

splendidly unfunctional (in symbolism at least) and expressed a determination to refuse to be swayed by circumstance. The German reaction was very different. Writers like Treitschke had long been contemptuous of England's addiction to games instead of to 'noble arms', as a symbol of her decadence. They held that 'the flag can never degenerate into a soccer ball'. The incidents were consequently in the paradoxical and revealing position of receiving interested publicity from both sides. If Caton Woodville saw fit to produce a poem celebrating the most famous such football attack, 'The Surreys Play the Game', the Germans seized upon it and circulated it in ten languages as propaganda for the Central Powers.[111]

'Playing the game', in fact, stood symbol for a whole attitude, of which good-natured equanimity in the face of hardship and danger was only part. It stood also for extreme endurance and a determination not to let the 'side' down:

> 'E takes 'is chance in the Fire Trench—
> with the shells a buzzin' about,
> 'E's quiet as mice in a night attack, and
> 'e shouts when it's needful to shout
> And he sticks 'is job with 'ardly a grouse
> —a damn tough bullet to chew.
> It's now as was always, 'is Majesty's Tommy
> —soldier and sportsman too.[112]

In war where the 'side' was the section or platoon, this idea acted to reinforce the cohesion of the primary group. Sport was the model:

that a man should strive to win credit for himself is natural, that he should seek to gain honour for other people is sublime. It is the quality of the British race, and essentially of Lancashire. Cannot Bolton then, the home of the Wanderers, put into its battalion the same spirit that it puts into its football? . . . Let every man look to himself and watch by no carelessness he renders himself unfit, and so weakens the battalion of which he is a member.[113]

Great Adventure, p. 103; Seligman, *Salonika Sideshow*, p. 86; Fussell, *Great War and Modern Memory*, pp. 27–8.

[111] Kiernan, 'Conscription and Society', p. 151; L. Farago (ed.), *German Psychological Warfare* (New York, 1942), 112; Brown, *Tommy Goes to War*, p. 171.

[112] *The Mudlark*, 3 (June 1916), 12.

[113] *Carry On*, 2 (Jan. 1916), 8.

Nor was the model without effect. According to one soldier, although disillusioned with the mistreatment of the infantry and the pointlessness of the war, 'men of my thinking did their job and did not let the side down'.[114]

Army sport was in a sense a refresher course in a set of values, not absolutely or universally accepted but none the less influential, and these values were of a sort to bolster compliance, stoicism, and even confidence. We may be reluctant to accept this concept. The cult of games as the school of virtue attained such overblown proportions, and a voice so extravagantly bombastic, that the reaction has all but swept it away. We may be inclined to deride Newbolt and his like today. Even in their heyday, the crude equation of warrior virtues with sporting virtues invited a *reductio ad absurdum*:

when the battalion goes in the attack you find all the battalion team in the first wave going ahead and doing all the work. In the next wave come the company teams—they are not quite so good. Then come the platoon teams, and so on . . .
Is it true? IS IT HELL!!!
Anyway the moral is that you should play football. If they want you to do it, do it. That is simply common sense.[115]

Yet, stripped of all elaboration, the fact remains that organized sport must embody some value system. The very fact of there being rules forms the lowest tier of such a system:

in the heat of competition a player may feel intensely frustrated, humiliated, angry, or depressed yet can neither come out hitting the opponents nor run away from them. Characteristically, the player may not even display his or her feelings. Within the confines of strict rules, the player just has to serve the next ball . . . take on the next batter, or simply line up again with his or her team mates.[116]

Sport may be 'an alternative source of ethical values to those founded in production and work', or it may be 'a dramatization of life at large' in which the ruling values of the society are rehearsed, reinforced, and spread.[117] At all events, it communi-

---

[114] Groom, *Poor Bloody Infantry*, p. 82.
[115] *The Outpost*, 4/1 (Nov. 1917), 8.
[116] D. Zillman, J. Bryant, and B. S. Sapolsky, 'The Enjoyment of Watching Sports Contests', in J. H. Goldstein (ed.), *Sports, Games and Play* (New York, 1979), 301.
[117] S. Parker, *The Sociology of Leisure* (1976), 29; J. W. Loy, B. D. McPherson, and G. Kenyon, *Sport and Social Systems* (1978), 381–92, 415.

cates values, and in Britain and the Dominions the value systems of the organized sports with a mass following tended to be, because of their roots in the public schools, quite strongly supportive of the status quo.

An important part of the sportsmanship creed, for example, was the belief that the British (and their Dominion offshoots) were more sportsmanlike than other nations, and that this in turn implied a moral superiority. 'I honestly do believe', wrote an Australian serving in the British ranks, 'that the British Empire stands for the best principles in mankind. I really do believe that they are the best sportsmen in the world.'[118] A corporal convalescing in England watched a boxing contest in camp, and 'gloried in the skill and sportsmanship of both crowd and combatants. No other country in the world, I thought, could aspire to such heights of enlightenment.'[119] Sportsmanship was held to bewilder the French. It was 'that baffling quality which no other country quite understands'. It demonstrated the moral superiority of the British and therefore stood, in theory at least, as a powerful argument for the justice of their cause: 'Britain conquers less for herself than for humanity.'[120]

If many in fact lost faith in the notion of the war as a crusade, still they were held to their duty by their own ideas of sportsmanlike behaviour. The individual's conduct still mattered more than the result it produced. It still behoved the soldier to do the right thing himself, however much the betrayals and deceptions of others might rob his action of its benefits. Troop journals echoed the sentiments of a man of the 16th Battalion CEF: 'there is no doubt in my mind that I did the right thing in coming over; whether the war was wrong or not does not alter the fact'.[121]

For the front-line soldiers, whatever might be going wrong at home *we* were still all right. Faith in England and English values was not lost. It was just that 'to find the real England you have to come to France';

---

[118] *The Outpost*, 4/4 (Feb. 1917), 136.

[119] Morrow, *Iron in the Fire*, p. 105.

[120] Owen, *Salonica and After*, p. 141; *The Dagger*, 1 (Nov. 1918), 19. A Dane serving in Canadian ranks thought this view ironic in the face of Ireland's oppression over seven centuries, and found it 'hard not to comment a bit upon the arrogance of the British race when they take it as a matter of course that we should all look upon the Empire as the salt of the earth': Dinesen, *Merry Hell*, p. 47.

[121] Urquhart, *History of the 16th Bn.*, p. 341.

> That England one by one had fled to France
> Not many elsewhere now save under France;

that the real England was 'not an island or an empire, but a wet populous dyke stretching from Flanders to the Somme'.[122] Despite all betrayals, the British private soldier had to keep plugging away, stay true to himself, and then not only would he finish the job here, but he would set everything to rights when he got back to Blighty.[123] In a very real sense, as Tawney told the civilians, 'we are your ghosts': 'when, as has happened in the present war, men have taken up arms under the influence of some emotion or principle, they tend to be ruled by the idea which compelled them to enlist long after it has been yielded, among civilians, to some more fashionable novelty'.[124] The war acted in this way precisely to reinforce certain values and to foster a cultural conservatism which made the troops in many ways the last of the Edwardians rather than the first of the moderns, as they are so often depicted.

Sporting values, in fact, could give some pattern to a war which, as idealism and enmity both faded, was hard to comprehend in any other terms. It was as a competition between sides, unapologetic and fiercely fought, but with little rancour and with place for respect for a worthy foe, that it appeared to many men. According to one Canadian ranker,

I honestly believe the average Canadian soldier's feeling—when considering the enemy—to be almost identical with the mixture of vexation and grudging admiration he feels towards a football team which has knocked him and his Club hollow. 'Keep your head down Fritzie boy! If you want to see your Vater in your Vaterland, keep your head down, Fritzie boy!' we sing to him. And when he does not keep his head down, he may get hit one day—but apart from that we feel no animosity other than the natural feeling against the man who is going to answer your shot.[125]

The idea of such a contest, in which lives were forfeit for no larger reason than rivalry, was sufficiently absurd, but it was as

[122] R. Farrer, *The Void of War* (1918), 25; J. Silkin (ed.), *First World War Poetry* (1979), 195; R. H. Tawney, *The Attack and Other Papers* (1953), 21.
[123] *The Whizz Bang*, 3 (Mar. 1916), 1; *The Outpost*, 4/1 (Nov. 1916), 40; *The Gasper*, 17 (Mar. 1916), 2.
[124] Tawney, *The Attack and Other Papers*, pp. 22–3.
[125] Dinesen, *Merry Hell*, pp. 172–3.

just such a mad contest of nations, arranged and staged by the politicians, that the war appeared to many men. If the war was not to be perceived as a crusade, and fewer and fewer front-line soldiers did so perceive it, the idea of contest did at least give it an understandable shape, and suggested, in side-loyalty, 'sticking it', and keeping cheerful, a pattern of ethics for men whose disillusionment from unrealistic preconceptions had left them lost and adrift. It was these values, according to a Dane serving in Canadian ranks, which upheld his comrades in the face of fear.[126]

The Dominion troops, in fact, were well to the fore in their use of the sportsmanship ethic. Among the Australians, even as the war proceeded and it became clear that this was very far from being a game, the language of sport survived:

there were 'sides', an action was a 'stunt', men had an 'innings' between leave or wounds, men killed were 'knocked' or 'knocked out', men defeated or dead 'took the count', men winning easily 'had a walkover'. Early in 1917 a veteran of Fromelles wrote that he was about to leave England 'to help knock out old "Bill" in the last round of the championship', in 1918 troops chosen for an attack 'got their guernsey', and at Menin Road a brave man dying told his mates that he was still playing and still had a jersey.[127]

No one any longer called the war 'the greatest game the world has ever known', but the deeper personal linkage between sport as a test of character and war as another test, even more exacting, was too deeply ingrained to be easily cast aside. Men no longer viewed their task as play, but they did see it as calling for the same qualities of courage, endurance, and team-work as had been tested in sport in happier days:

The gong has sounded, you take your stand
In the midst of the ring of life,
'Box on' is your first and your last command
As you enter the worldly strife.

'Box on' Lend a hand to the man who's down,
Strike not, assist him to rise,
'Tis as easy to smile as it is to frown—
The smile brings you nearer the prize.

---

[126] Ibid. 216.
[127] Gammage, *Broken Years*, pp. 90–4, 218.

'Box on' Play fair, though the fight be long
And the punishment be severe,
If your cause be just and your heart be strong
The verdict you need not fear.[128]

The Dominion troop journals in fact fully matched the British obsession with 'playing the game', and imbued this phrase with the same comprehensive range of values. It meant doing one's duty: 'Retrospective 1933' imagined the veteran, in years to come, reflecting,

But thank the Lord who made us men
We knew the game and played it then.[129]

It stood for stoic endurance:

You're sick of the game? Well, now that's a shame!
You're young, and you're brave, and you're bright
You've had a raw deal? I know but don't squeal
Buck up, do your damnedest, and fight.[130]

It stood for selflessness and playing for the team. Above all, it called for cheerfulness in adversity:

Be cheery and you'll find life's jake
If you but play the game.[131]

The Dominion troop journals just like the British exhorted their readers to 'keep smiling', 'keep cheerful', 'play the joker'. They had the same determination to find humour in trench existence and the same poignant faith in the power of humour. As *The Dead Horse Corner Gazette* in its 'Hints to Young Soldiers' advised, 'when you are feeling homesick, sing or whistle a comic song. Mirth is the old reliable tonic.'[132]

Humour

Sport and music hall were two important elements in the humour of the British troops, which many writers seized on as character-

---

[128] *Aussie*, 1 (Jan. 1918), 9.
[129] *Anzac Records Gazette*, 3 (Jan. 1916), 11.
[130] *The Canadian Sapper*, 3 (Apr. 1918), 81.
[131] *Dead Horse Corner Gazette*, 2 (Dec. 1915), 21.
[132] Ibid. 3 (June 1916), 38.

istic. There may have been others. For example, the relatively unmilitary nature of the society, compared to Imperial Germany or indeed to France, facilitated the association of humour and the military life. The Volunteer, who subsequently became the Territorial, had long been a subject for popular caricature. For everyone from Mr Punch to street urchins, he was the butt of unmalicious, but remorseless, ridicule. The gap between military pretension and humble civilian reality proved irresistible: in this sense, the Volunteers were an earlier 'Dad's Army', and in reaction, 'uncertain of their own status and conscious of a gap between their patrons' public and private opinion of the Force, the Volunteers in self protection and escape from reality, laughed at themselves'.[133] The 'Saturday Afternoon Soldiers', who were to form the bulk of the early BEF after the virtual destruction of the Regulars, were used to not taking themselves entirely seriously, just as the British public were used to the idea of finding humour in amateur soldiering. In Germany the reserve forces might command respect, in France on occasion antagonism, but only in Britain such derision.[134]

Whatever its exact pedigree, the important fact is that a style of humour which helped to smooth over rather than to open up divisions, to console rather than to subvert, carried over from civilian society into the war sectors. Humour can play an important part in maintaining morale. A study of GI humour in the next war was to show that it helped American troops to 'achieve a frame of mind in which it was possible . . . to endure and accept what could not be avoided. Humour allowed a safe discharge of dangerous tensions . . . [it] helped the men to achieve a kind of distance from their threatening experiences.'[135]

All these claims were similarly made for British humour on the Western Front. As war weariness mounted in the winter of 1917, 'only humour helped. Humour that made a mock of life and scoffed at our own frailty. Humour that touched everything with ridicule and had taken the bite out of the last thing, death. It was a working philosophy that carried us through the day.'[136] Mockery, however forced, served to humanize the horrors. With a

[133] Cunningham, *Volunteer Force*, pp. 78–80, 83–4.
[134] Porch, *March to the Marne*, p. 27.
[135] Stouffer (ed.), *The American Soldier*, ii. 190.
[136] Moran, *Anatomy of Courage*, pp. 143–4.

song like 'Hush! Here comes a whizz bang', 'the very knowledge of such songs may well have reduced the emotional distress caused by fear, and aided [the soldier], after the experience, to pick his uncertain way back to sanity'.[137] Similarly, to satirize a feeling of homesickness was to deny its intensity, and in some degree to reduce it. Songs like 'I don't want to be a soldier' or 'Far, far from Ypres I long to be' 'satirized more than war: they poked fun at the soldier's own desire for peace and rest, and so prevented it getting the better of him. They were strong bulwarks against défaitisme.'[138] In just the same way, troop journals made a joke of the seeming endlessness of the war, and in soldiers' slang 'irony is frequent, almost prevalent. It is the typically English irony of understatement and ridicule. Some of the terror disappeared, together with the pomp, from war and military glory, when the soldier decided to call his steel helmet a Tin-hat, his bayonet a Tooth-pick, his entrenching tool handle a Piggy-stick.'[139]

The troop journals introduced a note of ridicule into even the most bitterly felt grievances. Anger at the monotony and shortcomings of the army diet became comic hostility towards the eponymous Mr Maconochie (of Maconochie stews) and Mr Tickler (of Tickler's jam). A certain 'Will Bashem (Corporal)' sought 'the residential address of Mr Machonachie [*sic*] as when next on leave I wish to call and pay my compliments'; the enquiry of one 'Poetic Justice' was answered, 'yes we have heard that the man who invented the guillotine met his fate by it. We believe Mr Machonochie [*sic*] is still alive.'[140]

Many observers believed that this outlook helped to insulate the British troops against great swings of mood caused by hopes dashed. The French mutinies of 1917 owed something to the initial widespread belief in Nivelle's promised new strategy. The men of the 370th Regiment, for example, when they moved up from Alsace to take part in the new offensive, were 'dans un enthousiasme indescriptible . . . croyant qu'ils allaient poursuivre les Allemands'.[141] From this enthusiasm came 'the terrible shock

---

[137] Brophy and Partridge, *The Long Trail*, p. 18.
[138] J. Brophy and E. Partridge, *Songs and Slang of the British Soldier* (1931), 8.
[139] Brophy and Partridge, *The Long Trail*, p. 210.
[140] *The Limit*, 1 (Dec. 1917), inside front cover; *The Mudhook*, 8 (Oct. 1918), 14.
[141] Pedroncini, *Les Mutineries*, p. 152.

of disappointment', and the consequent belief that the war could never be won by these methods. The British troops, on the other hand, seemed to be armoured against such fluctuations by 'the traditional half ironic, wholly philosophic spirit of the British Army'; by their tendency to take refuge 'in a lighthearted cynicism [which] assumed that the worst always happens and that nothing goes right beneath the sun'.[142] They could no more take themselves entirely seriously as warriors than they could the business and artefacts of war. Ford Madox Ford's hero, 'Tietjens', is at times irritated, then amused, by the inability of his men to look and act like a serious military force, instead of like a collection of back-chatter men and pantomime drolls. Later, however, he begins to see that this is in fact one of their greatest strengths. As the tide turns in 1918, and he hears of the numbers of Germans struck down by influenza, he reflects:

Germans were the sort of people that influenza would bowl over. They were bores because they came for ever true to type. You read their confounded circulars and they made you grin whilst a little puking. They were like continual caricatures of themselves and they were continually hysterical ... Hypochondriachal ... Corps of Officers ... Proud German Army ... His Glorious Majesty ... Mighty Deeds ... Not much of the Rag-time Army about that, and that was welling out continuously all the time ... Hypochondria! A rag-time army was not likely to have influenza so badly. It felt neither its moral nor its physical pulse.[143]

The British soldiers, it was often remarked, did not strike attitudes: a private, newly drafted, 'marvelled at the calm acceptance of the war by these Lancashire men. No fuss or flurry; nothing at all to suggest they had been in action. You'd to question them directly about the battle to get any information at all; even then you weren't sure whether they were joking.'[144] They wore their role lightly and not as self-aware heroes. To Aldington's 'Winterbourne', 'part of their impressiveness was this very triviality, their complete unconsciousness that there was anything extraordinary or striking about them'.[145] It was also part

---

[142] Kelly, *39 Months*, p. 66; A. D. Gristwood, *The Somme and the Coward* (Bath, 1968), 132.
[143] Ford, *The Bodley Head Ford Madox Ford*, iv. 345.
[144] Tilsley, *Other Ranks*, p. 8.
[145] R. Aldington, *Death of a Hero* (1929), 293.

of their strength, for they saw themselves as cogs rather than as the machine itself: humour and cynicism oiled the turning, but turn they must. According to 'Winterbourne' again,

they had no feeling of hatred for their enemies . . . Nor in general were they long duped by the War talk. They laughed at the newspapers. Any newcomer who tried to be high-falutin was at once snubbed with 'For Christ's sake don't talk patriotic!' . . . the real soldiers, the front-line troops, had no more delusions about the War than he had. They hadn't his feeling of protest and agony over it all, they hadn't tried to think it out. They went on with the business, hating it, because they had been told it had to be done and believed what they had been told . . . they went on in their stubborn despair, with their sentimental songs and cynical talk and perpetual grousing; and it's my belief that if they'd been asked to do so, they'd still be carrying on now.[146]

Furiously as Wyndham Lewis had attacked the Englishman's sense of humour in *Blast!*, during the last months of peacetime London, he paid tribute to its value in time of war:

the Englishman has what he calls 'a sense of humour'. He says that the German, the Frenchman, and most foreigners do not possess this attribute, and suffer accordingly. For what does 'the sense of humour' mean but an ability to belittle everything? Not only does the Englishman not 'make a mountain out of a molehill', he is able to make a molehill out of a mountain. That is an invaluable magic to possess. The most enormous hobgoblin becomes a pygmy on the spot. Or such is the ideal of this destructive 'humorous' standpoint, which has played such a great part in anglosaxon life—just as its opposite, 'quixotry', has played a great part in Spanish life.

Of course, 'the sense of humour' played a very great part in the War. 'Old Bill' was the real hero of the World War, on the English side, much more than any V.C.. A V.C. is after all a fellow who does something heroic; almost unEnglish. It is taking things a bit too seriously to get the V.C. The really popular fellow is the humorous 'Old Bill' à la Bairnsfather. And it was really 'Old Bill' who won the war—with all that that expression 'won the war' implied.[147]

Many depicted the French troops as baffled, and sometimes angered, by the formless and unsparing comedic spirit of their British allies. R. H. Mottram, whose work as a claims officer gave him some experience of the war zone beyond the insular world of

[146] Ibid. 291.
[147] P. W. Lewis, *Blasting and Bombardiering* (1967), 37–8.

the battalion, contrasted his observations of French troops with his knowledge of his own men: 'they did not laugh much as a rule, they frowned, stared, or talked rapidly with gestures, and then if they did laugh, it was uproariously, brutally at someone's misfortunes, Satire they understood. But they missed entirely the gentle nag, nag, nag of ridicule that he used to hear from his own platoon or company.'[148]

With all its supposed advantages, British humour was to many the war-winning quality, the key to understanding how the troops had endured so long. A private soldier's poem in *The Rising Sun* explained 'Why we shall win':

> Not because our hearts are stouter
> Not that we're better men
> Not because we mock the doubter
> Fighting battles with his pen.
>
> Not because our Empire's peerless
> Not that we have got more 'tin'
> But—when things look worse than cheerless
> We can set our teeth and grin.[149]

This was the answer which R. H. Mottram supplied to the question of why the British troops, as he saw it, outlasted their allies and enemies. His hero 'Skene' watches the men on the troopship carrying them home after victory: they are 'singing together with precisely the same lugubrious humour as in the days of defeat, of stalemate or of victory: "Old soldiers never die. They only fade away".' The verse takes us back to the last time we heard it, when 'Dormer' had proclaimed: 'this War depends on turning a crank. The side that goes on turning it efficiently the longer will win. Our chaps look like lasting.' Lasted they have, and because of this unvarying 'lugubrious humour'.[150]

The idea that the British really enjoyed some sort of national monopoly of humour is clearly insupportable. However, it is not unreasonable to suppose that there were cultural differences between and within the national armies in view of the very different backgrounds of the men which composed them. The

---

[148] Mottram, *Spanish Farm Trilogy*, p. 466.
[149] *The Rising Sun*, 12 (Feb. 1917), 4.
[150] Mottram, *Spanish Farm Trilogy*, pp. 530, 509.

peasants struck their comrades in the French army by their taciturnity, and they made up something like three-quarters of the infantry.[151] The British, by contrast, came overwhelmingly from the cities. Men from agricultural occupations made up only 8.4 per cent of the recruits to the British forces before February 1916. Exemptions, and the need for appropriately skilled men in the transport corps and sappers, only accentuated a pre-existing difference. In 1911, manufacturing and transport occupations had engaged 89 per cent of the working population in Britain, but only 34 per cent in France.[152] Even if the 'culture of consolation' was not a unique product of conditions in Britain but one manifestation of a generalized response to industrialized urban society, it is clear that this response would have marked the lives of far fewer of the men who made up the French armies.

The occupational background of the Australian forces was closer to that of the British than the French. Examination of attestation papers suggests a figure of approximately 17 per cent for men in the AIF previously engaged in primary production. Allowance for miners and quarrymen reduces the figure for men from agricultural pursuits to something under 14 per cent.[153] This total is striking in relation to the popular conception of Australia of that period, but *Aussie* reflected just how false that conception was:

The Romantic Young Thing [with visions of Bushrangers, Explorers, Boundary Riders, Prickly Pear Estates, etc]. And what were you in Australia before the War?
Truthful Aussie (V.C., D.C.M., M.M.). I was a clerk in an office in Melbourne![154]

Most were not so truthful:

> He was a dinkum Aussie Bloke
> On London leave and thus he spoke
> To a big John Hop on duty there:
> Digger, give's the oil for Nelson's Square.

[151] Meyer, *La Vie quotidienne*, pp. 28–9, 357.
[152] J. M. Winter, 'Britain's "Lost Generation" of the First World War', *Population Studies*, 31 (1976), 454; P. N. Stearns, *Lives of Labour* (1975), 24.
[153] L. L. Robson, 'Origin and Character of the First AIF', *Historical Studies*, 15 (1973), 741–5; *Census of the Commonwealth of Australia 1911*, iii. 1283.
[154] *Aussie*, 7 (Sept. 1918), 10.

> For they tell the tale in the North of France
> That those lions will bark if by a chance
> An Aussie soldier should pass some day
> Who hasn't a station out Queensland way
>
> For that's the tale that the Aussies spun
> To the Tabs, each was a Squatter's son.
> Most of our swaddies are city-bred
> Don't know a sheep from a shearing shed.[155]

In fact, Australia was already one of the most highly urbanized societies in the world.[156] The predominance of the city-bred was perhaps even greater in the CEF, since the large French-speaking farm population in Quebec, together with the prairie farmers of diverse European origins, proved notably unresponsive to appeals for recruits.[157]

This preponderance of men from an urban and often industrial background in the British and Dominion forces might be expected to bring with it an increased risk of concerted resistance to the military authorities. There were many men here with experience of organized action in response to grievance. However, offsetting this fact to some extent, there were other elements to the culture which transferred to the war fronts and took strong root there, supported by copies, in the shape of army sports and concert parties, of the institutions which had supported them at home. These institutions had evolved in response to the conditions of urban society and now proved appropriate to the new conditions of mass warfare. In the case of sport at least, they were familiar also to some of the smaller number of French troops from the cities, and made a similar but less spectacular transference. It does not seem unreasonable in the circumstances to give some credence to contemporary testimony that the attitudes which had evolved in association with these institutions also crossed over to the war fronts.

All this is not to say that the contemporary newspaper depiction of the soldier, 'represented as invariably "cheerful", as revelling in the excitement of war, as finding "sport" in killing other

---

[155] *Aussie*, 3 (Mar. 1918), 9.
[156] Lawson, *Brisbane in the 1890s*, pp. 3–4.
[157] C. P. Stacey, *Canada and the Age of Conflict*, i (Toronto, 1977), 236–7.

men',[158] was in any sense accurate. The troop journals dissented bitterly from this picture:

> You write about the 'fray',
> From some place miles away,
> You're giving us what Tommy calls the 'dirts'.
> With your 'majesty of war',
> And our 'eagerness for more'—
> Remember that this rubbish sort of hurts.[159]

'Bilge about Blighties' parodied a war correspondent's report, concluding: 'inset is a typical photo of one of our troops who has been in the great advance and is longing to get at them again'. The inset was blank.[160] In the same vein, *The 5th Glo'ster Gazette* caricatured a glowering, thoroughly fed-up soldier, with the caption ' "our Tommies are always cheerful"—from the Daily Liar'.[161] And *The Whizz Bang* summed up the whole feeling with a parody of 'If':

> If you can see your parapet subsiding
> And dig it out and build it up anew,
> If you can sit all night your soul confiding
> To soaking humps of mud and not feel blue . . .
>
> .   .   .   .
>
> If you can lead your men to sodden trenches
> And loose your spleen by writing rotten
> rhymes,
> You're wasted in this land of putrid stenches
> You're wanted writing leaders for the Times.[162]

Yet there is a paradox here. The correspondents' depiction of cheeriness is being attacked, but in a form and place most likely to confirm it. Alongside the 'more serious and sentimental' productions of the French active service press, these magazines were seen as a tribute to the cheeriness of the British troops.[163] According to a student of this output, 'the keynote of the British journals was humour'.[164] They preached the virtues of cheerfulness, urg-

---

[158] Tawney, *The Attack and Other Papers*, pp. 24–6.
[159] *The Pennon*, 1 (Sept. 1918), 1.
[160] *The 5th Glo'ster Gazette*, 14 (Sept. 1916), 6.
[161] Ibid. 21 (Nov. 1917), 7.
[162] *The Whizz Bang*, 2 (Feb. 1916), 14.
[163] *Illustrated London News*, 15 May 1915, 622.
[164] Yates Smith, 'They Laughed at War', pp. 13–14.

ing their readers to 'keep smiling', 'be cheerful', 'smile', 'smile awhile', and so on.[165] A cheerful spirit was not seen as impossible or inappropriate to the front-line soldier. On the contrary, it was the only attitude to take:

> It helps you when the world seems dark and dreary
> It cheers you up when everything goes wrong
> It livens you when hours are sad and weary,
> And seem for endless time to drag along.[166]

Humour, in fact, was 'the greatest possible asset to any man serving his country at the front'.[167]

Cheerfulness was presented by the journals as a special British virtue, which 'helps to make Tommy Atkins what he is':

Where Fritz grates out his 'hymn of hate' Tommy sings snatches from a popular air entirely irrelevant to the occasion. It is this capacity for appreciating the humour of every situation that places the Britisher streets ahead of stodgy Herman;

like the man in the musical comedy 'we've gott-er mott-er, always merry and bright' . . . Remember you have a wonderful advantage over Fritz. He hasn't any sense of humour. You have. MAKE THE BEST OF IT.[168]

This faith in the power of 'cheeriness' was sufficiently widespread among the men themselves for a troop journal edited by other-ranks to poke gentle fun at it:

Officer on duty. You seem cheerful Jones.
Jones [whistling exuberantly]. You've got to be cheerful Sir; if you aren't cheerful you get depressed, so you've got to be cheerful.[169]

The troop papers thus supported the idea of 'cheeriness' at the very time that they attacked the press depiction of it. The apparent paradox is resolved when it is realized that the attack was concentrated on two specific aspects of the press picture which were felt grossly to misrepresent the truth. Firstly, the troops were very far from being always cheerful:

[165] *The Whizz Bang*, 3 (Mar. 1916), 1; *The Swell*, 2 (Jan. 1916), 1; *The Moonraker*, 3 (Dec. 1917), 38–9; *The Dump*, 2 (Dec. 1916), 32.
[166] *The Swell*, 2 (Jan. 1916), 1; *The Leadswinger*, 1/6 (Dec. 1915), 28–9.
[167] *The Outpost*, 3/6 (Sept. 1916), 61.
[168] *Stray Shots*, 8 (Aug. 1916), 1; *The Pennon*, 1 (Sept. 1918), 1; *The Very Light*, 1 (Mar. 1917), 3.
[169] *The Brazier*, 4 (July 1916), 6.

This front line stuff
Is pretty tough
In spite of what the papers say;
Newspaper bluff
And kindred guff
Make out we're ALWAYS feeling gay.

SOMETIMES we are
We never bar
A hearty laugh in camp or trench
But it would jar
An armoured car
To take it ALL without a wrench.[170]

As a Ministry of Information memorandum on the effects of air raids was to state in the next war, 'morale should never be over-played. The raid will have made many people frightened and far from heroic. They will resent a standard being set up which they know to be impossible.'[171] This first element in the men's hostility towards the newspaper picture had within it the seeds of the second: from the representation of cheerfulness as the habitual mood of the men sprang also, they thought, something of the civilian underestimation of the trials of life at the front, which was equally bitterly resented.

Lest the evidence of the troop journals be doubted, writers more usually associated with the school of 'disenchantment' also noted the men's strange cheerfulness. Sassoon wrote that 'I could never understand how they managed to keep as cheery as they did through such drudgery and discomfort with nothing to look forward to but going over the top or being moved up to Flanders again'.[172] He crystallized the sense of what the newspapers said, and, in the saying, left unsaid:

it was queer how the men seemed to take their victimization for granted. In and out; in and out; singing and whistling, the column swayed in front of me . . . A London editor driving along the road in a Staff car would have remarked that the spirit of the troops was amazing. And so it

[170] *The Listening Post*, 24 (Apr. 1917), 158.
[171] I. McLaine, *Ministry of Morale* (1979), 129.
[172] Sassoon, *Complete Memoirs of George Sherston*, pp. 310–11. Cf. R. Hart-Davis (ed.), *Siegfried Sassoon Diaries 1915–1918* (1983), 47–8, 151.

was. But somehow the newspaper men always kept the horrifying realities of the War out of their articles.[173]

Blunden too paid tribute to

man, ruddy-cheeked under your squat chin-strapped iron helmet, sturdy under your leather jerkin, clapping your hands together as you dropped your burden of cold steel, grinning and flinging old home repartee at your pal passing by . . . It is time to hint to a new age what your value, what your love was; your Ypres is gone, and you are gone; we were lucky to see you 'in the pink' against white-ribbed and socket-eyed despair.[174]

In retrospect Sassoon concludes, 'wonderful indeed had been that whimsical fortitude of the men who accepted an intense bombardment as all in the day's work and then grumbled their cigarette ration was one packet short'.[175] There is a remarkable congruity here with the 'culture of consolation' at home and it is apparent that the symbols of this culture which were replicated in the improvised theatres and sports grounds behind the lines were not stranded totems in an alien environment but cathedrals of a living faith.

Persistence and Change in the Soldiers' Outlook

The fact that there was a large decree of continuity in enthusiasms and attitudes from civilian to military life is significant not only in its effects but also in what it says about the nature of the war experience. It suggests that for many men the war was not quite the chasm, cutting across individual and collective experience and sundering past from future, that it is sometimes depicted. E. J. Leed, for example, compares the experience of the soldier encountering for the first time the world of the trenches, where normal peacetime categories were broken down or reversed, to that of a neophyte undergoing rites of passage.[176]

Much, no doubt, was overturned. A personal mode of life, more or less gracious, gave way to the primitive conditions of the

---

[173] Sassoon, *Complete Memoirs of George Sherston*, pp. 363–4.
[174] Blunden, *Undertones of War*, p. 145.
[175] Sassoon, *Complete Memoirs of George Sherston*, p. 540.
[176] Leed, *No Man's Land*, pp. 1–29.

trenches. Security was displaced by a nagging threat of death. Civilian taboos were broken, including the greatest taboo against killing, after which 'all other and minor prohibitions must tend to become still more negligible'.[177] All external marks of civilian identity and individuality vanished. The soldier became a number, identically dressed with his fellows, stripped of status and reduced to common subjection to another's will, deprived of the right to shape his own actions. The context of family and civilian community disappeared. This was a very different world, calling, it must have seemed, for rather different values and attitudes.

The troop journals commented on the revolution in habits which was often observed. Teetotallers found themselves no longer able to resist the temptation of escape into the forgetfulness or euphoria of drink.[178] Even swearing offered some relief from unbearable stress and tension. A candidate for the ministry joined Frank Richards's battalion and within three months, 'nobody would have thought who came into contact with him that he had ever studied for the ministry. His bad language won universal approval and he also became highly proficient in drinking a bottle of ving blong.'[179]

Besides swearing and drinking, many men stole property from the army, from civilians, and even, in the time-honoured army way of making up deficiencies in kit, from other soldiers. The euphemisms which disguised the nature of this act were legion, and its prevalence, 'by men who, before the War would not have dreamed of taking anything to which they were not legally entitled', was a joke to the troop journals.[180] However, 'this army method, if practised in civil life, would be described plainly as theft'.[181]

Religion also suffered, partly in consequence of these shifts in behaviour. Christianity, to many men, meant first and foremost 'godly habits'. A religion conceived of as being one of moral conduct and ultimate reward seemed scarcely appropriate to the soldier's life, alternating between the killing and profanity of the forward trenches, and the compensatory pleasures of sex, drink,

---

[177] A. Osborn, *Unwilling Passenger* (1932), 339.
[178] *The Incinerator*, 1 (May 1916), 13.
[179] Richards, *Old Soldiers*, p. 239.
[180] *Invicta Gazette*, 9 (Mar. 1917), 5–7; *The Outpost*, 3/1 (Mar. 1916), 9.
[181] Harvey, *Red and White Diamond*, p. 78.

or gambling behind the lines. It was mocked by the confident appeal of both sides to the same God: '*God Mit Uns*' read the belt buckles of the dead or captured enemy. Above all, it presented the problem of understanding how a beneficent God could allow this horror to happen.

The chaplains, in putting forward the Christian point of view, were distanced from their putative flock by their officer status. Quite apart from the antagonism between the ranks, this association with officialdom forced them into a false position, which could be perceived as such by all with even the rudest grasp of the tenets of the Christian faith. Chaplains found themselves preaching against feelings of goodwill towards the German common soldier, even, ironically enough, at Christmas, when such sentiments carried with them the abhorrent (to the authorities) suspicion of Christmas truces. Sufficiently removed already from 'love thine enemy', the officer cleric had either to adopt wholeheartedly the official viewpoint, eschewing contradictions so that 'in the whole blood-and-iron province of talk he would not only outshine any actual combatant—that is quite easy to do—but he would outshine any colonel who lived at a base',[182] or else attempt a compromise, loving one's fellow man even whilst trying to kill him, which must have seemed to those less accustomed to fine distinctions patently absurd. A chaplain of the 63rd Division was parodied in this way:

> I do not wish to hurt you
> But (Bang!) I feel I must.
> It is a Christian virtue
> To lay you in the dust.
>
> You—(Zip! That bullet got you)
> You're really better dead.
> I'm sorry that I shot you—
> Pray, let me hold your head.[183]

Understandably, official religion achieved very little success, and chaplains found themselves more eagerly sought after 'to get up some sports for us' or 'find out the local talent and arrange a concert'.[184] Their religion gave place to a proliferation of simple

[182] Montague, *Disenchantment*, pp. 56–8. Cf. M. Moynihan (ed.), *God on Our Side* (1983), 16.
[183] *The Mudhook*, 5 (May 1918), 12.
[184] R. Keable, *Standing By* (1919), 37.

superstitions shaped to a soldier's need. The padre editor of *The 5th Glo'ster Gazette* was moved to protest: 'it is high time that attention be drawn to the childish belief in "mascots". It is nothing less than rank paganism and silly superstition to believe that the "lucky charm" is going to protect one from danger.'[185]

Several of the popular justifications for fighting the war also lost credibility. The extravagant Germanophobia of the civilians, sustained neither by deep roots of enmity nor by the sight of a devastated homeland, declined, as has been seen, probably more than among the French. Some men, contemptuous of the French, forced to respect by the proficiency of the Germans, and angered by the rapaciousness of the peasants, actually began to question whether they were 'fighting on the wrong side'.[186]

There remained the idea of 'the War to end War'. British and French troop journals alike dressed up the struggle in this manner. The Allies would smash militarism, demonstrate that aggression could not pay, and, by ending autocracy, ensure that the decent, peace-loving sentiments of the majority would hence-forth be paramount. Some no doubt believed this to be the truth, and were helped to keep going accordingly. However, for many men it seems to have been progressively undermined as a motive for pursuing the war, by a growing hostility to their own regime which made the idea of a crusade difficult to sustain. Theirs was the regime which starved the soldier of food and munitions, perhaps of reinforcements, let 'shirkers' keep well-paid jobs in safety, pandered to the strikers who were stabbing him in the back, and all the while feather-bedded its functionaries and preached a fight to the finish, when others were bearing the brunt. Was one set of politicians, men were inclined to wonder, any worse than any other? With this hostility grew the suspicion that the 'greed, ignorance, incompetence and ambition' of the rulers of both sides was all that lay behind the war: 'there was, I think, an underlying feeling that we were all, friend and foe alike, helpless victims caught in the same net of inexorable circum-stances, and that, as the Prime Minister said—though in a much wider and more catholic sense than he intended—our real

---

[185] *The 5th Glo'ster Gazette*, 6 (Sept. 1915), 3. On superstition, see Fussell, *Great War and Modern Memory*, pp. 114–54.
[186] Croney, *Soldier's Luck*, p. 94; S. Rogerson, *Last of the Ebb* (1937), 85.

enemies were not the people, but those in high places who misled them'.[187]

The sense of hostility and mistrust towards Parliament can hardly be missed in the troop journals:

Tommy regards the M.P. with the same bewilderment as Hodge is stricken by when a glib and plausible cheap jack, furry of collar and brass-and-glassy of fingers, sells him gold watches for a shilling in the fair. The worthy fellow knows there is a catch somewhere, he knows the other for a rogue, and he knows he can refuse to buy, but he is easy going and sanguine; rhetoric impresses him, importunity he is weak against; in a tangle of specious volubility he cannot quite grasp the fallacy he knows to be there . . . bang goes his shilling![188]

The journals railed against political corruption, incompetence, and narrow party factionalism, and were even on occasion allowed to suggest that the whole party system should be swept away after the conclusion of peace.[189] As some symbol of present discontent with the war's conduct, battalions in France, even of guardsmen, were by 1918 refusing to sing the national anthem, or to give three cheers for the king.[190] In the same spirit the Dominion troops gave their politicians a rough reception whenever they dared to visit the battlefront in the later years of the war.[191]

The media of propaganda available to the State and the army to counteract this drift of feeling were of very limited effect. The national press lost in wartime much of its opinion-forming power. Its misrepresentations, not only of the soldiers' mood but of the 'success' of the various offensives, and of the 'inhumanity', 'cowardice', and 'faithlessness' of 'the Hun', were palpable to the troops. 'Can't believe a word you read' became a watchword among them: 'with a grin at the way he must have been taken in up to now, the fighting soldier gave the Press up'.[192] As bridges to

---

[187] Tucker, *Johnny Get Your Gun*, pp. 141–2; Noakes, *Distant Drum*, pp. 180–1.

[188] *The Gasper*, 16 (Apr. 1916), 2.

[189] *The 5th Glo'ster Gazette*, 21 (Nov. 1917), 3, and 22 (Mar. 1918), 4; *The Outpost*, 4/6 (Apr. 1917), 216; *The Emergency Ration*, 1 (Dec. 1916), 6.

[190] Noakes, *Distant Drum*, pp. 193–4. Cf. S. A. Bartlett, *From the Somme to the Rhine* (1921), 49; Gibbons, *Roll On Next War*, pp. 16–17.

[191] Burton, *Silent Division*, p. 282; Dawes and Robson, *Citizen to Soldier*, pp. 204–5.

[192] Montague, *Disenchantment*, p. 77. Cf. *The Outpost*, 4/4 (Aug. 1917), 121; *The Gasper*, 15 (Mar. 1915), 3; *The 5th Glo'ster Gazette*, 10 (Mar. 1916), 1–2.

home the newspapers continued to be read, but with scepticism. The troop journals vigorously lampooned their commentaries upon the war.

The army itself provided no significant flow of official propaganda. Unlike in the Second World War, it undertook no systematic programme of education in war aims. The orthodoxy encouraged among officers depicted 'the Hun' as an enemy evil and uncivilized in nature, needing to be put down by force, but the 'fire-eaters' who expounded this line often appeared more rabid than any 'Hun' and aroused only ridicule among the men.[193] The corps news-sheets which represented the only regularly circulated propaganda, being posted in each unit, embraced the orthodox line. Their only attempt to answer the question of 'why fight?' was the recounting of ever more fantastic German atrocities. Thus dismissing the problem, they concentrated rather on proving that victory was always just about to be won. But the tales of Russian triumphs, herds of prisoners, demoralization and starvation in the enemy camp were received by the troops with equal scepticism. 'Comic Cuts' was the popular name the corps sheets were given.[194]

Given this underlying lack of faith and the tremendous power of the war as an engine of change, one can perhaps better appreciate the value of creeds which, backed up by the structure of army entertainments, bound the soldier to his civilian past and preached the virtues of stoicism and compliance. They were all the more effective for being subliminally communicated. The element of continuity which they represented may even have played a part in the relatively smooth reintegration of British veterans after the war. The British troops had always remained 'citizens first',[195] never quite discarding a set of attitudes which distanced them from the profession of arms and allowed them to assimilate and diminish their experience through the operation of humour.

[193] Montague, *Disenchantment*, pp. 110–11; Andrews, *Haunting Years*, p. 205.
[194] Richards, *Old Soldiers*, pp. 128–9; Tuohy, *Crater of Mars*, p. 99; Sansom, *Letters from France*, pp. 122, 126, 131, 140. In the East, *The Egyptian Gazette*, an official production, attempted a similar aim and met with like response: see Idriess, *Desert Column*, p. 263.
[195] Ward (ed.), *The War Generation*, p. 34.

10

Homogeneity of the British and Dominion Forces

Affinities and Differences

To say that the majority of the men shared a common urban background is not, of course, to suggest that there were no differences between them. The ubiquity of sports and music hall does seem, however, to have signified a considerable degree of common culture. A striking feature of war memoirs is the rarity with which regional differences are alluded to, at least among English troops. As cross-drafting began the process of 'nationalizing' the various formations, men were confronted, often for the first time, by their countrymen from distant parts. The experience seems rarely to have been a surprising one. To take the most extreme case, men coming to a first-line Territorial battalion from outside might be struck by the narrowness of the men's viewpoint, by their shared local knowledge and intense suspicion of 'foreigners' from the nearest towns or counties, but they were not presented with an entirely unfamiliar welter of customs, attitudes, and recreations.[1] Men played the same games, sang mainly the same songs, cherished like jokes and popular idols. The Dominion troops, observers from outside, did not distinguish between the men of the different English regions, or favour one against another; all, in fact, were damned alike.

English troops were the largest single element in the British and Dominion forces, and in fact constituted a majority of the whole. The United Kingdom provided sixty-four out of the seventy-four British and Dominion Divisions which served in the major active war theatres, and England provided some 81 per

---

[1] Gladden, *The Somme*, p. 126; Behrend, *Make Me a Soldier*, p. 26; Andrews, *Haunting Years*, pp. 30, 187.

cent of total United Kingdom forces.[2] Haig's army was therefore predominantly an English one.

Looking at the other nations within the United Kingdom, and the extent to which they shared this common culture, evidence for the Irish and Welsh troops is unfortunately too scanty for conclusions to be drawn with any confidence. This is perhaps not entirely surprising in view of their smaller numbers. Out of the sixty-four United Kingdom Divisions serving in the major active war theatres, only two were Welsh, two Irish, and one Ulster. There are indications of differences. L. Wyn Griffith, for example, remembers a company of his battalion of the Royal Welch Fusiliers

waiting to go up into the trenches on relief, waiting, 'always bloody well waiting' . . . They start singing, in harmony, being Welsh, a fine old Welsh hymn tune in a minor key. The brigadier general asks me, 'Why do they always sing these mournful hymns? Most depressing—bad for morale. Why can't they sing something cheerful, like the other battalions?'

I try to explain to him that what they are singing now is what they sang as children, as I did, in chapel, in the world to which they really belong. They are being themselves, not men in uniform. They are back at home, with their families, in their villages. But he does not understand. Nor can he, with his background.[3]

Such glimpses are all too rare.

Evidence is more plentiful for the rather more numerous Scots, not least in the comments of the Dominion troops. Whereas the Anzacs were contemptuous and pitying towards the 'Tommy', they admired 'the Jocks' and recognized a 'kinship' with them.[4] Fellow-feeling may have played a part in the Etaples mutiny, where 'the presence of both Scottish and Anzac . . . soldiers gave the mutiny a cohesiveness which a riot could not have otherwise attained'.[5]

In Palestine too, Scots and Anzacs together were responsible for the worst breach of discipline in the theatre, when they

[2] *Statistics of the Military Effort*, opp. p. 28; Winter, 'Britain's "Lost Generation" ', p. 451.
[3] Panichas (ed.), *Promise of Greatness*, p. 288. Cf. Graves, *Goodbye to All That*, p. 81.
[4] Bean, *Official History*, iii. 754; Smith, *The Anzacs*, p. 153; Gammage, *Broken Years*, p. 208.
[5] Gill and Dallas, 'Mutiny at Etaples Base', p. 99.

descended upon the Arab village of Surafend in bloody reprisal for the shooting of a New Zealander.[6] Specifically, their comradeship was founded upon an affinity of spirit, the Australians seeing their own vigorous egalitarianism reflected in the Scottish troops' 'independent stalwart outlook' and 'rugged sincerity'.[7] In contrast, the Tommies' unquestioning acceptance of authority was a subject for parody. A cartoon in *Aussie* pictured a small, inoffensive looking soldier, imprisoned in an elaborate barbed-wire cage, and watched over by two armed guards, whilst in the foreground an Australian questions another Englishman:

The Digger. What did the cove in the clink do to be kept in a separate cage and a special guard over him?
The Choom. Ah! Choom, 'e's an out and out crook 'un 'e is; 'e give some cheek to our Lance-Corporal, 'e did.[8]

The evidence of the mutinies, scanty as it is, suggests that there was some foundation for the idea of a similarity between Scots and Australians. In the two wartime base mutinies, it was the men of the 51st (Highland) Division who staged the Calais disturbance, whilst at Etaples it was the shooting of a man of the 1/4th Battalion Gordon Highlanders which sparked the rioting, and 'if the insubordination of the Anzacs played an important part on the first day of the mutiny, it was the Scottish troops, present in far greater numbers, who gave the mutiny its force',[9] Curiously, in the Second World War too, it was men of the 51st Division, together with others from the 50th (Northumbrian), who were to be responsible for the largest and best-known British mutiny of that conflict, at Salerno in 1943.[10] These were all actions of men of the Highland battalions. The Australians did not define precisely whom they subsumed under the heading 'Jocks', but it is tempting to suppose that the most conspicuous of Scots, the distinctively uniformed, renowned, and lionized Highlanders, played a disproportionate part in establishing the image of their nationality in the Dominion troops' minds. The affinity could, then, be presented as a telling

[6] Smith, *The Anzacs*, p. 239.
[7] Bean, *Official History*, vi. 1087; Smith, *The Anzacs*, p. 153.
[8] *Aussie*, 9 (Dec. 1918), 2.
[9] Calais Base War Diary, WO 95/4018, 3 Apr. 1918, 21–22 July 1918; Gill and Dallas, 'Mutiny at Etaples Base', pp. 91, 100.
[10] D. Fraser, *And We Shall Shock Them* (1983), 108.

illustration of the importance of 'industrial discipline' to the obedience of the British army: here were men from the crofts and sheep stations, used to being, in greater or lesser part, masters of their own time, and now alike untameable and unamenable to rule.

However, we have seen how wrong it would be to suppose that the Australian Divisions were notably 'rural' in character, and the same is true for the Highlanders. Even at the outset, less than 30 per cent of the men in the 51st (Highland) Division came from the half of Scotland, including the Western Isles, lying north of a line along the southern boundaries of Banff, Inverness, and Argyll. These were men truly out of the mainstream. After their move to England, they were swept by an epidemic of measles, which 91 per thousand contracted, and from which 11 per thousand died. For the other 71 per cent of the division, however, the figures were 4 per thousand sick and 0.46 per thousand deaths.[11] The mass of the division was simply Scottish, and not Highland or rural. For Scotland as a whole, the percentage of the population engaged in agriculture, fishing, and forestry was, at 13.1 per cent, not significantly different from the figure for England and Wales of 10.2 per cent.[12] There were, then, many in the division who might laugh at the Bedford citizens of their first billets who, with ideas of wild Highlanders, 'gravely showed us how to flush a lavatory and how to turn a gas jet out'.[13]

Moreover, even the small truly Highland element steadily diminished. Back home, men were scarce, agriculture could spare only a limited proportion of its labour force, and the Highlands, with few focuses of social life, had already before the war enlisted a higher proportion of the population in the Territorials than any other region.[14] When these first battalions wasted, there were few Gaels to replenish them. The 1/4th (Ross and Cromarty) Seaforth Highlanders had started the war with at least 25 per cent of the battalion having Gaelic as their mother tongue. Already, by the end of 1915, 'it was less characteristically a Highland battalion and was becoming more like a Regular unit, filled with

---

[11] Bewsher, *History of the 51st Division*, pp. 3–5.
[12] PP 1913, LXXX, Cd. 6896: *Report on the Twelfth Decennial Census of Scotland 1911*, 129–39; PP 1913, LXXIX, Cd. 7019: *Census of England and Wales 1911*, 10.
[13] Rule, *Students under Arms*, p. 13.
[14] Cunningham, *Volunteer Movement*, pp. 46–9.

men from all parts of the country'. Thereafter, it assumed many
natures, as drafts came and went. In mid-1917, for example,
'cricket matches were very popular, for the Battalion at this time
numbered many Yorkshiremen'.[15] In all, some eighty-six out of
Scotland's 143 active list battalions had the appellation 'Highland', even though the population north of the Highland line was
only about 8 per cent of the whole.[16]

It is not therefore surprising to see the 'Lowland' troops
exhibiting the same attitude to discipline as their 'Highland'
countrymen. It was the CO and adjutant of the base depot of a
Lowland regiment, the Royal Scots, who were dismissed in the
wake of the Etaples mutiny.[17] When the 1/6th Battalion Scottish
Rifles 'demurred' at the proposal to put them in a Highland
Brigade, this may have revealed more about common attitudes to
authority than it did about the existence of historic
antagonisms.[18]

There does seem to have been a quality of initiative which
distinguished Scots and Dominion troops alike. The idea crops
up again and again. According to the official historian of the AIF,
it was to the initiative and self-reliance of the men that the
Australians' successes were first and foremost attributable.[19] For
the New Zealanders,

what were the causes which conduced to these successes? Firstly, the
New Zealander was endowed to a marked degree with bravery,
individuality and initiative. Every man fought intelligently. If a portion
of the attacking line was checked, the remainder worked their way
forward, dealt with the enemy opposing the advance, or relieved the
situation so that an advance was possible on the whole front.[20]

A private in the Auckland Regiment wrote that this was a war
where 'the close order fighting of the Napoleonic wars in which a
general surveyed his whole field, and everything depended upon
rapid, unquestioning, mechanical obedience, was giving way to
methods of fighting in which the initiative and intelligence of the
private soldier were becoming more and more factors in the

[15] Haldane, *History of the 4th Bn.*, pp. 142, 213.
[16] James, *British Regiments*, pp. 123–4; G. S. Pryde, *Scotland from 1603 to the Present Day* (1962), 257.
[17] Gill and Dallas, 'Mutiny at Etaples Base', p. 106.
[18] Blake (ed.), *Private Papers*, p. 123.
[19] Bean, *Official History*, vi. 1081–8.
[20] Stewart, *New Zealand Division*, p. xiv.

gaining of victory'. Consequently, he had no hesitation in attributing the élite status of the New Zealand troops to the high general
standard of education in their country, and to the egalitarian
spirit of the society, which encouraged men to think for themselves.[21] The Canadians, too, were men 'better schooled, more
boldly interested in life, quicker to take means to an end and to
parry and counter any new blow of circumstance', than either the
'battalions of colourless, stunted, half-toothless lads from hot,
humid Lancashire mills', or the 'battalions of slow, staring faces,
gargoyles out of the tragical-comical-historical-pastoral edifice of
modern English rural life'.[22] Fourth and least of the Dominion
contingents was the South African Brigade, and here too

the level of education and breeding was singularly high. The Brigade
resembled indeed the famous 51st Division of Highland Territorials . . .
In the slow intricacies of a modern campaign there is need of intelligence
and responsibility and power of initiative in every man . . . The possession of some education in no way lessens dash and tenacity in the field.
This was the moral of the Highland Territorials who were given first
place in Germany's catalogue of her most formidable opponents, and it
was also the moral of the South African Brigade.[23]

The Scots would probably not have dissented from this view of
their success. One of the great virtues of the ordinary soldier of
the 51st, according to the division's historian, was that 'in battle
he did not "see red" or lose his head, but coolly and intelligently
put into practice what he had learnt in his training . . . the
Division was trained throughout to act intelligently. It had learnt
to fight scientifically by the combination of skill and gallantry,
and not by animal courage alone, untempered by intelligence.'[24]
A history of one of the division's battalions echoed this
conclusion:

one of the chief things that struck the Royal Engineers and other officers
who had to do with training the men in special duties was their extraordinary keenness to learn and the thoroughness with which they had
learned. Long after the war was over a distinguished Irish General
expressed the hope that if ever he had troops under him again they

---

[21] Burton, *The Silent Division*, pp. 192–3, 123–4.
[22] Montague, *Disenchantment*, p. 115.
[23] J. Buchan, *History of the South African Forces in France* (1919), 17–18. Cf. 'Notes
on Certain Lessons of the Great War', WO 32/3116, p. 27.
[24] Bewsher, *History of the 51st Division*, pp. 47, 262, 410.

might be Scots. A Scotsman present expressed surprise at his preference for foreigners, to which the General replied that he held that hope because of the high standard of Scottish education, which ensured that the youngest lance-corporal would intelligently try to carry on his Commander's intentions even after all his officers were killed.[25]

The 51st perhaps owed its pre-eminence among Scottish Divisions in part to the fact that it was, until April 1918, the only Scottish Territorial Division on the Western Front: the 52nd (Lowland) was lost in the comparative backwater of the Palestine theatre. That left only the 9th and 15th Divisions which, as Kitchener formations, could not of course match the 51st. Nevertheless, among their peers they made a good showing, recovering from the effect of heavy casualties in their baptism of fire at Loos, to become two of the best Kitchener Divisions.[26]

The rebelliousness and independent spirit of the Scottish troops suggest an interesting parallel to the phenomenon, however exaggerated, of 'Red Clydeside'. Given the wealth of particular circumstance surrounding developments there, the comparison should not be pushed too far. Nevertheless, there is one suggestive point of similarity. Organization on Clydeside was aided by the Scottish Labour Party's emphasis on education classes in Marxism and industrial unionism.[27] On the Western Front, such political education cannot specifically be demonstrated to have been of significance, but the same generalized faith in, and enthusiasm for, education, sufficed to produce an unusual degree of independence of thought.

This enthusiasm and its consequences were characteristic of the Scotland of that period. The Presbyterian heritage, and the need to make the most of manpower resources in a country which, for centuries, had had little else, had given education in Scotland a high prestige, and influenced the development of a system which, traditionally, aimed at a fair general standard of education throughout, instead of devoting resources overwhelmingly to the instruction of an élite. For much the same reasons, Scottish education historically had embodied a strong democratic spirit.[28] The effect was to match the strongly egalitarian impulse

[25] Haldane, *History of the 4th Bn.*, p. 58.
[26] *Statistics of the Military Effort*, opp. p. 28; Green, *British Army*, p. 65.
[27] J. Hinton, *The First Shop Stewards' Movement* (1973), 124.
[28] J. Scotland, *The History of Scottish Education*, ii (1970), 257–60, 263–6.

of the Dominion countries, where there was a similar stress upon 'fair average quality standards' in education for all the population.[29] And the result was that ordinary Scots enjoyed education of a generally higher standard than in England, throughout the nineteenth and early twentieth centuries.[30]

Intelligent other-ranks, educated in a democratic tradition, were at once more accomplished troops than the English, and more inclined to question. Dominion troops and Scots alike did not share the complacency, passivity, and narrow obsession with comforts often shown by the 'Tommies'. The historian of the New Zealand Division contrasted the keen awareness shown by its men with 'the boyish insouciance of the English soldier'.[31] At home, wrote an officer of the division, education for all 'nurtures the seed of independence', so that all feel fit for leadership: consequently, in the field, the men in the ranks exhibit 'a native inquisitiveness . . . they seem to want to know all about their surroundings, and to have the intelligence to grasp the situation. A certain mental restlessness will not leave them content with only sufficient information to carry out their duties; they find out more.'[32]

For the Australian too, 'the world's business was the average Digger's business', whereas 'the English soldier, accustomed to leave external affairs to his officers, was constantly oblivious of what was happening half a mile away'.[33] An Australian subaltern noted that 'the Tommies don't seem to take much interest in the war outside their own part in it . . . whereas our chaps are always speculating on this, arguing on that, or giving biscuit tin orations on something else'.[34]

The English attitude struck the Dominion troops as curiously bovine, and, already unimpressed by their fighting performance, they were ready to make of the 'Tommy' a stock figure of humour. A cartoon in *Aussie* exemplified the outlook. Two English private soldiers were depicted, huddled close to a brazier, a few yards from a crossroads with a lamp-post, standing

---

[29] A. Barcan, *A History of Australian Education* (Melbourne, 1980), 235.
[30] Scotland, *History of Scottish Education*, ii. 261.
[31] Stewart, *New Zealand Division*, p. 73.
[32] Weston, *Three Years*, pp. 249–50.
[33] Bean, *Official History*, vi. 7.
[34] Gammage, *Broken Years*, p. 249.

amid windswept devastation, from which hung a sign saying 'Lamp-Post Corner':

Aussie [passing by]. Ay, Digger, is this Lamp-Post Corner?
Tommy. Don't know, Choom. I've only bin 'ere a month.[35]

This was an attitude not without advantages. The English were troops who might, more readily than most, go on fighting until they were told to stop. According to one officer, 'it is very curious to hear some of the answers that the men give to the question: "What are you fighting for?" Some have not the foggiest idea, while others who don't know, also don't care.'[36] There were many among the Dominion troops, however, and perhaps among the Scots, who were sure to ask the question 'why?', just as they had repeatedly asked themselves why saluting and button-polishing were necessary, why the regime at Etaples had to be so harsh, or why they had to make repeated and fruitless attacks while less reliable troops were spared them. In the first flush of enthusiasm, the Australians at 'The Nek' above Anzac Cove had obeyed orders with something of the Light Brigade spirit: 'after seeing the first attacking line mown down within a few yards by a whirlwind of rifle and machine-gun fire, the second, third and fourth lines each charged after its interval of time, at the signal of its leaders to certain destruction'. However, 'in 1918 such an incident as the charge at The Nek could not have happened. Australian leaders knew, and British commanders above them came to know, that these troops had the habit of reasoning why and not merely of doing and dying.'[37]

The Australians

The Scots and the Dominion troops had much in common which distinguished them from the English. There remains the problem of understanding why the Australians, almost from the outset, stood out from the other Dominion troops as exceptionally turbulent and unamenable to strict discipline. During the first half of 1917, their desertion rate was four times higher than the aver-

---

[35] *Aussie*, 3 (Mar. 1918), inside front cover.
[36] J. E. H. Neville, *The War Letters of a Light Infantryman* (1930), 52.
[37] Bean, *Official History*, vi. 1083.

age for the other Dominion Divisions. In March 1918, the British troops had less than one man per thousand in prison, the Canadians, New Zealanders, and South Africans 1.6, but the Australians almost nine.[38] All started out as amateurs, but whereas the Canadians became progressively more 'soldierly' in the eyes of the Command, the Australians kept throughout to their rejection of saluting, spit, and polish, and the whole notion of strict obedience. Haig visited the Canadians in February 1918 and noted 'they are really fine disciplined soldiers now and so smart and clean. I am sorry to say that the Australians are not nearly so efficient.'[39] The New Zealanders, too, 'had a higher discipline (measured by the old army standard)' than the Australians.[40]

Haig himself put the differences down to Birdwood, the first commander of the AIF, 'who, instead of facing the problem, had gone in for the easier way of saying everything is perfect and making himself as popular as possible'.[41] The official historian was inclined rather to attribute the lapses in discipline, which led to the mutinies, to the policy of Monash, Birdwood's successor, in stressing prestige as a sustaining force instead of the 'high moral issues' preached by his predecessor.[42] This allowed an explanation which evaded confronting the negative aspects of the egalitarianism and individualism which his official history lauded so highly. The CO of the 1st Battalion, on the other hand, preferred to blame the lax punishment of offenders by the new regime, reflecting the faith of orthodox military men of the period in the universal efficacy of rigid discipline, for all situations and all troops, regardless of the risks of riding with a hard rein.[43] Yet this ignores the experience of the Boer War, where the Australians had not enjoyed any separate organization, but had been integrated under British command: still their discipline had been heavily criticized, and the tactlessness of the British general commanding the column in which the 5th Victorian Mounted

[38] Bean, *Official History*, v. 28–30.
[39] Blake (ed.), *Private Papers*, p. 290.
[40] Williams, *Gallant Company*, p. 149.
[41] Blake (ed.), *Private Papers*, p. 290.
[42] Bean, *Official History*, vi. 876, 940.
[43] War Diary of the 1st Bn. AIF, WO 95/3217, Sept. 1918, Appendix 'CO's report to brigade 20 Sept. 1918'.

Rifles were included had driven this regiment to the verge of mutiny even in that very much less exacting war.[44]

Moreover, Australian indiscipline was apparent almost from the outset in the Great War, and it is hard to believe that it could have been produced in so short a time simply by some policy of the AIF. Already before Gallipoli, the day-to-day behaviour of the troops, dramatized by incidents like 'the battle of the Wazzir' in which Cairo's brothel quarter was sacked, was reducing the authorities in Egypt to despair.[45] In fact, even as the first two convoys set out from Australia en route to Egypt, the men regularly went absent without leave at the ports of call, and troops kept under special guard on board serenaded their officers with such songs as 'Britons Never Shall Be Slaves' and 'Every Dog Has His Day'.[46]

One factor of probable importance in the more serious later manifestations was the absence of the death penalty for desertion in the AIF, alone of British or Dominion forces.[47] Even before the long attrition of the continuing offensive from 8 August 1918, the CO of the 57th Battalion AIF was reduced to parading his men before they marched up to the line, and warning them that

concerning the matter of those men who went absent without leave or deserted on the eve of our operation, he wished all present to know that any man who acted in that manner would be paraded before a muster parade of the battalion and asked to explain his reason for such action, but he hoped that no man would be so base as to desert his comrades at such a time.[48]

Despite all that has been written about military groups, many found such ignominy insufficient deterrent when, by deserting, their lives might be saved.

Yet this could not have been responsible for the differences in smartness, saluting, and the respect and willingness shown in carrying out orders. The behaviour of the Australian troops in these respects may have owed something of its uniqueness to the unusual number of Dominion-born men to be found in the ranks

[44] G. Souter, *Lion and Kangaroo: The Initiation of Australia 1901–1919* (Sydney, 1976), 58–61.

[45] Gammage, *Broken Years*, pp. 33–40.

[46] Smith, *The Anzacs*, pp. 54–7.

[47] Bean, *Official History*, v. 32.

[48] War Diary of the 57th Bn. AIF, WO 95/3647, 5 Aug. 1918.

TABLE 5. *British-born members of the Dominion forces*

Contingent	% of population British-born (1911)	% of troops British-born
Canada	10.9	41.6
New Zealand	22.2†	n.a.
Australia	13.3†	18.1*

*Estimated from a sample of 2,291 attestation papers.
†Excluding Maoris and Aborigines.

Sources: *The Canada Year Book 1914*, p. 63; *New Zealand Official Year Book 1914* (Wellington, 1914), 118; *Official Yearbook of the Commonwealth of Australia 1901–1914* (Melbourne, 1915), 98; E. H. Armstrong, *The Crisis of Quebec 1914–1918* (New York, 1937), 248; L. L. Robson, 'The Origin and Character of the First AIF', *Historical Studies*, 15 (Oct. 1973), 744.

of the AIF. All the Dominion contingents contained a large number of recent immigrants from Britain, but the AIF less than the CEF or, in all probability, the NZEF (see Table 5).

This striking discrepancy in representation raises doubts about the accuracy of the estimate for the AIF. In fact, however, it is entirely in accordance with reasonable expectation once one takes into account the low volunteering rates of French Canadians and of the large numbers of immigrants of non-British origins in Canada; the fact that recent British immigration had favoured Canada so that a higher proportion of Canadians of British birth were of military age; and the higher proportion of Irish among the British-born in Australia.[49] In view of the very high proportion of British-born in the population of New Zealand, it seems reasonable to suppose that the percentage of British-born in the ranks of the NZEF was also considerably higher than in the AIF.

Aggregate figures, including all who served in the course of the war, do not reflect the full picture, for the British-born volunteered not only in disproportionate numbers but also unusually

[49] Armstrong, *Crisis of Quebec*, pp. 104, 248–50; *The Canada Year Book 1914*, p. 63; *Official Year Book of the Commonwealth of Australia 1901–1910* (Melbourne, 1911), 123, and *Official Year Book of the Commonwealth of Australia 1901–1914* (Melbourne, 1915), 98; Robson, 'Origin and Character of the First AIF', p. 741; Ward, *History of Australia*, p. 162; *New Zealand Official Year Book 1914*, p. 118; *Statistics of the Military Effort*, p. 363.

early.[50] They therefore played a larger part than the aggregate totals would suggest in establishing the original character of units and of the national contingents as a whole; they were numerous in that veteran core to which reinforcements would look for example; they were a large part of the group which suffered longest and most heavily, and which had most reason to rebel.

It perhaps owed something to the relative weakness of this element in the AIF that the Australians evolved a strongly distinctive character which in many ways matched closely the archetype of the bushman as he was drawn by popular Australian writers of the day. The bushman was

a practical man, rough and ready in his manners and quick to decry any appearance of affectation in others. He is a great improviser, ever willing 'to have a go' at anything, but willing to be content with a task done in a way that is 'near enough'. Though capable of great exertion in an emergency, he normally feels no impulse to work hard without good cause. He swears hard and consistently, gambles heavily and often, and drinks deeply on occasion. Though he is 'the world's best confidence man', he is usually taciturn rather than talkative, one who endures stoically rather than one who acts busily. He is a 'hard case', sceptical about the value of religion and of intellectual and cultural pursuits generally. He believes that Jack is not only as good as his master but, at least in principle, probably a good deal better, and so he is a great 'knocker' of eminent people unless, as in the case of his sporting heroes, they are distinguished by physical prowess. He is a fiercely independent person who hates officiousness and authority, especially when these qualities are embodied in military officers and policemen. Yet he is very hospitable and, above all, will stick to his mates through thick and thin.[51]

Add humour and these were almost exactly the characteristics so frequently ascribed, in praise or blame, to the men of the AIF.[52] They received clear expression in the pages of *Aussie*, printed for the AIF in France by the Corps Ammunition Park. No other magazine had quite the same fondness for tall stories, the deflation of authority, and making light of the running warfare against the Military Police. Started in January 1918, it proved 'much better suited to the taste of the "diggers" than the previous year's

[50] Armstrong, *Crisis of Quebec*, pp. 103–4.
[51] Ward, *Australian Legend*, pp. 1–2.
[52] Ibid. 212–17.

Rising Sun', which was a far more conservative journal. *Aussie*'s first issue had a run of 10,000 copies, the second of 60,000 and the third of 100,000, when the total strength of the Australians in France was only 110,000.[53] It seemed to reflect an image of the 'Digger' which accorded with that held by most of the 'Diggers' themselves. Some few complained that its use of slang was demeaning to Australians, and showed them in a poor light.[54] Most seem to have been only too happy with the 'rough and ready', unaffected image.

The bush legend had already achieved wide familiarity and acceptance in Australia. Whether this was a genuine transmission from country to city may be doubted. In large degree it appears to have been the creation of city publicists seeking to erect an idealized figure of the Australian as the sense of separate nationality began to be felt.[55] The society of the bush provided the germ to the minds of writers like Lawson, Furphy, and Paterson, but they built upon an egalitarian ethos already fostered by the social mobility of Dominion society.[56] To this ethos they added important, country-influenced glosses like 'work and burst' and a fiercer hostility to authority. For although the national and country traditions in Australia included the hard-working, sober, and virtuous settler farmer, as in New Zealand and Canada, uniquely the migrant pastoral worker predominated. As a result, when the men of the cities looked to the country for a national, rural, and egalitarian ideal compatible with their experiences and wishes, it was no 'sodbuster' ethos that they found.

As in Britain, the combination of socially conditioned attitudes with an effective, if not always neutral, interpreter and publicist of them, proved a potent force. As with Britain too, medium and attitudes transferred to the Western Front. *Aussie*, in a sense, took up where the Sydney *Bulletin* left off. It regularly carried verse by Australian writers like Paterson and Lawson. A verse of

[53] Bean, *Official History*, v. 20.
[54] *Aussie*, 2 (Feb. 1918), 1.
[55] Ward, *Australian Legend*, pp. 233–4; G. Davison, 'Sydney and the Bush: An Urban Context for the Australian Legend', *Historical Studies*, 18 (1978), 191–210. On the controversy surrounding *The Australian Legend*, see the whole of this volume and R. Lawson, 'The "Bush Ethos" and Brisbane in the 1890s', *Historical Studies*, 15 (1972), 276–83.
[56] Lawson, *Brisbane in the 1890s*, pp. 320–1.

Paterson's was particularly praised as 'full of good, staunch Australianism':

> The narrow ways of English folk
> Are not for such as we;
> They bear the long accustomed yoke
> Of staid conservancy.
> But all our roots are new and strange
> And through our blood there runs
> The vagabonding love of change
> That drove us westward of the range
> And westward of the suns.[57]

The bush ethos, by reason of the publicity which it had received in daily life in Australia, reached far beyond that section of the AIF composed of men from country occupations. For many city men it was an accepted national self-image.[58] Such a self-image, once firmly established, has as Russel Ward observes a considerable active potential and 'often modifies current events by colouring men's ideas of how they ought "typically" to behave'.[59] The stereotype continued to gather force between the Wars, reinforced by the record of the AIF in the Great War, and in the opinion of the official historian of the Australians, 'damaged' the Second AIF which served in World War II.[60] It is easy to see how it could have been corrosive of strict discipline also in the earlier conflict.

[57] *Aussie*, 2 (Feb. 1918), inside back cover, and 3 (Mar. 1918), inside back cover.
[58] Bean, *Official History*, i. 46.
[59] Ward, *Australian Legend*, p. 1.
[60] Bean, *Official History*, vi. 1085, n. 6.

Conclusion

The evidence of the troop journals, backed up by other sources, suggests that the British and Dominion troops in the First World War carried over from civilian life many institutions and attitudes which helped them to adjust to, and to humanize, the new world in which they found themselves. The literary evidence is supported by the fact that a great network of entertainments paralleling those at home existed behind the lines, extending to units of all types. These entertainments, as we have seen, were not the artificial creations of upper- or middle-class officers, but drew upon a wide base of support. It is significant that the dominant forms were association football, not rugby or cricket, and music hall, not the more fashionable and middle-class musical comedy. The recreations of mass society proved now appropriate to mass warfare. Regular army traditions of control and keeping the men always busy created scope for the translation of these forms from civilian life to take place, but it remained a translation none the less, the product of innumerable initiatives arising out of habits and enthusiasms which had been learned in peacetime.

A number of implications follow from this. Firstly, in military terms, the strength of the mores associated with sport and music hall, the usefulness of these institutions for enhancing periods of rest and recuperation, and the success of their translation to the war zones, may have played a part in upholding the morale of the British and Dominion troops. Many contemporary soldier observers certainly thought that this was the case and, as we have seen, there is evidence to support their view. There were of course many other factors operating on morale. Submarine warfare had less effect on the material conditions of the British army than the blockade on the German. Spared to a large extent the demographic anxieties of pre-war France and the hecatombs of 1914 and 1915, the British perhaps had less feeling of being a nation bleeding to death. But it should not be forgotten that the improvised British and Dominion armies entered the war with many disadvantages and no reasons for persisting in the struggle so vivid as an invasion of their soil. As the war developed into a test of endurance, mentalities were to become a critical area for all the combatants, and it was in this area that entertainments were to have their effect.

The implications for the longer term are more difficult to assess. The British and Dominion soldiers, it is apparent, did not entirely cut their ties to the civilian world and create a wholly autonomous 'trench culture'. Changes there were, but continuities also. Certainly these troops, like those of other nations, felt that their experience was inadequately understood at home and experienced the same anger towards complacent politicians, war profiteers, strikers, conscientious objectors, and the other enemies of the soldier who appear alike in French and British troop journals. Certainly too, as with the French troops, the condemnation was never general, for soldiers and civilians retained much in common, and the ties to family and friends were not severed.[1] The continuing strength of civilian cultural values, and the transfer of the institutions which supported them, may have helped to diminish the sundering and to ease the assimilation of the soldiers back into the mainstream after the war. This army at least did not experience the war as something totally outside traditional frames of reference.

From all points of view, it is clear that the soldiers' experience cannot be understood without a knowledge of time behind the lines as well as time in the trenches. The intention of this study is not to deny the horror of the war for those British and Dominion soldiers caught up in it: rather, the reverse. It was precisely because the war was so terrible, so hideous a reality after the civilians' dreams of glory, that men to survive had periodically to escape. Partly it was escape to a world before the war, partly to a wished-for world in which the war did not overthrow all mental bounds, but could be diminished and contained, a butt for jokes, scarcely more terrifying than mothers-in-law or seaside landladies, scarcely more momentous than a sporting contest. Beyond this, the activities of rest periods fulfilled the myriad other purposes of peacetime recreation. Human needs did not disappear simply through putting a man in uniform.

[1] Audoin-Rouzeau, 'Les Soldats français', pp. 68–9, 75–6.

The social historian, as others have argued, must cease to treat
the soldier as being somehow different in nature from the
civilian.[2] If he was too human to be the wartime journalists'
'Tommy', blissfully happy and revelling in death, neither was he
the wretched automaton, permanently sunk in pathetic passivity
and despair, sometimes depicted by the literature of disenchantment.[3] No more than other men was he capable of endless
unprotesting endurance: he kicked out at the system by myriad
minor offences. He sought intervals of pleasure to relieve the
suffering, and exercised ingenuity to create islands of sanity in
the midst of the horror.

The neglect of the soldiers' time behind the lines in favour of
a concentration upon the surreal and fantastic world of the
trenches is perhaps not surprising. The concert party troupes in
the midst of war are in a sense hardly less surreal, but the failure
to perceive their importance may also owe something to the poor
reputation of troop entertainments in the Second World War.
ENSA, officially Entertainments National Service Association
but more familiarly Every Night Something Awful, entered the
national memory as a standing joke in a way that eclipsed the
achievements of the concert parties in the First World War.

This is particularly ironic in view of the fact that it was from
recognition of this achievement that ENSA sprang. At the meeting of four theatre men in 1938 which set itself to consider the
question 'What shall the Theatre do if there is a second world
war?', and at which ENSA was conceived, two of the four were
motivated by memories of organizing concert party shows in the
First World War.[4] Less esoterically, it was the managerial frame-
work supplied by the Navy, Army, and Air Force Institutes
(NAAFI) which was to allow the infant to be more than an idea,
and this co-operation was forthcoming because 'the Corporation
had continued to provide small concert parties and music-hall
turns in special circumstances, such as the summer canvas
camps, ever since the First War. So their acceptance involved no
new principle, merely an extension of existing practice.'[5]

But whatever the common background, circumstances were

---

[2] Englander and Osborne, 'Jack, Tommy and Henry Dubb', pp. 594–5.
[3] Kelly, *39 Months*, pp. vii–viii; D. Jerrold, *The Lie About the War* (1930), *passim*.
[4] B. Dean, *The Theatre at War* (1956), 21, 29.
[5] Ibid. 34.

Conclusion

now different. These soldier-entertainers of the First World War were now out of uniform, proposing to supply entertainment chiefly by civilians. Moreover, the fact that the great part of the army spent most of the war in the British Isles not only exposed the soldier to the attentions of the well-meaning civilian amateur, but meant that these had to compete against commercial entertainments. The burgeoning of the film industry and of wireless had both decreased the tolerance for amateur or improvised entertainments. Now, ENSA found, 'the most popular form of entertainment for the troops is the cinema'.[6]

Yet the fate of ENSA should not be allowed to overshadow the greatly increased emphasis placed on entertainments in the Second World War, by all the armies which had behind them the experience of static warfare on the Western Front in the Great War. The Nazis were attentive in this as in all spheres of mass psychology. They boasted, not without foundation, that provision for the German soldier's entertainment was the best in the world. The troop welfare organization, 'Truppenbetreuung', directed the activities of some 14,000 artistes during the peak months of 1942. By the summer of 1944, concert parties, theatrical troupes, operatic ensembles, and orchestras had performed before military audiences totalling 275,000,000, making a considerable contribution to military morale.[7] The French army too, during the period of the 'Phoney War', had devoted much effort to keeping the troops amused: more, some felt, than to preparations for defence.[8] The collapse at Sedan was to show, just as the mutiny of the 5th Division twenty-three years earlier, that entertaining the troops was in itself no magic solution. As embodiment and reminder of a particular outlook, it had served the British well a generation before. Even without this singular function, it had a more limited value in combating demoralization. But it could not by itself conjure up high morale in the context of an unfavourable national mood.

For the British armies of the Second World War, the War Office created, alongside ENSA, the Directorate of Army Welfare, headed by a lieutenant-general, to organize entertainers

[6] Dean, The Theatre at War (1956), 47.
[7] R. Grunburger, A Social History of the Third Reich (1971), 140, 372, 375, 405.
[8] A. Horne, To Lose a Battle (1969), 172; W. L. Shirer, The Collapse of the Third Republic (1970), 513.

drawn from within the ranks of the armed services. Established after Dunkirk, the Directorate had little opportunity to create, in the campaigns of movement which characterized the Second World War, anything resembling the range and variety of entertainments which flourished in the First World War. Even had this been possible, central direction tended to foster a rather different line of development, with entertainers less closely tied to a parent formation.[9] In fact, none of the armies in the Second World War produced the kind of large-scale, improvised programmes of entertainments characteristic of Haig's armies in the First. The phenomenon was peculiar to them, product of the height of music hall's popularity, the immobility of the war fronts, and the initial paucity of concern about recreation at the highest level. Now German, French, and British authorities alike organized their entertainers and took them to the troops. Something, perhaps, was lost.

In the Great War, however, the British national enthusiasms were not entirely without their costs. Vitally needed training time was lost. At a deeper level, the 'sporting' approach was the negation of professionalism and serious-minded application. It may, for example, have contributed to the bungling of British staff work and to the slowness to adapt and innovate. The inverse of scepticism and phlegm may have been a lack of *élan* in attack; the inverse of narrow obsession with comforts a failure to develop self-reliance and enterprise; the inverse of confidence complacency. Thus Gibbs wrote of 'that cheery confidence which has never deserted the British soldier throughout this war, except in hours of supreme tragedy, and has been the cause of some of our weakness and most of our strength'.[10] For stability and endurance, however, which ultimately were the qualities that counted in the First World War, the British citizen soldiers, and the culture which shaped them, proved surprisingly well-adapted.

The different contingents which made up the armies of the British Empire had each their own character, but sufficient of this culture was common to all for humour and sceptical stoicism to characterize the whole force. The structure of entertainments was the same for Dominion and Imperial troops, though the

---

[9] Dean, *Theatre at War*, pp. 145, 231–3.
[10] P. Gibbs, *Open Warfare: The Way to Victory* (1919), 7.

attitudes they represented might differ as to shading. These attitudes should not be caricatured. It would be very far from the truth to fall into the newspaper depiction of the troops, 'representing them as glad and cheerful when they had reached the extreme of human suffering'.[11] They were not 'invariably cheerful'; they did not 'revel' in the 'excitement' of war; they were not 'light-hearted as children . . . charmed from the transient melancholy of childhood by a game of football or a packet of cigarettes'.[12] They had, though, learned from long experience that it was better to concentrate on pleasures than hardships, that the best way to render tolerable the worst of conditions was to make a joke of them, that moments of escape, such as games and concerts could provide, should be exploited to the full. To deny their humanity, to fail to recognize the way in which they adjusted to their appalling environment and made it endurable, is to belittle their achievement.

[11] Voigt, *Combed Out*, p. 140.
[12] Tawney, *The Attack and Other Papers*, pp. 24–6.

Appendix A. Troop Journals

This Appendix lists troop journals produced in active war theatres which have served as sources for this book. The following information is given (where available) for each magazine:

Title

Front(s) on which the journal was produced

Rank of editorial staff (O stands for officer and OR for other-rank)

Unit type

Collection in which a complete series of extant issues is held. Where a series is not available at a single location, more than one collection is given.

Abbreviations used are CUL (Cambridge University Library), BL (British Library), IWM (Imperial War Museum), PRO (Public Record Office).

Date of first appearance

Number of issues known to have been produced overseas

(i) Infantry Journals

Another Garland from the Front (also *A Christmas Garland from the Front*): France; O and OR; Canadian; BL and IWM; 1915; 4.

Anzac Book: Gallipoli; O; Australian and New Zealand; CUL; 1915; 1.

Aussie: France; O; Australian; CUL; 1918; 13.

The Bankers' Draft: France; OR; New Army (Bankers Bn.); BL; 1916; 2.

Bairns Gazette: Egypt; second-line Territorial; CUL; 1917; 1.

The Billon Valley Baloonist:[1] France; O; New Army; PRO WO 95/2050; 1916; 2.

The Brazier: France; OR; Canadian; BL; 1916; 9.

The Cherrybuff: France; O; New Army; IWM; 1917; 1.

Chronicles of the White Horse: Egypt; second-line Territorial; CUL and BL; 1916; 3.

The Cinque Ports Gazette: France; O; first-line Territorial; CUL; 1916; 1.

The Dagger: France; first-line Territorial; CUL; 1918; 2.

The Dardanelles Driveller: Gallipoli; Royal Naval Division; IWM; 1915; 1.

---

[1] Nichols, *The 18th Division*, p. 40.

The Dead Horse Corner Gazette: France; OR; Canadian; CUL; 1915; 3.

The Desert Rag: Egypt; OR; New Zealand; BL; 1.

Dicksey Scrapings: France; OR; first- or second-line Territorial; BL; 7.

The Dud: France; New Army; IWM; 1916; 1.

The Dud (Argyll and Sutherland): France; New Army; BL; 1916; 1.

The Dug Out Despatch: France; OR; Regular; IWM; 1915; 1.

Dug Out Gossip: Gallipoli; Royal Naval Division; IWM; 1915; 1.

The Dump: France; Civilians, O and OR; New Army; CUL and IWM; 1915; 3.

F.S.R.: France; first-line Territorial; BL; 1916; 1.

The Forty-Niner: France; O and OR; Canadian; BL; 1915; 6.

The Gasper: France (from Dec. 1915); OR; New Army (Universities and Public Schools Brigade); CUL and BL; 1915; 12.

The 20th Gazette: France (from Dec. 1915); OR (O from May 1916); Canadian; IWM; 1915; 12.

The 5th Glo'ster Gazette: France (Italy from Nov. 1917); O; first-line Territorial; CUL and IWM; 1915; 25.

The Growler: France; O; Canadian; IWM; 1916, 1.

The Honk (also *Rising Sun*): Troopship and France; OR; Australian; BL; 1915; 19.

The Incinerator: France; O; New Army (Belfast Young Citizens Bn.); BL; 1916; 2.

The Judean: Egypt; New Army (Jewish Bn.); IWM; 1918; 1.

The 6th K.S.L.I. News: France; New Army; BL and IWM; 1917; 1.

The Listening Post: France; O and OR; Canadian; CUL and BL; 1915; 32.

The 7th Manchester Sentry: Egypt; O and OR; first-line Territorial; BL and IWM; 1915; 6.

The Mesopoluvian (also *Martini Times*): Mesopotamia; O; New Army; IWM; 1917; 15.

The Minden Magazine: France; O; Regular; CUL; 1915; 8.

The Moonraker: Salonika; New Army; IWM; 1917; 3.

The Morning Rire: France; O; Regular; BL; 1915; 6.

The Mudhook: France; O; Royal Naval Division; CUL and BL; 1917; 10.

The Mudlark: France; O; Regular; BL; 1916; 1.

A New Year Souvenir of the Welsh Division: France; O; New Army; CUL; 1917; 1.

Old Doings:[2] France; OR; first-line Territorial; BL; 1918; 1.

The Old Firm Unlimited: Italy; O; first-line Territorial; IWM; 1918; 2.

The Outpost: France (from Jan. 1916); OR; New Army (Glasgow Commercial Bn.); IWM; 1916; 42.

---

[2] Smith, *Four Years*, p. 128.

Pelican Pie: France; second-line Territorial; BL; 1917; 1.
The Pennon: France; Regular; BL; 1918; 1.
Posh Stew: France; OR; first- or second-line Territorial; BL; 1917; 1.
The Quaysider: France (from Nov. 1915); New Army; BL; 1915; 1.
The Red Feather: France (from June 1915); O and OR; New Army; BL; 1915; 2.
The Rum Issue: France; O; first-line Territorial; CUL; 1917; 1.
The Salient:[3] France; O; VI Corps; CUL; 1915; 1.
The Shell Hole Advance: France; O; Canadian; BL; 1917; 1.
The Standard of C Company: France; O; Australian; CUL; 1918; 1.
Sub Rosa: France; first-line Territorial; BL; 1917; 2.
The Swell: France; OR; New Army; BL; 1915; 2.
The Third Bn. Magazine: France; Australian; CUL; 1918; 1.
The Trench Echo: France; O; Canadian; CUL, BL, IWM; 1915; 4.
The Very Light: France; New Army (3rd Manchester Pals); BL; 1917; 1.
The Vic's Patrol: France; O and OR; Canadian; BL; 1916; 3.
The 23rd: Voice of the Bn.: France; OR; Australian; IWM; 23.
The Western Scot: France (from July 1916); O and OR; Canadian; IWM; 1916; 6.
The Whizz Bang: France; O; first-line Territorial; CUL and BL; 1916; 6.
The Wipers Times (also *B.E.F. Times, Kemmel Times, New Church Times, Somme Times, Better Times*): France; O; New Army; 1930 fac. edn.; 1916; 21.

(ii) Cyclists

The Limit: France; BL; 1917; 1.

(iii) Cavalry

The Duration: France; Regular; BL; 1.
The Emergency Ration: France; BL; 1916; 1.
The Middlesex Yeomanry Magazine: Egypt; Yeomanry; IWM; 1917; 3.

(iv) Artillery

The Archie Gazette: France; BL; 1.
Gunfire: Italy; IWM; 1918; 1.
Kamp Knews: France; first-line Territorial; CUL; 1.
Mules Monthly: France; BL; New Army; 1916; 1.
Night Lines: France; BL; 1917; 1.

[3] Tuohy, *Crater of Mars*, p. 109.

O Pip: France; Canadian; IWM; 1.
The Periscope: France; BL; 1916; 1.
Spit and Polish: France; BL; 1916; 4.
The Ypres Times and Tombstones Journal: France; BL; 1916; 1.

(v) Engineers

The Akakar Magazine: France; OR; BL; 1917; 7.
Lines: Egypt; CUL; 1917; 1.
Stray Shots: France; O and OR; first-line Territorial; BL; 1915; 9.
The Switchboard: France; OR; New Army; BL; 1916; 6.
White and Blue: Palestine; first-line Territorial; CUL; 1918; 1.
The Wiggle Waggle: France; BL; 3.

(vi) Transport

At the Back of the Front: France; BL; 1.
Illustrated 718: France; O; CUL; 1916; 4.
The Jackdaw: France; OR; BL; 1917; 12.
The Open Exhaust: France; OR; BL; 1916; 9.
The Packing Note: France; O and OR; BL; 1916; 1.
The Fuze: France; second-line Territorial; BL; 1916; 3.

(vii) Field Ambulances

All Abaht It: France; OR; Australian; BL; 1916; 1.
The Iodine Chronicle: France; O and OR; Canadian; CUL and BL; 1915;
16.
The Leadswinger: France; O and OR; first-line Territorial; CUL; 1915;
15.
The Linseed Lance: France; OR; second-line Territorial; BL; 7.
M & D: France; OR; Canadian; BL; 1917; 5.
Now and Then: France; OR; Canadian; CUL; 1915; 1.
N.Y.D.: France; O and OR; Canadian; BL; 1916; 6.
The Poultice: France; first-line Territorial; BL; 1916; 2.
The Sling: France; Canadian; CUL; 1917; 2.
The Splint Record: France; O; Canadian; CUL; 1915; 1.
The Tabloid: France; OR; BL; 1.
The Wormlet: France; CUL; 1918; 1.

(viii) Base Units

The A.O.C. Workshops Gazette: France; OR; BL; 1916; 11.
Anzac Records Gazette: France; Australian; BL; 1915; 3.

The B.H.T.D. Summer Annual: France; BL; 1.
Hangar Happenings: France; OR; CUL; 1917; 4.
The Jackass: France; OR; Australian; CUL; 1918; 5.
The Hangar Herald: France; O; BL; 1.
The Racite: Egypt; BL; 1915; 1.
The Splinterproof: France; O; BL; 1.
The Strafer: France; BL; 1915; 1.

Appendix B. Concert Parties and Cinemas

Divisions listed are the total number (excluding Indian) of British Empire Infantry Divisions which served in the major war theatres (France/Belgium, Italy, Salonika, Gallipoli, Egypt/Palestine, Mesopotamia). The lists of concert parties and cinemas are not necessarily complete, but represent only those that are known.

I. Divisional

Divisions	Date of arrival (or of formation if formed overseas)	Divisional concert party	Date formed	Divisional cinema
Regular				
1	Aug. 1914			★
2	Aug. 1914	★		
3	Aug. 1914	★		
4	Aug. 1914	★	Dec. 1914	★
5	Aug. 1914	★	autumn 1915	★
6	Sept. 1914	★	Feb. 1915	★
7	Oct. 1914	★		
8	Nov. 1914	★	Nov. 1915	★
27	Dec. 1914			
28	Jan. 1915			
29	Mar. 1915	★	May 1917	
New Army				
9 (Scottish)	May 1915	★		★
10 (Irish)	July 1915			
11 (Northern)	July 1915			
12 (Eastern)	May 1915	★	summer 1916	★
13 (Western)	July 1915			
14 (Light)	May 1915			
15 (Scottish)	July 1915	★		
16 (Irish)	Dec. 1915	★		★

Divisions	Date of arrival (or of formation if formed overseas)	Divisional concert party	Date formed	Divisional cinema
17 (Northern)	July 1915	★	autumn 1916	★
18 (Eastern)	July 1915			
19 (Western)	July 1915	★	Dec. 1915	★
20 (Light)	July 1915	★	autumn 1916	
21	Sept. 1915	★		
22	Sept. 1915			
23	Aug. 1915	★		★
24	Aug. 1915	★		
25	Sept. 1915	★		
26	Sept. 1915	★		
30	Nov. 1915	★		
31	Dec. 1915	★		
32	Nov. 1915	★		
33	Nov. 1915	★		
34	Jan. 1916	★	Mar. 1916	★
35 (Bantam)	Jan. 1916	★		
36 (Ulster)	Oct. 1916	★	Jan. 1916	★
37	July 1915	★		
38 (Welsh)	Jan. 1916	★		
39	Mar 1916	★		
40 (Bantam)	June 1916	★		★
41	May 1916	★		
First-line Territorial				
42 (E. Lancs.)	Sept. 1914	★	summer 1917	
46 (N. Midland)	Feb. 1915	★	Dec. 1916	★
47 (London)	Mar. 1915	★	Feb. 1916	
48 (S. Midland)	Mar. 1915	★	Jan. 1916	★
49 (W. Riding)	April 1915	★	spring 1916	
50 (Northumbrian)	April 1915	★		★
51 (Highland)	April 1915	★	early 1916	★
52 (Lowland)	June 1915	★	late 1917	
53 (Welsh)	Aug. 1915	★	summer 1917	
54 (Wessex)	Aug. 1915			
55 (W. Lancs.)	Jan. 1916	★		

Divisions	Date of arrival (or of formation if formed overseas)	Divisional concert party	Date formed	Divisional cinema
56 (London)	Feb. 1916	★	May 1916	★
Second-line Territorial				
57 (W. Lancs.)	Feb. 1917	★		
58 (London)	Jan. 1917	★	Dec. 1916	★
59 (N. Midland)	Feb. 1917	★	Dec. 1916	
60 (London)	June 1916	★	spring 1916	
61 (S. Midland)	May 1916	★		★
62 (W. Riding)	Jan. 1917	★		
66 (E. Lancs.)	Feb. 1917	★		
Other British				
Guards	Aug. 1915			★
63 (Royal Naval)	Mar. 1915	★		
74 (Yeomanry)	Mar. 1917	★		
75	Mar. 1917			
Australian				
1	Mar. 1915			★
2	Aug. 1915			★
3	July 1916	★	Dec. 1916	★
4	Feb. 1916	★		★
5	Feb. 1916	★	Sept. 1916	★
New Zealand				
1	Jan. 1915	★		★
Canadian				
1	Feb. 1915			
2	Sept. 1915	★		
3	Dec. 1915	★	Dec. 1917	
4	Aug. 1916	★	Dec. 1916	
Totals				
74		59		28

At least 80 per cent of the divisions which served in the active war theatre therefore employed a divisional concert party. Breaking down the total of seventy-four divisions into those which served a year or more in France (sixty-four) and those which did not (ten), the percentages are 87 per cent and 50 per cent respectively.

Sources

For dates of arrival see *Statistics of the Military Effort*, opp. p. 28. The date for the New Zealand Division is that of the formation of the joint New Zealand/Australian Division, from which the New Zealand Division subsequently evolved. For concert parties and cinemas:

1st Division: J. Smythe, *In This Sign Conquer* (1968), 195.

2nd: E. Wyrall, *History of the 2nd Division 1914–1918*, i (1921), 197.

3rd: Dolden, *Cannon Fodder*, p. 122.

4th: War Diary of the 4th Division, WO 95/1449, 30 Dec. 1914 and Routine Orders 12 Jan. 1915.

5th: D. S. Inman and A. H. Hussey, *The 5th Division in the Great War* (1921), 96; Fairclough, *1st Birmingham Bn.*, p. 51.

6th: War Diary of the 6th Division, WO 95/1585, bundle marked 'Miscellaneous', 'Issued With Routine Orders dated 12 Feb. 1915' and Routine Order No. 170 8 Sept. 1915.

7th: G. H. Greenwell, *An Infant in Arms* (1972), 184.

8th: Boraston and Bax, *The 8th Division in War*, p. 60.

29th: Gillon, *Story of the 29th Division*, p. 102.

9th: Ewing, *History of the 9th Division*, pp. 75, 416.

12th: Scott and Brumwell, *History of the 12th Division*, pp. 29, 257–8.

15th: Feilding, *War Letters*, pp. 223, 301.

17th: A. H. Atteridge, *History of the 17th Division* (Glasgow, 1929), 165; Nicholson, *Behind the Lines*, p. 257.

19th: Wyrall, *History of the 19th Division*, pp. 23–4.

20th: Inglefield, *History of the 20th Division*, pp. 110–11.

21st: Middlebrook, *Kaiser's Battle*, pp. 154–5.

23rd: Sandilands, *The 23rd Division*, pp. 228–9; Gladden, *Across the Piave*, p. 33.

24th: Dolden, *Cannon Fodder*, p. 157.

25th: M. Kincaid-Smith, *The 25th Division in France and Flanders* (1920), 42.

26th: H. C. Day, *Macedonian Memories* (1930), 150.

30th: Anon., *16th: 17th: 18th: 19th Bns. The Manchester Regt. (First City Brigade): A Record 1914–1918* (Manchester, 1923), 133.

31st: Anon., *History of the 10th Bn. E. Yorks Regt.*, p. 173.

32nd: C. H. Cooke, *Historical Records of the 16th (Service) Bn. Northumberland Fusiliers* (Newcastle, 1923), 77.

33rd: Richards, *Old Soldiers*, p. 280.

34th: J. Shakespear, *The 34th Division* (1921), 305–7; Mack, *Letters from France*, p. 24.

35th: C. H. Cooke, *Historical Records of the 19th (Service) Bn. Northumberland Fusiliers* (Newcastle, 1920), 50.

36th: Falls, *History of the 36th Division*, pp. 135–7; H. Samuels, *With the Ulster Division in France* (Belfast, 1921), 35–7.
37th: Weetman, *The Sherwood Foresters*, p. 145.
38th: Richards, *Old Soldiers*, p. 280.
39th: Blunden, *Undertones of War*, p. 157.
40th: F. E. Whitton, *History of the 40th Division* (Aldershot, 1926), 171.
41st: Aston and Duggan, *History of the 12th Bn.*, pp. 64–6.
42nd: Gibbon, *The 42nd Division*, p. 95.
46th: T. E. Sandall, *A History of the 5th Bn. the Lincolnshire Regt.* (Oxford, 1922), 98; Weetman, *The Sherwood Foresters*, p. 162.
47th: Maude, *The 47th Division*, pp. 223–4.
48th: *The 5th Glo'ster Gazette*, 9 (Feb. 1916), 9; P. L. Wright, *The 1st Buckinghamshire Bn. 1914–1919* (1920), 101.
49th: Bales, *History of the 1/4th Bn.*, p. 66.
50th: A. L. Raimes, *The 5th Bn. The Durham Light Infantry 1914–1918* (1930), 35.
51st: Nicholson, *Behind the Lines*, p. 251; Bewsher, *History of the 51st Division*, p. 269.
52nd: Thompson, *The 52nd Division*, pp. 353, 504.
53rd: C. H. D. Ward, *History of the 53rd (Welsh) Division 1914–1918* (Cardiff, 1927), 118.
55 J. Shakespear, *A Record of the 17th and 32nd Bns. Northumberland Fusiliers (NER) Pioneers* (Newcastle, 1926), 61.
56th: C. H. D. Ward, *The 56th Division* (1921), 140; Bailey and Hollier, *The Kensingtons*, p. 145.
57th: Wurtzburg, *History of the 2/6th Bn.*, p. 55.
58th: Grimwade, *War History of the 4th Bn.*, p. 236; Grey, *2nd City of London Regt.*, p. 277.
59th: Hall, *The Green Triangle*, p. 46.
60th: P. H. Dalbiac, *History of the 60th Division* (1927), 38.
61st: E. C. Matthews, *With the Cornwall Territorials on the Western Front* (Cambridge, 1921), 32; Gauld, *Truth from the Trenches*, p. 175.
62nd: E. Wyrall, *History of the 62nd (W. Riding) Division 1914–1919* (1925), i. 169.
66th: Bales, *History of the 1/4th Bn.*, p. 156.
Guards: C. Headlam, *History of the Guards Division in the Great War 1915–1918* (1924), i. 101–2.
63rd: *The Mudhook*, 1 (Sept. 1917), 11.
74th: Hill, *Chauvel of the Light-Horse*, p. 114.
1st–5th Australian: *Aussie*, 4 (Apr. 1918), 5; 5 (June 1918), 12; 9 (Dec. 1918), 20; Cuttriss, *Over the Top*, pp. 112–13; A. D. Ellis, *The Story of the 5th Australian Division* (1920), 121.
New Zealand: Stewart, *New Zealand Division*, p. 142.

1st–4th Canadian: Wood, *With the 5th Glo'sters*, p. 100; Hodder-Williams, *Princess Patricia's Canadian Light Infantry*, i. 282–3; Russenholt, *Six Thousand Canadian Men*, pp. 103–4.

II. Brigade Concert Parties

Brigade	Date of concert party formation	Front on which formed
Regular		
87 Brigade		
New Army		
89		France
92	Sept. 1916	France
122	late 1916	France
First-line Territorial		
139	mid 1918	France
145		
147	Jan. 1918	France
Second-line Territorial		
179	Mar. 1917	Salonika
181		
Australian		
7		
8		
9		
10		

Sources

87th Bgd.: Gillon, *Story of the 29th Division*, p. 102.
89th: Grey, *2nd City of London Regt.*, p. 171.
92nd: Anon., *History of the 10th Bn. E. Yorks. Regt.*, p. 73.
122nd: Russell, *History of the 11th Bn.*, p. 176.
139th: Carrington, *War Record of the 1/5th Bn.*, p. 17.
145th: Wood, *With the 5th Glo'sters*, p. 93.
147th: Bales, *History of the 1/4th Bn.*, p. 185.
179th: Bailey and Hollier, *The Kensingtons*, p. 271.
181st: Anon., *War Record of the 21st London Regt. (First Surrey Rifles) 1914–1919* (1927), 217.
7th, 8th, 9th Australian: Cutlack (ed.), *War Letters*, p. 125.
10th Australian: F. C. Green, *The Fortieth* (Hobart, 1922), p. 144.

III. Battalion Concert Parties

Battalion	Date of concert party formation	Front on which formed
Regular		
1st Coldstream Guards		France
2nd Dorset with 1st Manchester		Mesopotamia
2nd Royal Fusiliers		France
New Army		
15th Cheshire		France
6th Durham Light Infantry		France
7th East Kent		France
9th King's Liverpool	July 1916	France
21st Northumberland Fusiliers	Dec. 1916	France
11th Royal Scots		France
12th East Surrey		France
First-line Territorial		
1/5th Durham Light Infantry	May 1917	France
1/4th King's Liverpool		France
1/5th London		France
1/13th London		France
1/18th London		France
Second-line Territorial		
2/5th Gloucestershire	June 1917	France
2/6th King's Liverpool	Sept. 1918	France
2/4th Royal Fusiliers		France
2/8th Royal Warwickshire	May 1917	France
Dominion		
24th Australian	late 1918	
26th Australian		
16th Canadian	May 1917	France
Princess Patricia's Canadian Light Infantry	June 1916	France

Sources

1st Coldstream: Noakes, *Distant Drum*, p. 163.
2nd Dorset: *The Mesopoluvian*, 2 (June 1917), 6.
2nd Royal Fusiliers: Grey, *2nd City of London Regt.*, p. 221.
15th Cheshire: Cooke, *Historical Records of the 19th Bn.*, pp. 83–4.

6th Durham: R. B. Ainsworth, *The Story of the 6th Bn. The Durham Light Infantry* (1919), p. 44.

7th E. Kent: War Diary of the 7th Buffs, WO 95/2049, 17 Sept. 1917.

9th King's: E. H. G. Roberts, *The Story of the '9th King's' in France* (Liverpool, 1922), 47.

21st Northumberland: Ternan, *Story of the Tyneside Scottish*, pp. 139–40.

11th Royal Scots: Croft, *Three Years*, pp. 140–2.

12th E. Surrey: Aston and Duggan, *History of the 12th Bn.*, pp. 64–6.

1/5th Durham: Raimes, *The 5th Bn. The Durham Light Infantry*, pp. 97, 108–9.

1/4th King's: Russell, *With the Machine-Gun Corps*, p. 27.

1/5th London: Smith, *Four Years*, p. 345.

1/13th London: Tucker, *Johnny Get Your Gun*, p. 20.

1/18th London: F. Dunham, *The Long Carry* (Oxford, 1970), 210.

2/5th Gloucs.: Barnes, *Story of the 2/5th Bn.*, pp. 67, 152.

2/6th King's: Wurtzburg, *History of the 2/6th Bn.*, p. 219.

2/4th Royal Fusiliers: Grimwade, *History of the 4th Bn.*, p. 236.

2/8th Royal Warks.: H. T. Chidley, *Black Square Memories* (Oxford, 1924), 126.

24th Australian: Harvey, *Red and White Diamond*, p. 218.

26th Australian: *The Standard of C Company*, 1 (July 1918), 12.

16th Canadian: Urquhart, *History of the 16th Bn.*, pp. 224–5.

PPCLI: Hodder-Williams, *Princess Patricia's Canadian Light Infantry*, i. 140.

Bibliography

All published works were published in London unless otherwise stated.

I. Primary Sources: Unpublished, Manuscript, and Trench Journals

Public Record Office, Kew

CAB. 23, CAB. 24 (Cabinet Papers and Memoranda)
WO. 32, WO. 95 (War Office Papers)

Cambridge University Library

British and Dominion Troop Journals (for details see Appendix A)
Concert Programmes
A Souvenir of 'The Goods' Divisional Concert Party
French Troop Journals:
  La Baionette
  Le Claque à Fond

British Library

British and Dominion Troop Journals (for details see Appendix A)
The Ladysmith Bombshell
French Troop Journals:
  La Bourguignotte
  120 Court
  Le Canard de Boyau
  L'Echo des Guitounes
  Le Klaxon
  Marmita
  Le Midi au Front
  Le Parpaing
  Le Plus-que-Torial
  Le Poilu

Imperial War Museum

British and Dominion Troop Journals (for details see Appendix A)
Concert Programmes
The Ladysmith Lyre

II. Parliamentary Papers

PP. 1913, LXXX, Cd. 6896: *Report on the Twelfth Decennial Census of Scotland.*
PP. 1913, LXXIX, Cd. 7019: *Census of England and Wales 1911.*
PP. 1914–16, XXXIX, Cd. 8168: *Report of Recruiting in Ireland.*
PP. 1919, X, Cmd. 174: *Report of the Work of the Camps Library.*
PP. 1921, XX, Cmd. 1193: *General Annual Reports of the British Army (including of the Territorial Force) for the period from 1 October 1913 to 30 September 1919.*

III. Official Publications

(i) Statistical Reports

The Canada Year Book 1914 (Ottawa, 1915).
Census of the Commonwealth of Australia 1911 (Melbourne, 1914) 3 vols.
Official Year Book of the Commonwealth of Australia 1901–1910 and 1911–1914 (Melbourne, 1911 and 1915).
Statistics of the Military Effort of the British Empire during the Great War 1914–1920 (1922).

(ii) Official Histories

BEAN, C. E. W., *et al.*, *Official History of Australia in the War of 1914–1918* (Sydney, 1923–42).
BUTLER, A. G., *The Australian Medical Services in the War 1914–1918* (Melbourne, 1938–43).
DREW, H. T. B., *The War Effort of New Zealand* (Auckland, 1923).
DUGUID, A. F., *Official History of the Canadian Forces in the Great War 1914–1919* (Ottawa, 1938).
EDMONDS, J. E., *et al.*, *History of the Great War Based on Official Documents* (1920–49)
NICHOLSON, G. W. L., *Official History of the Canadian Army in the First World War, Canadian Expeditionary Force, 1914–1919* (Ottawa, 1962).
POWLES, C. G., *The New Zealanders in Sinai and Palestine* (Auckland, 1923).
STEWART, H., *The New Zealand Division 1916–1919* (Auckland, 1921).
WAITE, F., *The New Zealanders at Gallipoli* (Auckland, 1921).

IV. Contemporary Newspapers and Periodicals

(i) Newspapers
Daily Mail
Illustrated London News
The Times
The Times Literary Supplement

(ii) Periodicals
The Bystander
John Bull
The Nation
The Tatler

V. Books and Articles

Published in London unless otherwise stated. In Sections i–iii, the rank of the author, where apparent from the text, is recorded in brackets after the title according to the following key: (R) served in the ranks; (O) served as an officer; (RO) served in the ranks until commissioned; (U) served but rank unknown; (Misc.) several contributors of different ranks; (F) served in a foreign army; (C) civilian; (N) no information; (B) born after the war or too young to serve.

(i) Memoirs

ADAMS, H. M., *A War Diary 1916–1918* (Worcester, 1922) (R).
ALDINGTON, R., *Life for Life's Sake* (New York, 1941) (O).
ANDREWS, W. L., *Haunting Years* (1930) (R).
ASHWELL, L., *Modern Troubadours: A Record of the Concerts at the Front* (1922) (C).
BARTLETT, S. A., *From the Somme to the Rhine* (1921) (O).
BEHREND, A. F., *Nine Days* (Cambridge, 1921) (O).
——*Make Me a Soldier* (1961).
——*As from Kennel Hill* (1963).
BEN ASSHER (pseud.), *A Nomad Under Arms* (1931) (O).
BIDDER, H. F., *Three Chevrons* (1919) (R).
BISCOE, J. T., *Gunner Subaltern 1914–1918* (1971) (O).
BLACK, D., *Red Dust* (1931) (R).
BLACK, E. G., *I Want One Volunteer* (Toronto, 1965) (R).
BLASER, B., *Kilts Across the Jordan* (1926) (R).
BLUNDEN, E., *Undertones of War* (1965) (O).
BOMBARDIER X (pseud.), *So This Was War!* (1930) (R).

Bowra, C. M., *Memories* (1966) (O).
Boyd, D., *Salute of Guns* (1930) (O).
Brenan, G., *A Life of One's Own* (1975) (O).
Burrage, A., *War is War* (1930) (R).
Burton, O. E., *The Silent Division* (1935) (RO).
Caldicott, R., *London Men in Palestine* (1919) (O).
Campbell, P. J., *The Ebb and Flow of Battle* (1977) (O).
——*In the Cannon's Mouth* (1979).
Carrington, C. E., *A Subaltern's War* (1930) (O).
——*Soldier from the Wars Returning* (1965).
Casson, S., *Steady Drummer* (1935) (O).
Chapman, G. P., *A Kind of Survivor* (1975) (O).
Clarke, A. O. T., *Transport and Sport in the Great War Period* (1938) (O).
Cloete, S., *A Victorian Son* (1972) (O).
Colwill, R. A., *Through Hell to Victory* (Torquay, 1927) (O).
Coppard, G., *With a Machine Gun to Cambrai* (1980) (R).
Croft, W. D., *Three Years with the 9th Division* (1919) (O).
Croney, P., *Soldier's Luck* (Ilfracombe, 1965) (R).
Cuddeford, D. W. J., *And All for What?* (1933) (O).
Cutlack, F. M. (ed.), *War Letters of General Monash* (Sydney, 1935) (O).
Cuttriss, G. P., *Over the Top with the 3rd Australian Division* (1918) (O).
Dalton, H., *With British Guns in Italy* (1919) (O).
Davis, A. H., *Extracts from the Diaries of a Tommy* (1932) (R).
Dawson, C., *Living Bayonets* (1919) (O).
Day, H. C., *Macedonian Memories* (1930) (O).
Dearden, H., *Medicine and Duty* (1928) (O).
Delamain, F. (ed.), *Going Across* (Newport, 1952) (O).
de Wiart, A. C., *Happy Odyssey* (1950) (O).
Dinesen, T., *Merry Hell! A Dane with the Canadians* (1929) (R).
Doc (pseud.), *Letters from Somewhere* (1918) (O).
Dolden, A. S., *Cannon Fodder* (Poole, 1980) (R).
Douie, C. O. G., *The Weary Road* (1929) (O).
Dugdale, G., *Langemarck and Cambrai* (Shrewsbury, 1932) (O).
Dunham, F., *The Long Carry* (Oxford, 1970) (R).
Dunn, J. C. (ed.), *The War the Infantry Knew, 1914–1919* (1938) (O).
Durrell, J. C. V., *Whizzbangs and Woodbines* (1918) (C).
Eberle, V. F., *My Sapper Venture* (1973) (O).
Edmunds, G. B., *Somme Memories* (Ilfracombe, 1955) (R).
Empey, A. G., *From the Fire Step* (1917) (R).
Eyre, G. E. M., *Somme Harvest* (1938) (R).

FEILDING, R., *War Letters to a Wife* (1929) (O).

FENNAH, A., *Retaliation* (1935) (R).

FRASER-TYTLER, N., *Field Guns in France* (1929) (O).

FRENCH, A., *Gone for a Soldier* (Kineton, 1972) (RO).

FRYER, E. R. M., *Reminiscences of a Grenadier 1914–1919* (1921) (R). *Fusilier Bluff* (1934) (O).

GAULD, H. D., *The Truth from the Trenches* (1922) (R).

GIBBON, M., *Inglorious Soldier* (1968) (O).

GIBBONS, J., *Roll On Next War* (1935) (R).

GIBBS, P., *Realities of War* (1929) (C).

GLADDEN, E. N., *Ypres 1917* (1967) (R).

——*Across the Piave* (1971).

——*The Somme 1916* (1974).

GLUBB, J., *Into Battle* (1978) (O).

GOODCHILD, G., *Behind the Barrage* (1918) (O).

GORDON, H., *The Unreturning Army* (1967) (O).

GOSSE, P., *Memoirs of a Camp Follower* (1950) (O).

GOWLAND, J. S., *War Is Like That* (1933) (O).

GRAHAM, S., *Private in the Guards* (1919) (R).

GRAVES, R., *Goodbye to All That* (1980) (O).

GRAY, F., *Confessions of a Private* (Oxford, 1920) (O).

GREENWELL, G. H., *An Infant in Arms* (1972) (O).

GREGORY, H., *Never Again* (1934) (R).

GRIFFITH, L. W., *Up to Mametz* (1931) (O).

GROOM, W. H. A., *Poor Bloody Infantry* (1976) (R).

HAIGH, R. H., and TURNER, P. W. (eds.), *Not for Glory* (1969) (R).

HARBOTTLE, G., *Civilian Soldier 1914–1919* (1981) (R).

HART, B. H. LIDDELL, *The Memoirs of Captain Liddell Hart*, i (1965) (O).

HART-DAVIS, R. (ed.), *Siegfried Sassoon Diaries 1915–1918* (1983) (O).

HARVEY, H. E., *Battle Line Narratives* (1928) (R).

HASLAM, A. D., *Cannon Fodder* (1930) (R).

HAWKINGS, F., *From Ypres to Cambrai* (1973) (RO).

HAWORTH, C., *March to Armistice 1918* (1968) (R).

HEAD, C. O., *No Great Shakes* (1943) (O).

HENSON, L., *My Laugh Story* (1926) (R).

HILL, J. A. S., *The Front Line and Beyond It* (1930) (R).

HISCOCK, E., *The Bells of Hell Go Ting-a-Ling-a-Ling* (1976) (R).

HITCHCOCK, F. C., *Stand To* (1937) (O).

HOPE, T. S., *The Winding Road Unfolds* (1937) (R).

HUTCHISON, G. S., *Footslogger* (1931) (O).

——*Warrior* (1932).

IDRIESS, I. L., *The Desert Column* (Sydney, 1933) (R).

JACOMB, C. E., *Torment* (1920) (R).
KEABLE, R., *Standing By* (1919) (O).
KELLY, D. V., *39 Months with the 'Tigers' 1915–1918* (1930) (O).
KELLY, R. B. T., *A Subaltern's Odyssey* (1980) (O).
KIERNAN, R. H., *Little Brother Goes Soldiering* (1930) (R).
LAMBERT, A., *Over the Top* (1930) (R).
LATHAM, B., *A Territorial Soldier's War* (Aldershot, 1967) (RO).
LAUDER, H., *A Minstrel in France* (1918) (C).
LAWRENCE, T. E., *Seven Pillars of Wisdom* (1981) (O).
LEWIS, P. W., *Blasting and Bombardiering* (1967) (O).
LLOYD, T., *The Blazing Trail of Flanders* (1933) (O).
LUCY, J., *There's a Devil in the Drum* (1938) (R).
LUDENDORFF, E. F. W., *My War Memories* (1919) 2 vols. (F).
MACK, I. A., *Letters from France* (Liverpool, 1932) (O).
MACKENZIE, C. N., *The Tale of a Trooper* (1921) (R).
MACMILLAN, H., *Winds of Change* (1966) (O).
MARKS, T. P., *The Laughter Goes from Life* (1977) (R).
MAXWELL, J., *Hell's Bells and Mademoiselles* (Sydney, 1932) (O).
MAY, E., *Signal Corporal* (1972) (R).
MELLERSH, H. E. L., *Schoolboy into War* (1978) (O).
MITCHELL, G. D., *Backs to the Wall* (Sydney, 1937) (RO).
MOLESWORTH, G. N. (ed.), *A Soldier's War* (Taunton, 1958) (R).
MONTAGUE, C. E., *Disenchantment* (Westport, Conn., 1978) (R).
MORAN, C. M. W., *The Anatomy of Courage* (1945) (O).
MORROW, E., *Iron in the Fire* (Sydney, 1934) (R).
MOTTRAM, R. H., *The 20th Century: A Personal Record* (1969) (O).
——*Journey to the Western Front* (1936).
MUGGE, M. A., *The War Diary of a Square Peg* (1920) (R).
MURRAY, J., *Gallipoli As I Saw It* (1965) (R).
——*Call to Arms* (1980).
NETTLETON, J., *The Anger of the Guns* (1979) (O).
NEVILLE, J. E. H., *The War Letters of a Light Infantryman* (1930) (O).
NICHOLSON, W. N., *Behind the Lines* (1939) (O).
NOAKES, F. E., *The Distant Drum* (Tunbridge Wells, 1952) (R).
NOYES, F. W., *Stretcher Bearers at the Double* (Toronto, 1936) (R).
OSBORN, A., *Unwilling Passenger* (1932) (O).
OWEN, H. C., *Salonica and After* (1919) (C).
PACKER, C., *Return to Salonika* (1964) (R).
PANICHAS, G. A. (ed.), *Promise of Greatness* (1968) (Misc.).
PARKER, E., *Into Battle* (1964) (RO).
PEACOCK, B., *Tinker's Mufti* (1974) (O).
PLOWMAN, M., *A Subaltern on the Somme* (1927) (O).
POLLARD, A. O., *Fire-Eater* (1932) (RO).

PRIESTLEY, J. B., *Margin Released* (1962) (RO).
PRIVATE 940 (pseud.), *On the Remainder of Our Front* (1917) (R).
PURDOM, C. B. (ed.), *Everyman at War* (1930) (Misc.).
QUIGLEY, H., *Passchendaele and the Somme* (1928) (R).
READ, H., *The Contrary Experience* (1963) (O).
REES, R. T., *A Schoolmaster at War* (1936) (O).
REID, F., *The Fighting Cameliers* (Sydney, 1934) (R).
REITH, J. C. W., *Wearing Spurs* (1966) (O).
REMARQUE, E. M., *All Quiet on the Western Front* (1977) (F).
RICHARDS, F., *Old Soldiers Never Die* (1933) (R).
ROGERSON, S., *Twelve Days* (1933) (O).
RORIE, D., *A Medico's Luck in the Great War* (Aberdeen, 1929) (O).
ROWLANDS, D. H., *For the Duration* (1932) (R).
RULE, A., *Students under Arms* (Aberdeen, 1934) (R).
RULE, E. J., *Jacka's Mob* (Sydney, 1933) (RO).
RUSSELL, A., *With the Machine Gun Corps* (1923) (R).
RUSSELL, H., *Slaves of the War Lords* (1928) (R).
SANSOM, A. J., *Letters from France* (1921) (O).
SCOTT, R., *A Soldier's Diary* (1923) (O).
SELIGMAN, V. J., *Macedonian Musings* (1918) (O).
——*The Salonika Sideshow* (1919).
SEVERN, M., *The Gambardier* (1930) (O).
SLACK, C. M., *Grandfather's Adventures in the Great War* (Ilfracombe,
    1977) (O).
SMITH, A., *Four Years on the Western Front* (1922) (R).
SULZBACH, H., *With the German Guns* (1973) (F).
TAWNEY, R. H., *The Attack and Other Papers* (1953) (R).
TAYLOR, F. A. J., *The Bottom of the Barrel* (1978) (R).
TERRAINE, J. (ed.), *General Jack's Diary* (1964) (O).
THOMAS, A., *A Life Apart* (1968) (O).
THORBURN, A. D., *Amateur Gunners* (Liverpool, 1933) (O).
THORP, C. H., *A Handful of Ausseys* (1919) (R).
TILLET, B., *Memories and Reflections* (1931) (C).
TILSLEY, W. V., *Other Ranks* (1931) (R).
TIVEYCHOC, A., *There and Back* (Sydney, 1935) (R).
TOWNSHEND, E. (ed.), *Keeling Letters and Recollections* (1918) (R).
TROOPER (pseud.), *The Four Horsemen Ride* (1935) (R).
TUCKER, J. F., *Johnny Get Your Gun* (1978) (R).
TUOHY, F., *The Crater of Mars* (1929) (O).
VAUGHAN, E. C., *Some Desperate Glory* (1981) (O).
VILLARI, L., *The Macedonian Campaign* (1922) (F).
VOIGT, F. A., *Combed Out* (1920) (R).
WADE, A., *Gunner on the Western Front* (1936) (O).

WEST, A. G., *Diary of a Dead Officer* (1919) (O).
WESTON, C. H., *Three Years with the New Zealanders* (1918) (O).
WILLEY, B., *Spots of Time* (1965) (O).
WILLIAMS, H. R., *The Gallant Company* (Sydney, 1933) (RO).
WILLIAMSON, H., *A Soldier's Diary of the Great War* (1929) (O).
WOOD, W. J., *With the 5th Glo'sters at Home and Overseas* (1925) (R).

(ii) Novels from Experience

ALDINGTON, R., *Death of a Hero* (1929) (O).
BARBUSSE, H., *Under Fire*, trans. W. F. Wray (1926) (F).
BENSTEAD, C. R., *Retreat* (1930) (O).
CHAPMAN, G. P., *A Passionate Prodigality* (1965) (O).
CLOETE, S., *How Young They Died* (1969) (O).
FORD, F. M., *The Bodley Head Ford Madox Ford*, iv (1963) (O).
GRISTWOOD, A. D., *The Somme and the Coward* (Bath, 1968) (U).
HAY, I. (pseud.), *The First Hundred Thousand* (1915) (O).
——*Carrying On: After the First Hundred Thousand* (1917).
HILL, H., *Retreat from Death* (1936) (R).
HODSON, J. L., *Grey Dawn—Red Night* (Bath, 1974) (R).
MACGILL, P., *The Red Horizon* (1916) (R).
——*The Great Push* (1917).
MANNING, F., *The Middle Parts of Fortune* (1977) (R).
MOTTRAM, R. H., *The Spanish Farm Trilogy* (1979) (O).
RAYMOND, E., *The Jesting Army* (1930) (O).
SASSOON, S., *The Complete Memoirs of George Sherston* (1972) (O).
SHERRIFF, R. C., *Journey's End* (1930) (O).
WILLIAMS, H. R., *Comrades of the Great Adventure* (Sydney, 1935) (RO).
WILLIAMSON, H., *The Patriot's Progress* (1930) (O).
——*How Dear Is Life* (1954).
——*A Fox Under His Cloak* (1955).
——*The Golden Virgin* (1957).
——*Love and the Loveless* (1958).
——*A Test to Destruction* (1960).

(iii) Unit Histories

AINSWORTH, R. B., *The Story of the 6th Bn. The Durham Light Infantry* (1919) (O).
ARTHUR, J. W., and MUNRO, I. S., *The 17th Highland Light Infantry* (Glasgow, 1920) (N).
ASHCROFT, A. H., *The History of the 7th South Staffordshire Regt.* (1920) (O).

ASTON, J. A., and DUGGAN, C. M., *The History of the 12th (Bermondsey) Bn. East Surrey Regt.* (1936) (O and R).

ATKINSON, C. T., *The 7th Division* (1927) (N).

ATTERIDGE, A. H., *History of the 17th (Northern) Division* (Glasgow, 1929) (N).

BAILEY, O. F., and HOLLIER, H. M., *The Kensingtons (13th London) Regt.* (1936) (R).

BALES, P. G., *The History of the 1/4th Bn. Duke of Wellington's (West Riding) Regt. 1914–1919* (Halifax, 1920) (O).

BARNES, A. F., *The Story of the 2/5th Bn. The Gloucestershire Regt.* (Gloucester, 1930) (O).

BEAUMAN, A. B., *With the 38th in France and Italy* (Lichfield, 1919) (O).

BERDINNER, H. F., *With the Heavies in Flanders 1914–1919* (1922) (R).

BEWSHER, F. W., *The History of the 51st (Highland) Division 1914–1918* (Edinburgh, 1921) (O).

BLACKWELL, E., and AXE, E. C., *Romford to Beirut* (Clacton-on-Sea, 1926) (R).

BORASTON, J. H., and BAX, C. E. O., *The 8th Division in War, 1914–1918* (1926) (O).

BRADBRIDGE, E. U., *The 59th Division 1915–18* (Chesterfield, 1928) (O).

BUCHAN, J., *The History of the South African Forces in France* (1919) (C).

BURTON, O. E., *The Auckland Regt.* (Auckland, 1922) (RO).

The 10th Bn. The Cameronians (Scottish Rifles): A Record and a Memorial, 1914–1918 (Edinburgh, 1923) (O).

CARRINGTON, C. E., *The War Record of the 1/5th Bn. The Royal Warwickshire Regt.* (Birmingham, 1922) (O).

CHALMERS, T., *A Saga of Scotland: The History of the 16th Bn. The Highland Light Infantry* (Glasgow, 1930) (N).

—*An Epic of Glasgow: The History of the 15th Bn. The Highland Light Infantry* (Glasgow, 1934).

CHIDLEY, H. T., *Black Square Memories: An Account of the 2/8th Bn. The Royal Warwickshire Regt. 1914–1918* (Oxford, 1924) (O).

CHURTON, W. A. V., *The War Record of the 1/5th (Earl of Chester's) Bn. The Cheshire Regt. 1914–1919* (Chester, 1920) (O).

COLLISON, C. S., *The 11th Royal Warwicks in France* (Birmingham, 1928) (O).

COOKE, C. H., *Historical Records of the 19th (Service) Bn. Northumberland Fusiliers (Pioneers)* (Newcastle, 1920) (O).

—*Historical Records of the 16th (Service) Bn. Northumberland Fusiliers* (Newcastle, 1923).

—*Historical Records of the 9th (Service) Bn. Northumberland Fusiliers* (Newcastle, 1928).

COOP, J. O., *The Story of the 55th (West Lancashire) Division* (Liverpool, 1919) (O).

CORBETT, E. C., *The Worcestershire Regt: War Story of the 1/8th (Territorial) Bn.* (Worcester, 1921) (R).

CORRIGALL, D. J., *The History of the 20th Canadian Bn. Canadian Expeditionary Force in the Great War 1914–1918* (Toronto, 1935) (O).

CRUTTWELL, C. R. M. F., *The War Service of the 1/4th Royal Berkshire Regt. (T.F.)* (Oxford, 1922) (O).

DALBIAC, P. H., *History of the 60th Division* (1927) (O).

DAVSON, H. M., *The History of the 35th Division in the Great War* (1926) (O).

EAMES, F. W., *The Second Nineteenth, Being the History of the 2/19th London Regt.* (1930) (O).

ELLIOT, G. F. S., *War History of the 5th Bn. King's Own Scottish Borderers* (Dumfries, 1928) (O).

ELLIS, A. D., *The Story of the 5th Australian Division* (1920) (O).

ELLIS, C., *The 4th (Denbighshire) Bn. The Royal Welch Fusiliers in the Great War* (Wrexham, 1926) (O).

EWING, J., *The History of the 9th (Scottish) Division 1914–1919* (1921) (O).

FAIRCLOUGH, J. E. B., *The 1st Birmingham Bn. in the Great War 1914–1919* (Birmingham, 1933) (U).

FALLS, C., *The History of the 36th (Ulster) Division* (Belfast, 1922) (O).

FETHERSTONHAUGH, R. C., *The 24th Bn. C.E.F., Victoria Rifles of Canada 1914–1919* (Montreal, 1930) (O).

FINDLAY, J. M., *With the 8th Scottish Rifles 1914–1919* (1926) (O).

FOLEY, H. A. (ed.), *Scrap Book of the 7th Bn. Somerset Light Infantry* (Aylesbury, 1932) (O).

GIBBON, F. P., *The 42nd (East Lancashire) Division 1914–1918* (1920) (N).

GILLON, S., *The Story of the 29th Division* (1925) (O).

GRANT, D. P., *The 1/4th (Hallamshire) Bn. York and Lancaster Regt. 1914–1919* (1927) (O).

GREEN, F. C., *The Fortieth* (Hobart, 1922) (O).

GREY, W. E., *The 2nd City of London Regt. (Royal Fusiliers) in the Great War (1914–19)* (1929) (O).

GRIMWADE, F. C., *The War History of the 4th Bn. The London Regt. (Royal Fusiliers) 1914–1919* (1922) (O).

HALDANE, M. M., *A History of the 4th Bn. The Seaforth Highlanders* (1928) (O).

HALL, W. G., *The Green Triangle, Being the History of the 2/5th Bn., The Sherwood Foresters (Notts. and Derby Regt.) in the Great European War 1914–1918* (Letchworth, 1920) (O).

HARVEY, W. J., *The Red and White Diamond* (Melbourne, 1920) (R).

HEADLAM, C., *History of the Guards Division in the Great War 1915–1918* (1924) 2 vols. (O).

HENRIQUES, J. Q., *The War History of the 1st Bn. Queen's Westminster Rifles 1914–1918* (1923) (O).

The 5th Bn. Highland Light Infantry in the War 1914–1918 (Glasgow, 1921) (O).

History of the 50th Infantry Brigade (Oxford, 1919) (N).

The History of the 8th Bn. Queen's Own Royal West Kent Regt. 1914–1919 (1921) (N).

The History of the 1/6th Bn. The Royal Warwickshire Regt. (Birmingham, 1929) (N).

The History of the 2/6th Bn. The Royal Warwickshire Regt. (Birmingham, 1929) (N).

History of the 1st and 2nd Bns. The North Staffordshire Regt. (The Prince of Wales') 1914–1923 (Longton, Staffordshire, 1933) (N).

A History of the 10th (Service) Bn. The East Yorkshire Regt. (Hull Commercials) (1937) (N).

HODDER-WILLIAMS, R., *Princess Patricia's Canadian Light Infantry 1914–1919* (1923) 2 vols. (C).

HOPKINSON, E. C., *Spectamur Agendo: 1st Bn. The East Lancashire Regt. August and September 1914* (Cambridge, 1926) (O).

HUTCHISON, G. S., *The 33rd Division in France and Flanders 1915–1919* (1921) (O).

INGLEFIELD, V. E., *The History of the 20th (Light) Division* (1921) (O).

INMAN, D. S., and HUSSEY, A. H., *The 5th Division in the Great War* (1921) (O).

JERROLD, D., *The Royal Naval Division* (1923) (O).

JOURDAIN, H. F. N., and FRASER, E., *The Connaught Rangers*, iii (1928) (O).

KEESON, C. A. C., *The History and Records of Queen Victoria's Rifles 1792–1922* (1923) (O).

KINCAID-SMITH, M., *The 25th Division in France and Flanders* (1920) (O).

——(ed.), *A War Record of the 21st London Regt. (First Surrey Rifles) 1914–1919* (1927) (O).

LOWE, C. E. B., *Siege Battery 94* (1920) (O).

LOWE, W. D., *The War History of the 18th (S.) Bn. Durham Light Infantry* (1920) (O).

MACKENZIE, D., *The 6th Gordons in France and Flanders* (Aberdeen, 1922) (O).

MAJENDIE, V. H. B., *A History of the 1st Bn. The Somerset Light Infantry (Prince Albert's) July 1st 1916 to the End of the War* (Taunton, 1921) (O).

16th, 17th, 18th, 19th Bns. The Manchester Regt. (First City Brigade): A Record 1914–1918 (Manchester 1923) (N).

MARDEN, T. O., *A Short History of the 6th Division* (1920) (O).

MARTIN, D. (ed.), *The 5th Bn. The Cameronians (Scottish Rifles) 1914–1919* (Glasgow, 1936) (O).

MATTHEWS, E. C., *With the Cornwall Territorials on the Western Front, Being the History of the 5th Bn. Duke of Cornwall's Light Infantry in the Great War* (Cambridge, 1921) (O).

MAUDE, A. H., *The 47th (London) Division 1914–1919* (1922) (N).

MEAKIN, W., *The 5th North Staffords and The Midland Territorials (The 46th and 59th Divisions) 1914–1919* (Longton Staffordshire, 1920) (O).

MESSENGER, C., *Terriers in the Trenches: The Post Office Rifles at War, 1914–1918* (Chippenham, 1982) (B).

MILNE, J., *Footprints of the 1/4th Leicestershire Regt.* (Leicester, 1935) (O).

MISSEN, L. R., *The History of the 7th (Service) Bn. Prince of Wales' (North Staffordshire Regiment) 1914–1919* (Cambridge, 1920) (O).

NICHOLS, G. H. F., *The 18th Division in the Great War* (Edinburgh, 1922) (O).

NICHOLSON, G. W. L., *Canadian Expeditionary Force 1914–1919* (Ottawa, 1962) (O).

——*The Fighting Newfoundlander* (Ottawa, 1964).

PICKFORD, P., *War Record of the 1/4th Bn. Oxfordshire and Buckinghamshire Light Infantry* (Banbury, 1919) (O).

RAIMES, A. L., *The 5th Bn. The Durham Light Infantry 1914–1918* (1930) (O).

ROBERTS, E. H. G., *The Story of the '9th King's' in France* (Liverpool, 1922) (N).

ROSE, G. K., *The Story of the 2/4th Oxfordshire and Buckinghamshire Light Infantry* (Oxford, 1920) (O).

ROSS, R. B., *The 51st in France* (1918) (O).

RUSSELL, R. O., *The History of the 11th (Lewisham) Bn. The Queen's Own Royal West Kent Regt.* (1934) (O).

RUSSENHOLT, E. S., *Six Thousand Canadian Men, Being the History of the 44th Bn. Canadian Infantry 1914–1919* (Winnipeg, 1932) (O).

RUTTER, O. (ed.), *The History of the 7th (Service) Bn. The Royal Sussex Regt. 1914–1919* (1934) (O).

SAMUELS, A. P., *With the Ulster Division in France* (Belfast, 1921) (O).

SANDALL, T. E., *A History of the 5th Bn. The Lincolnshire Regt.* (Oxford, 1922) (O).

SANDILANDS, H. R., *The 23rd Division 1914–1919* (Edinburgh, 1925) (O).

SANDILANDS, J. W., and MACLEOD, N., *The History of the 7th Bn. Queen's Own Cameron Highlanders* (Stirling, 1922) (O).

SCOTT, A. B., and BRUMWELL, P. M., *The History of the 12th (Eastern) Division in the Great War* (1923) (O).

SHAKESPEAR, J., *Historical Records of the 18th (Service) Bn. Northumberland Fusiliers* (Newcastle, 1920) (O).

——*The 34th Division* (1921).

——*A Record of the 17th and 32nd Bns. Northumberland Fusiliers (N.E.R.) Pioneers 1914–1919* (Newcastle, 1926).

A Short Account of 'The Nuggets' Pierrot Troupe (1919).

STEWART, J., and BUCHAN, J., *The 15th (Scottish) Division* (Edinburgh, 1926) (O and C).

SUTHERLAND, D., *War Diary of the 5th Seaforth Highlanders* (1920) (O).

TERNAN, T., *The Story of the Tyneside Scottish* (Newcastle, 1920) (O).

THOMPSON, R. R., *The 52nd (Lowland) Division 1914–1918* (Glasgow, 1923) (O).

TOPP, C. B., *The 42nd Bn., C.E.F., Royal Highlanders of Canada* (Montreal, 1931) (O).

URQUHART, H. M., *The History of the 16th Bn. (Canadian Scottish) C.E.F. in the Great War 1914–1919* (Toronto, 1932) (O).

WARD, C. H. D., *The 56th Division* (1921) (O).

——*The 74th (Yeomanry) Division in Syria and France* (1922).

——*History of the 53rd (Welsh) Division (T.F.) 1914–18* (Cardiff, 1927).

——*The Welsh Regt. of Foot Guards 1915–1918* (1936).

WEETMAN, W. C. C., *The Sherwood Foresters in the Great War 1914–1919: 1/8th Bn.* (Nottingham, 1920) (O).

WHEELER, C., *Memorial Record of the 7th (Service) Bn. The Oxfordshire and Buckinghamshire Light Infantry* (Oxford, 1921) (O).

WHITTON, F. E., *History of the 40th Division* (Aldershot, 1926) (O).

WILSON, S. J., *The 7th Manchesters July 1916 to March 1919* (Manchester, 1920) (O).

WREN, E., *Randwick to Hargicourt: The History of the 3rd Bn. A.I.F.* (Sydney, 1935) (O).

WRIGHT, P. L., *The 1st Buckinghamshire Bn. 1914–1919* (1920) (O).

WURTZBURG, C. E., *The History of the 2/6th (Rifle) Bn. 'The King's' (Liverpool Regt.) 1914–1919* (Aldershot, 1920) (O).

WYRALL, E., *The History of the 2nd Division 1914–1918*, i (1921) (O).

——*The History of the 62nd (West Riding) Division 1914–1919*, i (1925).

——*The History of the 19th Division 1914–1918* (1932).

——*The 17th (S.) Bn. Royal Fusiliers 1914–1919* (1930).

(iv) General Works

Aladdin in Macedonia: A Pantomime by Members of the 85th Field Ambulance (1917).

ARMSTRONG, E. H., *The Crisis of Quebec 1914–18* (New York, 1937).

ASCOLI, D., *The Mons Star* (1981).

ASHWORTH, T., *Trench Warfare 1914–1918: The Live and Let Live System* (1980).

ATKINS, J. B., *The Relief of Ladysmith* (1900).

AUDOIN-ROUZEAU, S., *14–18 Les Combattants des tranchées* (Paris, 1986).

BAILEY, P., *Leisure and Class in Victorian England* (1978).

BAMFORD, T. W., *Rise of the Public Schools* (1967).

BARCAN, A., *A History of Australian Education* (Melbourne, 1980).

BARKER, A. J., *The Neglected War: Mesopotamia 1914–1918* (1967).

BAYNES, J., *Morale* (1967).

BECKER, J. J., *The Great War and the French People*, trans. A. Pomerans (Leamington Spa, 1985).

BECKETT, I. F. W., and SIMPSON, K. (eds.), *A Nation in Arms: A Social Study of the British Army in the First World War* (Manchester, 1985).

BLAKE, R. (ed.), *The Private Papers of Douglas Haig, 1914–1919* (1952).

BOND, B., *The Victorian Army and the Staff College 1854–1914* (1972).

BOOTH, J. B., *A Pink 'Un Remembers* (1937).

BROPHY, J., and PARTRIDGE, E., *Songs and Slang of the British Soldier* (1931).

—— ——*The Long Trail: Soldiers' Songs and Slang, 1914–1918* (1965).

BROWN, M., *Tommy Goes to War* (1978).

CARRINGTON, C. E., *Rudyard Kipling: His Life and Work* (1955).

CHESHIRE, D. F., *Music Hall in Britain* (Newton Abbot, 1974).

CRU, J. N., *Témoins* (Paris, 1929).

CRUTCHLEY, C. E., *Machine Gunner 1914–1918* (Folkestone, 1975).

CUNNINGHAM, H., *The Volunteer Force* (1975).

DALLAS, G., and GILL, D., *The Unknown Army: Mutinies in the British Army in World War I* (1985).

DAWES, J. N. I., and ROBSON, L. L., *Citizen to Soldier* (Melbourne, 1977).

DEAN, B., *The Theatre at War* (1956).

ELLIS, J., *Eye-Deep in Hell: The Western Front 1914–1918* (1976).

ESSAME, H., *The Battle for Europe, 1918* (1972).

FALLS, C., *Caporetto 1917* (1966).

FARAGO, L. (ed.), *German Psychological Warfare* (New York, 1942).

FARSON, D., *Marie Lloyd and Music Hall* (1972).
FARWELL, B., *The Great Boer War* (1977).
——*For Queen and Country* (1981).
FRASER, D., *And We Shall Shock Them* (1983).
FUSSELL, P., *The Great War and Modern Memory* (1975).
GAMMAGE, B., *The Broken Years: Australian Soldiers in the Great War* (Canberra, 1974).
GARDNER, B. (ed.), *Up the Line to Death: The War Poets 1914–1918* (1976).
GERMAINS, V. W., *The Kitchener Armies* (1930).
GIBBS, P., *From Bapaume to Passchendaele* (1918).
——*Open Warfare: The Way to Victory* (1919).
GIRARDET, R., *La Société militaire dans la France contemporaine, 1815–1939* (Paris, 1953).
GOODSPEED, D. J., *The Road Past Vimy* (Toronto, 1969).
GORCE, P. M. DE LA, *The French Army*, trans. K. Douglas (1963).
GOUGH, H., *The Fifth Army* (Bath, 1968).
GREEN, H., *The British Army in the First World War* (1968).
GRUNBURGER, R., *A Social History of the Third Reich* (1971).
HALLIDAY, E. M., *The Ignorant Armies* (1961).
HAMILTON, I., *The Soul and Body of an Army* (1921).
HARRIS, H., *The Irish Regiments in the Great War* (Cork, 1968).
HART, B. H. LIDDELL, *History of the First World War* (1970).
HAYES, G. P., *World War One: A Compact History* (Folkestone, 1973).
HENSON, L., *My Laugh Story* (1926).
HILL, A. J., *Chauvel of the Light Horse* (Melbourne, 1978).
HINTON, J., *The First Shop Stewards Movement* (1973).
Hints on Training Issued by XVIII Corps (1918).
HOBSON, J. A., *The Psychology of Jingoism* (1901).
HOLMES, R., *Firing Line* (1987).
HOLT, R., *Sport and Society in Modern France* (1981).
HORN, D., *Mutiny on the High Seas* (1973).
HORNE, A., *The Price of Glory* (1964).
——*To Lose a Battle* (1969).
HOUSMAN, L. (ed.), *War Letters of Fallen Englishmen* (1930).
HOWARTH, P., *Play Up and Play the Game* (1973).
INNES, C. R., *With Paget's Horse to the Front* (1901).
JACKSON, R., *At War with the Bolsheviks* (1972).
JAMES, E. A., *British Regiments 1914–1918* (1978).
JAMES, L., *Mutiny in the British and Commonwealth Forces, 1797–1956* (1987).
JERROLD, D., *The Lie About the War* (1930).
KEEGAN, J., *The Face of Battle* (1976).

KIPLING, R., *Soldiers Three* (1899).

——*Barrack Room Ballads* (1973).

KOCH, T. W., *Books in Camp, Trench and Hospital* (1917).

LAFFIN, J. (ed.), *Letters from the Front* (1973).

LAWSON, R., *Brisbane in the 1890s* (Queensland, 1973).

LEED, E. J., *No Man's Land: Combat and Identity in World War I* (Cambridge, 1979).

LLOYD, A. L., *Folk Song in England* (St Albans, 1975).

LOWERSON, J., and MYERSCOUGH, J., *Time to Spare in Victorian England* (Sussex, 1977).

LOY, J. W., McPHERSON, B. D., and KENYON, G., *Sport and Social Systems* (1978).

McCAFFREY, D. W. (ed.), *Focus on Chaplin* (1971).

MACDONALD, L., *They Called It Passchendaele* (1978).

——*The Roses of No Man's Land* (1980).

——*Somme* (1983).

MacINNES, C., *Sweet Saturday Night* (1969).

MACK, E. C., *Public Schools and British Opinion Since 1860* (New York, 1941).

McLAINE, I., *Ministry of Morale* (1979).

MARSHALL, S. L. A., *Men Against Fire* (New York, 1947).

MASON, P., *A Matter of Honour: An Account of the Indian Army, Its Officers and Men* (1974).

——*Kipling: The Glass, the Shadow and the Fire* (1975).

MASON, T., *Association Football and English Society 1863–1915* (Sussex, 1980).

MEACHAM, S., *A Life Apart: The English Working Class 1890–1914* (1977).

MELLER, H. E., *Leisure and the Changing City 1870–1914* (1976).

MELLOR, G. J., *The Northern Music Hall* (Newcastle, 1970).

MEYER, J., *La Vie quotidienne des soldats pendant la grande guerre* (Hachette, 1966).

MIDDLEBROOK, M., *The First Day on the Somme* (1971).

——*The Kaiser's Battle* (1978).

MOORE, W., *See How They Ran* (1970).

——*The Thin Yellow Line* (1973).

MORRIS, J., *Heaven's Command* (1973).

MOYNIHAN, M. (ed.), *People at War 1914–1918* (Newton Abbot, 1973).

——*A Place Called Armageddon* (Newton Abbot, 1975).

——*God on Our Side: The British Padre in World War I* (1983).

MYERS, C. S., *Shell Shock in France* (Cambridge, 1940).

NEWSOME, D., *Godliness and Good Learning* (1961).

PAKENHAM, T., *The Boer War* (1979).

PALMER, A., *The Gardeners of Salonica* (1965).

PARKER, P., *The Old Lie: The Great War and the Public School Ethos* (1987).

PARKER, S., *The Sociology of Leisure* (Newton Abbot, 1973).

PEDRONCINI, G., *Les Mutineries de 1917* (Paris, 1967).

——*Pétain* (Paris, 1974).

PELLING, H., *Popular Politics and Society in Late Victorian Britain* (1979).

PITT, B., *The Crucible of War: Western Desert 1941* (1980).

POPE, W. M., *Carriages at Eleven* (1947).

PORCH, D., *The March to the Marne* (Cambridge, 1981).

PRICE, R., *An Imperial War and the British Working Class* (1972).

PRIESTLEY, J. B., *The Edwardians* (1970).

ROBERTS, R., *The Classic Slum* (Manchester, 1971).

ROBSON, L. L., *The First A.I.F.: A Study of Its Recruitment 1914–1918* (Melbourne, 1970).

ROTHSTEIN, A., *The Soldiers' Strikes of 1919* (1980).

SCOTLAND, J., *The History of Scottish Education*, ii (1970).

SETH, R., *Caporetto: The Scapegoat Battle* (1965).

SHIRER, W. L., *The Collapse of the Third Republic* (1970).

SILKIN, J. (ed.), *First World War Poetry* (1979).

SIMON, B., and BRADLEY, I. (eds.), *The Victorian Public School* (Dublin, 1975).

SIMON, E., *The Anglo-Saxon Manner* (1972).

SKELLEY, A. R., *The Victorian Army at Home* (1977).

SMITH, P. A., *The Anzacs* (1978).

SMYTHE, J., *In This Sign Conquer* (1968).

SOBEL, R., and FRANCIS, D., *Chaplin: Genesis of a Clown* (1977).

SOUTER, G., *Lion and Kangaroo: The Initiation of Australia 1901–1919* (Sydney, 1976).

SPICER, L. D. (ed.), *Letters from France* (1979).

SPIERS, E. M., *The Army and Society, 1815–1914* (1980).

STACEY, C. P., *Canada and the Age of Conflict*, i (Toronto, 1977).

STEARNS, P. N., *Lives of Labour* (1975).

STEWART, J. I. M., *Rudyard Kipling* (1966).

STONE, N., *The Eastern Front 1914–1917* (1975).

STOUFFER, S. A!, et al., *The American Soldier* (Princeton, 1949).

TERRAINE, J., *Douglas Haig: The Educated Soldier* (1963).

——*Impacts of War 1914 and 1918* (1970).

——*To Win a War: 1918: the Year of Victory* (1978).

——*The Smoke and the Fire: Myths and Anti-Myths of War 1861–1945* (1980).

——*White Heat: The New Warfare 1914–1918* (1982).

THOUMIN, R. (ed.), *The First World War*, trans. M. Kieffer (1963).

VAN CREVELD, M., *Fighting Power: German and U.S. Army Performance 1939–45* (1983).

VICINUS, M., *The Industrial Muse: A Study of 19th Century British Working Class Literature* (1974).

WADE, M., *The French Canadians 1760–1945* (1955).

WAITES, B., *A Class Society at War: England 1914–1918* (Leamington Spa, 1987).

WALVIN, J., *The People's Game: A Social History of British Football* (1975).

——*Leisure and Society 1830–1950* (1978).

WARD, R. (ed.), *The War Generation: Veterans of the First World War* (New York, 1975).

WATT, R. M., *Dare Call It Treason* (1964).

WEBER, E., *Peasants into Frenchmen* (1977).

WILKINSON, R., *The Prefects* (1964).

WILLIAMS, J., *The Home Fronts* (1972).

WILSON, A., *The Strange Ride of Rudyard Kipling* (1977).

WILSON, T., *The Myriad Faces of War: Britain and the Great War, 1914–1918* (Cambridge, 1986).

WINTER, D., *Death's Men: Soldiers of the Great War* (1979).

WINTER, J. M., *The Great War and the British People* (1986).

WINTRINGHAM, T. H., *Mutiny* (1936).

WOHL, R., *The Generation of 1914* (1980).

WOLFF, L., *In Flanders Fields* (1959).

WOODWARD, L., *Great Britain and the War of 1914–1918* (1967).

YAPP, A. K., *The Romance of the Red Triangle* (1919).

YOUNG, P. M., *A History of British Football* (1968).

YOUNGHUSBAND, G., *A Soldier's Memories* (1917).

(v) Articles

ANDREWS, B., 'The Willow Tree and The Laurel: Australian Sport and Australian Literature', in R. Cashman and M. McKernan (eds.), *Sport in History* (Queensland, 1979).

ASHPLANT, T. G., 'London Working Men's Clubs 1875–1914', in E. Yeo and S. Yeo (eds.), *Popular Culture and Class Conflict 1590–1914* (Brighton, 1981).

AUDOIN-ROUZEAU, S., 'Les Soldats français et la nation de 1914 à 1918 d'après les journaux de tranchées', *Revue d'Histoire Moderne et Contemporaine*, 34 (1987).

BAKER, W. J., 'The Making of a Working Class Football Culture in Victorian England', *Journal of Social History*, 13 (1979).

BARNETT, C., 'A Military Historian's View of the Great War', *Essays*

By Divers Hands, Being the Transactions of the Royal Society of Literature, 35 (1970).

BRAY, R. M., ' "Fighting as an Ally": The English-Canadian Patriotic Response to the Great War', *Canadian Historical Review*, 61 (1980).

DAVISON, G., 'Sydney and the Bush: An Urban Context for the Australian Legend', *Historical Studies*, 24 (1980).

DUNAE, P. A., 'Boys' Literature and the Idea of Empire 1870–1914', *Victorian Studies*, 24 (1980).

DUNNING, E., 'The Development of Modern Football', in E. Dunning (ed.), *The Sociology of Sport* (1971).

ENGLANDER, D., 'The French Soldier 1914–1918', *French History*, 1 (1987).

ENGLANDER, D., and OSBORNE, J., 'Jack, Tommy and Henry Dubb: The Armed Forces and the Working Class', *Historical Journal*, 21 (1978).

FERRO, M., 'Le Soldat russe en 1917: indiscipline, patriotisme, pacifisme et révolution', *Annales E.S.C.*, 26 (1971).

FIRTH, S. G., 'Social Values in the New South Wales Primary School 1880–1914: An Analysis of School Texts', *Melbourne Studies in Education* (Melbourne, 1970).

GILL, D., and DALLAS, G., 'Mutiny at Etaples Base in 1917', *Past and Present*, 69 (1975).

GOOCH, J., 'Attitudes to War in Late Victorian and Edwardian England', in B. Bond and I. Roy (eds.), *War and Society*, 1 (1976).

GURFEIN, M. I., and JANOWITZ, M., 'Trends in Wehrmacht Morale', *Public Opinion Quarterly*, 10 (1946).

JANOWITZ, M., and SHILS, E. A., 'Cohesion and Disintegration in the Wehrmacht in World War Two', in M. Janowitz (ed.), *Military Conflict* (1975).

KIERNAN, V. G., 'Conscription and Society in Europe before the War of 1914–18', in M. R. D. Foot (ed.), *War and Society* (1973).

——'Colonial Africa and Its Armies', in B. Bond and I. Roy (eds.), *War and Society*, ii (1977).

LAWSON, R., 'The "Bush Ethos" and Brisbane in the 1890's', *Historical Studies*, 15 (1972).

LEINSTER-MACKAY, D., and HANCOCK, G., 'Godliness, Manliness and Good Learning: Victorian Virtues and West Australian Exemplars 1891–1911'; *Melbourne Studies in Education* (Melbourne, 1979).

LITTLE, R. W., 'Buddy Relations and Combat Performance', in M. Janowitz (ed.), *The New Military* (New York, 1967).

MACINNES, C., 'Kipling and the Music Halls', in J. Gross (ed.), *Rudyard Kipling: The Man, his Work and his World* (1972).

McKernan, M., 'Sport, War and Society: Australia 1914–1918', in R. Cashman and M. McKernan (eds.), *Sport in History* (Queensland, 1979).

McKibbin, R., 'Work and Hobbies in Britain 1880–1950', in J. M. Winter (ed.), *The Working Class in Modern British History: Essays in Honour of Henry Pelling* (Cambridge, 1983).

Malone, E. P., 'The New Zealand School and the Imperial Ideology', *New Zealand Journal of History*, 7 (1973).

Mangan, J. A., 'Athleticism', in B. Simon and I. Bradley (eds.), *The Victorian Public School* (Dublin, 1975).

—— ' "Play Up and Play the Game": Victorian and Edwardian Public School Vocabularies of Motive', *British Journal of Educational Studies*, 23 (1975).

Marshall-Cornwall, J., 'Staff Officer 1914–18', *War Monthly*, 42 (1977).

Martineau, W. H., 'A Model of the Social Functions of Humour', in J. H. Goldstein and P. E. McGhee (eds.), *The Psychology of Humour* (1972).

Metcalfe, A., 'Organized Sport in the Mining Communities of South Northumberland 1880–1889', *Victorian Studies*, 25 (1982).

Morton, D., ' "Kicking and Complaining": Demobilization Riots in the Canadian Expeditionary Force 1918–19', *Canadian Historical Review*, 61 (1980).

Moskos, C., 'Behaviour of Combat Soldiers in Vietnam', in C. Moskos (ed.), *The American Enlisted Man* (New York, 1970).

Murray, W. W., 'How Trench Magazines Helped the Troops', *Our Empire*, 9 (1933).

Pedroncini, G., 'Le Moral de l'armée française en 1916', in *Verdun 1916: Actes du colloque international sur la bataille de Verdun* (Verdun, 1976).

Porch, D., 'The French Army and the Spirit of the Offensive 1900–14', in B. Bond and I. Roy (eds.), *War and Society*, i (1976).

Price, R. N., 'Society, Status and Jingoism', in G. Crossick (ed.), *The Lower Middle Class in Britain 1870–1914* (1977).

Robson, L. L., 'The Origin and Character of the First A.I.F.: Some Statistical Evidence', *Historical Studies*, 15 (1973).

Sandford, K. A. P., 'The Victorians at Play: Problems in Historiographical Methodology', *Journal of Social History*, 15 (1981).

Senelick, L., 'Politics as Entertainment: Victorian Music Hall Songs', *Victorian Studies*, 19 (1975).

Sloan, L. R., 'The Function and Impact of Sports for Fans', in J. H. Goldstein (ed.), *Sport, Games and Play* (Hillsdale, NY, 1979).

STEDMAN JONES, G., 'Working Class Culture and Working Class Politics in London, 1870–1900: Notes on the Remaking of a Working Class', *Journal of Social History*, 7 (1974).

SUMMERFIELD, P., 'The Effingham Arms and The Empire: Deliberate Selection in the Evolution of the Music Hall in London', in E. Yeo and S. Yeo (eds.), *Popular Culture and Class Conflict 1590–1914* (Brighton, 1981).

TURNER, I., 'The Emergence of Aussie Rules', in R. Cashman and M. McKernan (eds.), *Sport in History* (Queensland, 1979).

WARD, R., 'The Australian Legend Re-visited', *Historical Studies*, 18 (1978).

WESBROOK, S. D., 'The Potential for Military Disintegration', in S. C. Sarkesian (ed.), *Combat Effectiveness* (1980).

WHITTAM, J., 'War and Italian Society 1914–16', in B. Bond and I. Roy (eds.), *War and Society*, i (1976).

WINTER, J. M., 'Britain's "Lost Generation" of the First World War', *Population Studies*, 31 (1977).

YATES SMITH, L. P., 'They Laughed at War', *Defence* (1940).

ZILLMAN, D., BRYANT, J., and SAPOLSKY, B. S., 'The Enjoyment of Watching Sports Contests', in J. H. Goldstein (ed.), *Sport, Games and Play* (Hillsdale, NY, 1979).

Index